The Dragon, Image, and Demon

THE THREE RELIGIONS OF CHINA:
CONFUCIANISM, BUDDHISM, AND TAOISM -
GIVING AN ACCOUNT OF THE MYTHOLOGY,
IDOLATRY, AND DEMONOLATRY OF THE CHINESE

The Dragon,
Image,
and Demon

THE THREE RELIGIONS OF CHINA:
CONFUCIANISM, BUDDHISM, AND TAOISM -
GIVING AN ACCOUNT OF THE MYTHOLOGY,
IDOLATRY, AND DEMONOLATRY OF THE CHINESE

HAMPDEN C. DUBOSE

INTRODUCTION BY LOREN COLEMAN

COSIMOCLASSICS

NEW YORK

The **Dragon, Image, and Demon, Or, the Three Religions of China: Confucianism, Buddhism, and Taoism—Giving an Account of the Mythology, Idolatry, and Demonology of the Chinese.** First published in 1887. Current edition published by Cosimo Classics in 2014. Introduction © 2014 by Loren Coleman.

Cover copyright © 2014 by Cosimo, Inc. Cover design by popshopstudio.com. Cover illustration "The Emperor depicted as a Taoist magician." From Album of the Yongzheng Emperor in Costumes (1723), Palace Museum, Beijing/ Wikimedia Commons.

ISBN: 978-1-61640-938-8

HAMPDEN COIT DUBOSE was born on September 30, 1845, in Darlington, South Carolina. He was educated at the Presbyterian Theological Seminary in Columbia, and then became a missionary in the Presbyterian Church.

(On a personal ancestry note, the middle name of the maternal grandfather of my two New England-born sons is also *Coit*. The Coit family has an old New England legacy, tracking back to Salem, Massachusetts, in 1638, then on to Norwich, Connecticut, and Norwich, Vermont, as well as a branch that resettled in Georgia and South Carolina, when the Rev. George Henry Coit, moved from New England and settled locally after graduating from the Presbyterian Theological Seminary. The name is familiar to many today due to the California wing of the family that gave a 1929 bequest for Coit Tower, which continues to serve as an Art Deco memorial dedicated to Coit's beloved San Francisco firefighters.)

DuBose was an enthusiastic servant of God, and moved with his wife, Pauline Eliza McAlpine, on behalf of the American Presbyterian Mission (South), to China in 1872. They settled in Suzhou, along the Grand Canal of China.

As soon as the missionary couple arrived in China, they learned the language and settled down to understand the Chinese culture and the other religions than their own. Rev. Hampden Dubose apparently did this, completely and deeply. He went on to discover the wide-spread use and negative effects of opium in China, and co-founded and became the first president of the Anti-Opium League in China. Mrs. DuBose was a strong woman, also, and Rev. DuBose recorded how she once single-handedly calmed a large rioting crowd at their school, until the local authorities arrived.

Furthermore, DuBose wrote several books reflective of his study of the Chinese, including Biblical study aids (in Chinese), sermons (in Chinese), *Preaching in Sinim: The Gospel to the Gentiles, with Hints and Helps for Addressing a Heathen Audience* (1873), and *The Dragon, Image, and Demon, Or the Three Religions of China* (1886).

DuBose's book *The Dragon, Image, and Demon, Or the Three Religions of China*, here reprinted in the *Loren Coleman Presents Series*, was first published in London in 1886. It candidly discusses different facets of the Confucian, Buddhist, and Taoist religions, including mythology and demonology associated with them, especially the worship of dragons. As DuBose observes, "The fabulous dragon of China is a monster with scales like a crocodile and having five-clawed feet. He has no wings, and when he rises in the air, it is by a power he is supposed to possess of transforming himself at pleasure... The dragon, which is a flying reptile, seems to be an original Chinese creation."

Unlike other older cryptozoology titles, the author, the Rev. Hampden DuBose, places the unknown—demons, gods, dragons—and their importance, in a specific cultural context, within the Eastern religions. In addition to giving an overview of each religion, DuBose discusses the importance of nature, the idolatry and worship of dragons, and the various god- and demon-figures in Eastern mythology and religion, which are intertwined. The diversity within the book is wide-ranging, beyond dragons, could be found of what each system is. The "Dragon" is the emblem of China and its State Church; the "Image" is a synonym for the Indian religion—it matters little the size, colour, or name of the image; and the term "Demon" is Taoism in a nut-shell.

These dark chapters are written in the hope that some small impetus may, by the facts presented, be given to Christian missions in China. We now need 3,000 ordained men to go "two and two" to the 1,600 walled cities of the Empire. Oh, that some reader might hear the Macedonian cry! If the heart is touched, shall not the hand send a contribution to the mission treasury? How many might give $1000 a year to support a married missionary? How many churches might send out their own man? The *finance of missions* needs to be placed on a more definite basis; money to be raised by regular subscriptions, rather than depending on the collecting box. I write in a plain style so that boys may understand as well as men. When six years old, my father gave me a little red picture book, about Rev. R. Moffat in Africa; it took full possession of my soul, and in the "log parsonage" I resolved to go to the heathen. I trust that this book will follow every Christian boy that reads it like a policeman.

It is generally put down that when any one engages in a labour like this he does it to the neglect of mission work, so to exonerate oneself it is necessary to state that besides colportage, and constant street and tea-shop preaching, there has been an average of fifty sermons a month in the chapels. How can one expect the favour of God if he neglects what he is sent to do? The command is *not* "Go, *write* my Gospel." One of my teachers, an editor, gave the advice to the class "to save the *joinings* of time."

The suggestion is made to younger missionaries that they orally translate some of the chapters of this book with their teachers, so as to familiarise themselves with the *local idolatry.*

As this is not a comprehensive work on the middle kingdom, but simply on "Religion in China," there has been no opportunity to express my admiration for the many noble traits of national character,—the brightness of their intellects, the love of literature, the frugality and industry, the strength of the government, the solidity of their institutions, their peaceful dispositions, and their courtesy to foreigners. What a glorious country will the Land of Sinim—the land of promise—be, when they "turn to God from idols, to serve the living and true God, and to wait for His Son from heaven!"

H. C. D.

SOUTHERN (U.S.A.) PRESBYTERIAN MISSION,
Soochow, *September 30th,* 1885.

CONTENTS.

CHAPTER I.

THE THREE RELIGIONS DOVETAILED.

CHAPTER II.

THE CHURCH OF THE LEARNED.

CHAPTER III.

THE SEE OF PEKING.

CHAPTER IV.

THE HIGH-PRIEST OF CHINA.

CHAPTER V.

THE ADORATION OF NATURE.

CHAPTER VI

ANCESTRAL IDOLATRY.

CHAPTER VII.

CONFUCIUS : HIS CHARACTER AND INFLUENCE.

CHAPTER VIII.

THE CONFUCIAN SACRIFICES.

CHAPTER IX.

CONFUCIAN GODS.

CHAPTER X.

BUDDHA, THE LIGHT OF ASIA.

CHAPTER XI.

THE ORIENTAL BANYAN.

CHAPTER XII.

THE THEOLOGY OF BUDDHISM.

CHAPTER XIII.

THE WORSHIP OF BUDDHISM.

CHAPTER XIV.

THE IDOLATRY OF BUDDHISM.

CHAPTER XV.

MOUNTAINS, ISLANDS, AND FESTIVALS.

CHAPTER XVI.

WOMEN AND BUDDHISM.

CHAPTER XVII.

THE HEART OF BUDDHISM.

CHAPTER XVIII.

THE GODS OF BUDDHISM.

CHAPTER XIX.

GODS OF THE PEOPLE.

CHAPTER XX.

GODS OF TRADES.

CHAPTER XXI.

THE ABSURDITIES OF POLYTHEISM.

CHAPTER XXII.

TAOIST PHILOSOPHY.

CHAPTER XXIII.

TAOISM AS A RELIGION.

CHAPTER XXIV.

POPES, PRIESTS, AND TEMPLES.

CHAPTER XXV.

TAOIST GODS.

CHAPTER XXVI

MEDICAL DIVINITIES.

CHAPTER XXVII.

THE STAR GODS.

CHAPTER XXVIII.

THE IMMORTALS.

CHAPTER XXIX.

AFTER DEATH, THE SEVEN SEVENS.

CHAPTER XXX.

DEMONOLATRY.

LIST OF ILLUSTRATIONS.

THE DRAGON IMAGE, AND DEMON.

CHAPTER I.

THE THREE RELIGIONS DOVETAILED.

THERE are two considerations which make the study of religion in China of prime importance. One is the vastness of the population, say 350,000,000, one-fourth of the inhabitants of the globe, men with moral accountability, intellectual activity, and immortal destiny. Looking at this mighty host marching towards the grave, surely the Christian should give their eternal happiness or misery more than a passing or a passive thought. The other is the length of time the three religions have had for their operation,—Buddhism, one thousand eight hundred, Taoism two thousand five hundred, and Confucianism four thousand years: they have influenced sixty, eighty, and one hundred and twenty generations of men once living, but now sleeping in the tomb. The field of action has been in an empire where literature has been progressive, and the arts have flourished ; amidst a high order of civilisation ; and under a government which has seen Babylon fall, Nineveh destroyed, and Greece and Rome crumble to dust. Surely if man by searching could find out God, this land of Sinim would have found Him ages long since passed away, and rejoiced in Him as the living God. Alas! the people have been drifting farther and farther from the truth, and in their development these hoary systems have not had an upward but a downward tendency.

The thoughtful man asks: What are the religions of China? What relations do they bear one to the other? What do these pagan systems teach? What gods do the people worship? How do they worship them? What mediation do they offer for sin? What are their views about the immortality of the soul? What hopes have they beyond the grave? In the following pages an attempt will be made to answer these living questions.

No Arithmetical Division.— The words Confucianism, Buddhism, and Taoism are upon the lips of every man, woman, and child in the land, but the Chinese cannot be divided numerically among the three religions. Some writers have put down 180,000,000 Buddhists to China by the convenient method of halving the population. The Confucianists are the literary class, but they worship in Buddhist temples and use the Taoist ritual. According to popular reckoning, the priests of Buddhism and Taoism are the only real Buddhists and Taoists, as the people do not consider that they themselves belong to these faiths, though they worship regularly in the temples. look upon the priestcraft as their ministry, and contribute systematically to the support of these religions. To belong to the Church is " to eat the Church's rice." No Chinaman save a shaven-head or yellow-cap would say, " I am a Buddhist," or, " I am a Taoist." The gentry say, " I am a Confucianist," or more generally, " We Confucianists ; " but the term is not used by the mercantile or by the working classes. Ask a shopman, mechanic, or farmer to what religion he belongs, and his answer would be a look of astonishment, as he does not consider himself a member of any church, for he has not passed a literary examination, which is the rite of baptism of Confucianism, and he does not eat the rice of the priesthood, which is the only sacrament Buddhism and Taoism know.

It is a surprising phenomenon. " China is the only country in the world where three systems could stand side-by-side without one expelling or superseding the other." A European cannot understand how any one could belong to three religions at once, yet this is the case with the Chinese. The religions stand more in the relation of friendly denominations at home than of contending systems.

The Three in Partnership.—The three have entered into partnership in religious trade. For centuries Confucianism stood alone, with its worship of Heaven, its deification of ancestors, and its personification of nature, fearing equally to offend the spirits of the mountains or the genii of the hills. Next arose Taoism, like a tall giant, and gathering within the folds of his garments the wild beliefs which were floating in the impure atmosphere of heathenism, made them into a compound of polytheism, rationalism, and superstition, and sent his followers into the dark caves upon the mountain sides, seeking for the elixir of immortality.

Then came the Indian religion, with its images and
shrines, its fumes of incense and lighted candles, its
monks in livery, and ritual in Sanscrit, and, like a mighty
flood, it swept from the mountains to the sea-shore; the
people found it exactly adapted to their carnal minds,
and so Buddhism was accepted as an organised Church.
Taoism, scorning to be left behind in the race, and seeking to be "all things to all men," reached out its left hand

The Three Founders.

to Buddhism, and borrowed its legends and prayer-books,
and with its right hand it stole the state gods of Confucianism, and hid them among its "household stuff,"
and its devotees, leaving the speculations of the old
philosopher, betook themselves to charms, sorcery,
and spiritualism. At first Confucianism persecuted
Buddhism with fire and with sword, but as it had no
temple rites nor images to offer in its place, after

centuries these two became silent partners. Theoretically Confucianism opposes idol worship, but practically adopts it, as is strikingly illustrated in the case of the

Emperor K'anghe.—In the " Sacred Edict," under the maxim, " Degrade strange religions in order to exalt the orthodox doctrine," he says of the Buddhists, " The sum of what they do is to feign calamity and felicity, misery and happiness, in order to make merchandise of their ghostly and unexamined tales. At first they swindle people out of their money in order to feed themselves. By degrees they proceed to collect assemblies to burn incense."

In his celebrated letter to the priests at Poo-too, A.D. 1684, he says, " I sent an officer to offer a solemn sacrifice, and I wrote an inscription to be put up over the main gateway at the entrance of the island. I sent also money out of my own private treasury, to rebuild the temples and to beautify and adorn the surroundings. . . . Hereafter, trusting to the energy of Buddha and compassion of the goddess of mercy, perhaps we may have merciful clouds, seasonable rain, the sweet dew and balmy winds; thus the country will have peace and prosperity, and the people will have happiness and longevity."

The Three are Relatives.—The three are nearly related and are on similar bases. A priest pointed me to a tripod and said the three feet were symbolic of the three churches. All definitions are more or less defective, and it is difficult to make a description accurate; yet there are terms by which we can describe approximately the relationship of the three, though none of them present the case save in a one-sided light, and so are only partial views of truth.

Confucianism is based on morality, Buddhism on idolatry, and Taoism on superstition. The first is man-worship, the second image-worship, and the third spirit-worship. From another point of view the orthodox faith is characterized by an absence of worship, the Indian faith by the worship of the seen, and the native faith by the fear of the unseen. Confucianism deals more with the dead past, Buddhism with the changing future, while Taoism is occupied with the evils of the present.

Considered in their relations to philosophy, the three systems are ethical, physical, and metaphysical. Confucianism in its prominent characteristics was ethical, occupying itself mainly with social relations and civil duties. Taoism, "as developed by the followers of Laotsze, may be characterized as physical; without any conception of true science, it was filled with the idea of inexhaustible resources hidden in the elements of the material universe." Buddhism, as metaphysical, was engaged in "abstruse speculations and subtle inquiries into the nature and faculties of the human mind . . . . and the grounds of our delusive faith in the independent existence of an eternal world."

The three "occupy the three corners of a triangle," the moral, the ideal, and the material. Confucianism "discourses on virtue and vice, and the duty of compliance with law and the dictates of conscience." As to Buddhism, its "gods are personified ideas," its worship is "homage rendered to ideas," and not "reverence paid to beings believed to be actually existing." In Taoism " the soul is a purer form of matter, which gains immortality by a sort of chemical process, which transmutes it into a more ethereal substance, and prepares it for being transformed into the regions of immortality." " Supporting, instead of destroying each other, they bind the mind of the nation in three-fold fetters."

All Three National.—The three religions are all supported by national authority. Theoretically, Confucianism is the religion of the State, the Established Church of China. The mandarins are literary men, who owe their promotion to letters, the heritage Confucius has left the nation ; the Confucian temples are under Imperial patronage ; and the Confucian worship is conducted by Government officials and maintained at Government expense. Buddhism has also been accepted as a national religion, in that temples have been built by Imperial grants, monasteries endowed from the Government revenues, books have been written by emperors, and the religion acknowledged as one of the great integral parts of the State. Taoism becomes a State religion, in that the dead ministers and generals who are assigned rank in Hades have office given them by the Taoist pope, become gods in Taoist temples, have Taoist priests as their guardians, and are worshipped according to the forms of Taoism. The State gods and numerous patron deities of the cities and market towns are under the wing of Taoism, so practically it is a national religion.

One Man worships in Three Temples. — One person will conform to the three modes of worship. Were Confucianism true to her principles and to her utterances against idolatry, she would draw a line of demarcation between the religion which bears the name of the sage and the two polytheistic systems. But what is really the practice of the *literati?* On the one hand, they seek protection of the Taoist goddess of the Pole Star, while on the other they bend the knee before the Buddhist goddess of Mercy, in earnest supplication for the blessing of a son. In the funeral procession will be found priests of both orders, and in the masses for the dead Buddhist priests are employed on certain fixed days, while Taoist priests are called in to officiate upon others. A few years ago, in this city, praying for rain, on one side of the temple one hundred Buddhists, and on the other one hundred Taoists, were employed to chant, the mandarins worshipping between. The city temples are generally controlled by the Taoist priests, but sometimes the Buddhists are in charge. The celibate priests of Buddha by their vows leave their families, discard their progenitors, and have no descendants; but, strange to say, they observe the six feasts of the year, and join in the ancestral worship of Confucianism. Taoism, like Buddhism, teaches transmigration; both seek oracular responses, both are vegetarians, and both go to the idols in time of sickness. It seems to make little difference to the people to what temple they go or what god they worship.

Many of the gods are the Same.—In a Buddhist temple there are seen Taoist images, and in a Taoist temple Buddhist divinities are enshrined. The Buddhists call the goddess of Mercy "the great teacher to open the gate," and the Taoists call her "The self-existent Heaven-honoured." The Pearly Emperor is called " Imperial Ruler" by the Taoists, and " King of Indra's Paradise" by the Buddhists. The Confucianists call the god of War "Military Sage," the Buddhists call him the "god of Protection," and the Taoists call him the " Minister of Heaven." The Buddhists and Taoists have each the " Three Precious Ones,"—Buddha, the law. and the Church in the first ; and wisdom, the Scriptures, and the priests in the second. They both have the ten kings of hell, and sometimes in a Taoist temple there will be a double row of buildings with images representing the punishments in the " earth-prison" of the Buddhists.

It may be said that many of the lines of distinction drawn in this work are arbitrary ; some to facilitate classification, some to prevent needless repetition, and some because the position assigned seemed most appropriate. Religion in the heart of a Chinese is three-headed, and so looks for help on every side. " All are Confucianists, all Buddhists, and all Taoists."

Is the Union Beneficial ?—What deductions may we draw from this commingling of the three religions? (1) There is a total lack of desire to know what is true. The question never crosses the native mind, " What is truth?" To accept conflicting systems, and to receive passively their teachings is not ennobling to the intellect. (2) It does not produce a healthy state of religious sentiment. The expounders of the religions lack zeal for any, while the people become indifferent to all, and this is the worst state of mind the missionary has to deal with. (3) The treaty of peace established between the three is at the price of true religion; with the priests it becomes a matter of trade,—do not "rob my

business," and I will not "cut" your gains,—so it
becomes a question of a "living" between the bonzes
and yellow-caps, and they find that a united effort to
dupe the multitude is most successful in reaping a harvest
of "filthy lucre." If a practical thought might be recorded, it is this—the denominational differences of
Protestants tend to a healthy state of piety.

The Relative Influence.—It has been stated above
that there can be no arithmetical division of the Chinese
among the religions, so it is impossible to give the
numbers of adherents to each, as is done when the census
is taken among Western nations, and a tabulated statement is made of the followers of different faiths, and of
the membership of the several Protestant denominations.
A proximate estimate of the relative influence of the
three is all that can be reckoned. Confucianism is
certainly the religion of the scholars and the aristocracy.
The appointments of the State are many, and the ritual
very minute; and in the worship of ancestors, in which
all unite, "the heart of the nation reposes more upon
the rites offered at the family shrine than upon all the
rest." So, as far as this goes, all are Confucianists;
also many are ashamed of Buddhism and Taoism, while
all glory in Confucianism. Yet, save in the article of
ancestral idolatry, the women and the middle and lower
classes, the great mass of the people, have little or no
connection with the Church of the sages, while it is theirs
to chant and pray, to burn incense and candles, to visit
the shrines, go on pilgrimages, and worship the million
idols. In central China, it is calculated that Buddhism
has twice the influence of Taoism, as the priesthood is

more earnest; so if Confucianism and Buddhism were considered equal, they would stand in this section relatively two, two, and one. In north China there is much less idol worship, and Taoism ranks ahead of Buddhism, so that it would be impossible to form a judgment except by an unbiassed survey of the whole field. Taking this, probably the three are nearly equal in their hold upon the affections of the people. As to prestige, Confucianism is first in renown, and rises like the tall mountains, whereas the fertile plains of the other two systems are more productive in idolatrous rites.

CHAPTER II.

THE CHURCH OF THE LEARNED.

CONFUCIANISM is a foreign term, which covers the three departments of the State religion, ancestral idolatry, and the worship of Confucius. The Chinese term is *ju kiao*, or "Church of the learned."

Not Strictly a Religion.—There is in China no generic term for religion in the usual sense of that word, and it is difficult to discuss Confucianism as a religious system with the followers of that sect. The name embraces education, letters, ethics, and political philosophy. Its head was not a religious man, practised few religious rites, and taught nothing about religion. In its usual acceptation the term Confucianist means "a gentleman and a scholar;" he may worship only once a year, yet he belongs to the Church. Unlike its two sisters it has no priesthood, and fundamentally is not a religion at all; yet with the many rites grafted on the original tree it becomes a religion, and the one most difficult to deal with. Considered as a Church, the classics are its scriptures, the schools its churches, the teachers its priests, ethics its theology, and the written character, so sacred, its symbol.

No Creator.—It is often asked, "Have the Chinese

any idea of a Creator?" The question is distinctly answered in the negative. Dr. Legge presents one sacrificial prayer of the Emperor to Shangte in A.D. 1538, which speaks intelligently of creation. This prayer sparkles as a single gem among the million Chinese volumes, whereas English secular literature abounds in its allusions to the Creator. "Of old, in the beginning, there was the great chaos without form and dark. . . . In the midst thereof there presented itself neither form nor sound. Thou, O spiritual Sovereign, camest forth in Thy presidency, and first didst divide the grosser parts from the purer. Thou madest heaven, Thou madest earth, Thou madest man. All things got their being with their reproducing power." The minds of thinking men at this time are too "cumbered with much serving" their own material interests to be troubled about the origin of matter. There are three indefinite theories about the creation :—

1. That there was no prime agent, but all things came of themselves; they were spontaneously produced.

2. The second hypothesis is that all things were produced by the agency of the dual powers *Yang* and *Yin*, the male and female principles of nature. A native author says, "Heaven was formless, an utter chaos; the whole mass was nothing but confusion. Order was first produced in the pure ether, and out of it the universe came forth; the universe produced air, and air the milky way. When the pure male principle *Yang* had been diluted it formed the heavens; the heavy and thick parts coagulated and formed the earth. . . . From the subtle essence of heaven and earth the dual principles *Yang* and

Yin were formed; from their joint operation came the four seasons, and these, putting forth their energies, gave birth to all the products of the earth. The warm influence of the *Yang* being condensed produced fire, and the finest parts of the fire formed the sun. The cold exhalations of the *Yin* being likewise condensed produced water, and the finest parts of the watery substance formed the moon. By the seminal influence of the sun and moon came the stars. Thus heaven was adorned with sun, moon, and stars; the earth also received rain, rivers, and dust."

Pankoo.
Pankoo.—These explanations were "too subtle for the common people," so they ascribe the "dividing of heaven and earth" to the first man, Pankoo, who "had the herculean task to mould the chaos which produced him, and to chisel out the earth that was to contain him." This primal individual—looking like a dwarfish specimen of a man, and clothed like a bear—"they picture holding a chisel and mallet in his hands, splitting and fashioning vast masses of granite. Behind the openings his powerful hand has made are seen the sun, moon, and stars; monuments of his stupendous

labours. His efforts were continued 18,000 years, and by small degrees he and his work increased; the heavens rose, the earth spread out and thickened, and Pankoo grew in stature six feet every day, till, his labours done, he died for the benefit of his handiwork. His head became mountains, his breath wind and clouds, and his voice thunder; his limbs were changed into the four poles, his veins into rivers, and his flesh into fields; his beard was turned into stars, his skin and hair into herbs and trees, and his teeth, bones, and marrow into metals, rocks, and precious stones; his dropping sweat increased to rain; and lastly, *the insects which stuck to his body were transformed into people!*"

No Sabbath.—There is no day of rest in the Land of Sinim, and the requirements of the fourth commandment are the principal obstacle alleged by many in the way of accepting Christianity. The Chinese have a holiday of about two weeks at New Year, and a respite at the feasts; and in this city clerks are entitled to three half-days a month at the discretion of the employer. They have not suffered physically from the want of a day of rest as other people, because they do not exercise their minds on such high subjects as Western nations, neither do they work with such muscular activity; but no one can witness "the wearied condition of society" where there is no Sunday, and not long for the day when the seventh part of the time may be observed as a day of rest.

The Splendid Morality.—The moral code known as Confucian deserves the world-wide commendations bestowed upon it, for as a teacher of ethics the sage of China stands in the foremost rank of practical philo-

sophers.   It proves that the Gentiles " are a law unto
themselves," and " show the work of the law written in
their hearts."   The Confucian morality is one great
element of stability in Chinese institutions, and one
cause of the remarkable duration of this ancient empire.

"It would indeed be hard to over estimate the influence
of Confucius in his ideal *princely scholar*, and the power
for good this conception ever since has exerted over his
race.   It might be compared to the glorious work of
the sculptor on the Acropolis at Athens.—that matchless
statue more than seventy feet in height, whose casque
and spear of burnished brass glittered above all the
temples and high places of the city, and engaged the
constant gaze of the mariner on the near Ægean ; guiding his onward course, yet still ever beyond his reach.
The immeasurable influence in after ages of the character
thus portrayed proves how lofty was his own standard,
and the national conscience has ever since assented to the
justice of the portrait."

The *ideal teacher* is thus described : "He is entirely
sincere and perfect in love.   He is magnanimous,
generous, benign, and full of forbearance.   He is pure in
heart, free from selfishness, and never swerves from the
path of duty in his conduct.   He is deep and active, like
a fountain, sending forth his virtues in due season.   He
is seen, and men revere him ; he speaks, and men believe
him ; he acts, and men are gladdened by him.   He
possesses all heavenly virtues.   He is one with heaven."

The classics discourse on the " five relations " of prince
and subject, father and son, husband and wife, brother
and brother, friend and friend ; they expand the reciprocal

duties, and enforce the moral obligations resting on each party. The "five virtues" are upon the lips of the people, and daily they speak of "benevolence, righteousness, propriety, knowledge, and faith." The precepts of the sages have filtered down through the masses, and have become staple topics of common conversation.

Confucianism makes "rectify yourself" the leading dogma of political economy. "Wishing to order well their states, they first regulated their families. Wishing to regulate their families, they first cultivated their persons. Wishing to cultivate their persons, they first rectified their hearts. Wishing to rectify their hearts, they first sought to be sincere in their thoughts." "Their thoughts being sincere, their hearts were then rectified. Their hearts being rectified, their persons were cultivated. Their persons being cultivated, their families were regulated. Their families being regulated, their states were rightly governed."

The central sun of the Confucian ethics is filial piety; this is the keynote of the song the sages sing, the keystone of the moral arch, the key that unlocks the mystery of the antiquity of the nation and the stability of its institutions. The solid rock on which China is founded is that the son should honour his father, and the inferior should obey his superior.

Vice not Deified.—One remarkable trait of Chinese idolatry is that there is no deification of sensuality, which, in the name of religion, could shield and countenance those licentious rites and orgies that have enervated the minds of worshippers, and polluted their hearts in so many pagan countries. "The Chinese have not endeavoured to lead the votaries of pleasure—falsely so-called—further down the road to ruin, by making its path lie through a temple, and trying to sanctify the acts by putting them under the protection of a goddess, nor does the mythology teem with disgusting relations of the amours of their deities." "Vice is in a great degree kept out of sight, as well as out of religion." This is true of the three religions, and is owing chiefly to the commanding influence of Confucianism. However corrupt in practice the people may be, the precept is printed on their minds and repeated by their lips, and, *to a casual observer*, the condition of society in regard to virtue is as smooth as the placid bosom of a lake.

The Heart.—The first little primer put into the hands of a Chinese boy after he learns a few hundred "square characters" is the "Three Character Classic," which begins, "Man's nature is originally good." The philosopher Mencius discourses at considerable length on the goodness of human nature. He says, "The tendency of man's nature to good is like the tendency of water to flow downwards. There are none but have this tendency to good, just as all water flows downwards." In justice to the ancient teacher it should be said that he in a degree modifies this his most extreme statement, and holds that man's condition is owing to his education and surroundings. "The trees of the New Mountain were once beautiful. . . . They were hewn down by axes and bills, and could they retain their beauty? . . . Through the nourishing influence of the rain and dew, they were not without buds and sprouts springing forth, but then came the cattle and goats and browsed upon them. To these things is owing the bare and stript appearance of the mountain ; . . . but is this the nature of the mountain? And so also of what properly belongs to man ; shall it be said that the mind of any man was without benevolence and righteousness? The way in which a man loses his proper goodness of mind is like the way in which the trees are denuded by axes and bills. Hewn down day after day, can the mind retain its beauty? But there is a development of its life day and night, and in the calm air of the morning, just between night and day, the mind feels in a degree those desires and aversions which are proper to humanity, but the feeling is not strong, and it is fettered and destroyed by what takes place during the day."

The opinions of Mencius were controverted by the philosopher Seun, who took as his text, " The nature of man is evil." All the Chinese, however, accept the interpretation of Choofootsze, whose commentary is memorised in the schools, and he teaches in the baldest terms the essential goodness of human nature.

" THE HEART, THE HEART, THE HEART," is a motto often engraved in the solid walls of the temple, and the triple enunciation of the text is equal in force to a sermon. Glance above (on the sacred walls), and you will see the sign, " RECTIFY THE HEART," a solemn exhortation to morality.

The doctrine of Confucianism is, first, that the heart is good ; that it is good by nature, and that the thoughts of the heart, flowing in their natural channels, are pure. Second, that a man may rectify his own heart ; that he can exercise a control over it, and when it deviates from the right way he can, by his own power, nourish and restore it to the path of virtue.

Conscience.—The Church of the learned pronounces distinctly its teachings about conscience, that inward monitor in the soul of man which approves what is good and warns of the evil. Mencius says, "The heart of pity is the principle of benevolence; the heart which perceives shame and dislike is the principle of righteousness; a modest and complaisant heart is the principle of propriety; the heart which approves and disapproves (*i.e.*, conscience) is the principle of knowledge. Without the heart of pity he is not a man, without a heart to perceive shame and dislike he is not a man, without a modest and complaisant heart he is not a man, without a heart to approve and disapprove (*i.e.*, without a conscience) he is not a man." The people have many proverbs of similar import; for example, "Do not violate your conscience;" "Never do what your conscience cannot endure;" "Cheat your conscience, and a life's happiness is destroyed."

The Confucianist.—We are not simply to look at Confucianism as it is recorded in the sacred books,—its "Five Classics" bearing an exceedingly distant analogy to the Old Testament, and its "Four Books" to the New, —but at the religion as it is illustrated in the lives and characters of its professed followers. "The tree is known by its fruits" is a principle accepted not only by the adherents of Christianity, but a dogma of universal application. Let us measure the orthodox faith of China by this standard. The contempt towards the foreign barbarian, the opposition to Western progress, the looking backward instead of forward, is characteristic *number one*. The *second* characteristic is *pride*; the upturned nose, the scornful eye, the arched brow, the curled lip, the disdainful smile, reveal what the mind thinks of the foreigner. The *third* is *parade;* alms to be given in public, sparrows counted one, two, three, four, to seven hundred, when set free from the snare of the fowler at the front door, ancestors worshipped publicly, all "to be seen of men." *Number four* is a *picayune view of sin;* to misuse written paper, to trample on a grain of rice, to hold up wet clothes on the person to dry in front of the kitchen range (or god), these are the great sins of the Pharisees, who "tithe the mint and the anise." The *fifth* national characteristic is the *oppression of the poor* and perversion of justice, as is seen when there is a failure of the harvest, and the tenant, unable to pay the exorbitant rent of twelve dollars an acre, is beaten, and cangued for six months.

Want of Religion.—There is not a religion on the face of the globe where the followers have less religion than in the Church of the learned. The men of China! The prevailing malady is irreligion; happily the disease is not so widespread among the peasantry. One cause is that the Confucian books do not teach religion. Another is the opposition in former times of the Confucianists to idolatry. A third cause is the prevailing scepticism of the gentry; they do not believe in God, in heaven, in hell, or in future rewards and punishments. The neglect of worship is a fourth reason; some sacrifice simply at the feasts, others pray only once a year. As a fifth cause the great worldly-mindedness of the Chinese may be assigned; their hearts are fixed on gain; they are "carnal," of this "earth, earthy."

Failed to Elevate.—That Confucianism has exerted

a mighty influence for good cannot be denied, yet though it has been a conserving intellectual power in the land, it has failed to elevate the nation morally and spiritually. Confucianism teaches truthfulness, but do not the people "delight in lying" and "love a lie"? Is not their ceremonious etiquette a cover for mendacity, "the ancestor of all their sins," and the one of all others which makes Western nations hold them in contempt? Experience proves that this is not confined to the illiterate, but that the higher we go in the ranks of society the more skill is displayed in the disregard of truth. Honesty is taught in the scriptures of the "Five Classics and Four Books," and the glib tongues of the people show with what facility they can repeat the precepts of the ancients; but when the mandarins, the great lights in the Church of the learned, receive a salary of $600 per annum, and clear $30,000, it suggests doubts as to impeccability. This system of dishonesty, like a stream when traced back from the mouth to its source, runs backwards through all gradations of society, diminishing in its volume in proportion as the width of the channel narrows the opportunity for "squeezing." Emblazoned on door and gateway is the maxim, "Of ten thousand wickednesses fornication is the chief;" but in what country is the seventh commandment violated more in the heart, in the eye, or in the speech? Thus Confucianism, a moral system, pure and noble in its teachings, has failed to elevate and ennoble the race.

The Citadel.—The foremost opposition to the introduction of Christianity comes from those who esteem themselves the followers of Confucius. They assent to our views about the "emptiness" of Buddhism, the deceptions of Taoism, the character of the priesthood, the mud and stone of the images, but when we gently allude to ancestral idolatry, the worship of heaven and earth, and the sacrifices of the mandarins, they are offended. Also, the Confucianists do the thinking for the people; they have the minds, the books, the schools, and the offices. Without a long residence in the country it is hard to imagine the influence of a penniless scholar in his neighbourhood, and the mental control he exercises over the minds of the peasantry. More than this, the graduates at the Government examinations form a clique or "ring," and their voice is the unwritten law of China, their authority above that of His Excellency the Governor. The lamented Carstairs Douglas said at the Shanghai Missionary Conference of 1877, "Confucianism is the citadel; take it, and the war is ended.'

CHAPTER III.

THE SEE OF PEKING.

Heaven.—The Chinese often speak of Heaven, and at New Year, in the open courts of the houses, the worship of Heaven is conducted. The proverbs relating to Heaven are on every lip: "It is man's to scheme, it is Heaven's to accomplish;" "Nothing can escape the eye of Heaven;" "Man has a thousand schemes, but they are not equal to one scheme of Heaven;" "There is nothing partial in the ways of Heaven;" "Man does not know, but Heaven knows;" "You may deceive men, you cannot deceive Heaven;" "Riches and honour are appointed by Heaven."

"Relying on Heaven, we Eat Rice."

The most common proverb is, "We rely upon Heaven for our food;" and this picture of the character for Heaven, with a man, rice-bowl and chop-sticks in hand, leaning upon great Heaven, hangs in the post-offices, and suggests an humble trust in a higher power for our daily food. The solemn oath is taken by the finger pointing to Heaven. They say, " Above the heavens is Heaven," which tells of the striving of the immortal mind after the infinite. The term may be used very conveniently in preaching, as in the parable of the prodigal son the wanderer says, " I have sinned against Heaven."

The Son of Heaven.—The chief god of China is Heaven, and the Emperor of China is his earthly representative ; " he is regarded as the vicegerent of Heaven, especially chosen to govern all nations," and is co-ordinate with Heaven, from whom he directly derives his right and power to rule among men. His titles are "Son of Heaven," " Wise son of Heaven," " Heavenly Emperor," " Heavenly Sovereign,"—"terms which are given him as the ruler of the world by the gift of Heaven." The Emperor recognises Heaven as his Father, and the people recognise the Emperor as the correlative of Heaven, and no title do the subjects of His Imperial Majesty delight more to use than "The Son of Heaven."

The Emperor receives his *appointment* from Heaven. B.C. 2200 it was said to Yu the Great, " August Heaven regarded you with its favouring degree, and suddenly you obtained all within the four seas, and became sovereign of the empire." It is customary for a monarch, when he ascends the throne, or, as the Chinese say, " when he receives from Heaven and revolving nature the government of the world," to issue an inaugural decree. In

A.D. 1820, four thousand years after the date above, the Emperor Tao-kwang heralded his coronation day in the following language: "That Heaven's throne should not be long vacant, I purpose on October 3rd devoutly to announce the event to Heaven . . . and then shall sit down on the Imperial throne."

In the Celestial empire the terminology of the court accords with the appellation, "The Son of Heaven." The kingdom is "all under Heaven," the dynasty is "the Heavenly dynasty," the throne is the "Heaven-conferred seat," the revenues are the "Heaven-appointed emoluments," famine and pestilence are the "judgments of Heaven," and the emperors are to walk in "Heaven's way." "What's in a name?" Why, there is ancestry, and glory, and stability in this magic title "Son of Heaven."

The Son of Heaven as the Federal Head of His People.—"The idea of expiation is found in the earlier and later history of China." It is a solemn event when the Emperor, the vicegerent of Heaven, the high-priest of the nation, in his vicarious character descends from his throne, robes himself in sackcloth, makes public confession, becomes the substitute for his people, and appears as the sin-bearer. The doctrines of substitution and federal headship, as expounded by decree and example in the Established Church of the Middle Kingdom, are set forth in the two following proclamations, written thirty-six centuries apart:—

B.C. 1766, the Emperor Tang says: "When guilt is found anywhere in you who occupy the myriad regions, let it rest on me, the One Man. When guilt is found in me, the One Man, it shall not attach to you who occupy the myriad regions." During seven years of famine it was suggested that a human victim should be offered in sacrifice to Heaven. The Emperor said, " If a man must be the victim, I will be he." " He fasted, cut off his hair and nails, and in a plain cart drawn by white horses, clad in rushes, in the guise of a sacrificial victim, he proceeded to a forest of mulberry trees, and there prayed, asking to what error or crime of his life the calamity was owing."

In the time of a severe drought, the Emperor Taokwang, July 24th, 1832, offered the following prayer: "Oh! alas! Imperial Heaven! . . . this year the drought is most unusual. Summer is past, and no rain has fallen. . . . I, the minister of Heaven, am placed over mankind, and am responsible for keeping the world in order, and for tranquillizing the people. Although it is now impossible for me to eat or sleep with composure, although I am scorched with grief and tremble with anxiety, still, after all, no genial and copious showers have been obtained. . . . The sole cause is the daily deeper atrocity of my sins: but little sincerity and little devotion. . . . Hence I have been unable to move Heaven's heart, and bring down abundant blessings. . . . I examine myself and consider my errors, looking up and hoping that I may obtain pardon. . . . Prostrate I beg Imperial Heaven to pardon my ignorance and stupidity, and to grant me self-renovation, for myriads of people are involved by me, the One Man. My sins are so numerous it is difficult to escape from them."

The Minister of Religion.—In the Grand Council of

Peking there is a Minister of Religion, or rather a Minister of Religious Rites and Ceremonies, who has charge of the ritual of the State. One of the six Boards is the Board of Rites. Among the duties of this board is the superintendence of "the rites to be observed in worshipping deities and spirits of departed monarchs, sages, and worthies," and "in saving the sun and moon when eclipsed."

The Mandarin Priests.—Very few foreigners have any conception of the amount of religious worship required of the mandarins, and how they are the Levites of the Confucian dispensation. Take as an example the Governor of Soochow. He acts as chief priest twice a year at the sacrifices to Confucius, at the small altars of Heaven and Earth, at the temple of the Worthies, at the temples of the Crown Princes, and in time of drought at the temple of the Five Dragons. Twice a month he goes to see his apotheosis, the Governor of Hades, and also worships at the new and full moon at each of the temples of the god of Literature, War, Wind, the Sun, Fire, Agriculture, the Empress of Heaven, and the Chinese Æsculapius. Sometimes he sends a deputy. There is not one of the officials, whether high or low, who does not have his appropriate list of divinities to be adored, so that the State religion requires a good proportion of his time, and there are a number of temples committed to his special charge.

Imperial Gold.—Some estimate of how great are the sums spent by the Chinese Government in idolatry may be made by a view of the magnificent temples at the capital, for "there is nothing which more arrests the attention of a visitor to Peking than the number, size, and costliness of the temples which have been built by the Government, and which are supported by its revenues;" by a view of the Confucian temples throughout the empire, the city temples, the grants to Buddhist temples, and by the official rebuilding of temples; also by the money spent in animal sacrifices, in incense and candles, and in paper sycee, etc. There is a very lavish expenditure of silver in idolatry, and "it would be hard to say to which religion the Government patronage is most given, it is so freely given to them all." To carry out its architectural designs and maintain its religious services, there is required a constant drain on the national exchequer.

An Anchor to the Nation.—We naturally desire to inquire, "What are the reasons for the remarkable duration of the Chinese people?" The first that suggests itself is filial piety, the inculcation of obedience to parents, teachers, and rulers, "that thy days may be long in the land which the Lord thy God giveth thee." Another is the triple constitution of the government; a monarchy of the rulers, an aristocracy of the scholars, and a democracy of the people. A third and potent reason is their religion; their faith in the power or powers above, controlling the destiny of the empire and the fortunes of the people. As a reverse picture, behold unhappy France!

The Imperial religion has recognised Heaven as regulating the affairs of the Government, and so by the will of Heaven a dynasty may change, and by the will of Heaven a new emperor ascend the throne, and by the

will of Heaven the capital be removed, yet in this sense
of reference to a higher power there is permanency.
While recognising the control of Heaven, China has at
the same time avoided the evils of Church and State,
and also the evils of a hierarchy with its government
by a priesthood.

Religion in China is recognised in the State, in the
temple, and in the family. The first is a pompous
ritual, yet these ceremonials are a conserving power; the
second is a *wooden* (to use a native term for stolid,
blockish) homage, yet the worshipper is affected by the
external sounds and symbols; the third, family worship,
is formal, yet addresses itself more directly to the heart.
If an appeal for family religion in lands of light might
be presented, it may be based upon the fact that the
great conflict of Christianity here is not with the State
or temple worship, but with the Church in the home.
As the Samsonian strength of Chinese paganism lies in
its family altar,—though it is only erected a few times
a year.—so the power of Protestantism is not in denominational wealth or influence, nor in the numbers who
assemble at church, but in the faithfulness of the father,
the patriarch and priest of the home, in daily assembling
the household to read the word, sing the psalm, and bow
at the throne of grace.

CHAPTER IV.

THE HIGH-PRIEST OF CHINA.

THE city of Peking consists of three cities in one: the Tartar city to the north, about thirteen miles in circumference; the Chinese city to the south, twenty-two miles around, the south wall of the Tartar city forming the north wall of the Chinese city; and the Imperial or Forbidden city, which lies within the Tartar city, and in which are the palaces, royal park, lake, and artificial hill. In the southern part of the Chinese city is a park, a mile square, which contains the famous Temple and Altar of Heaven. " Within a second wall, which surrounds the sacred buildings, rises a copse of splendid and thickly growing cypress trees, reminding one of the solemn shades in the vicinity of famous temples in ancient Greece." Besides the Temple and Altar of Heaven, there are the Temple of Imperial Expanse, the Fasting Palace, halls for the royal retinue and musicians, and buildings for the sacrificial vessels and the slaughter of animals.

The Temple of Heaven.—The Temple of Heaven, as it is called by foreigners, or more properly "The Temple for Praying for a Propitious Year," is the chief attraction of the park. It is not built on the ground, but upon the top of the north altar, which consists of three marble terraces, twenty-seven feet in height,

with marble balustrades, the marble top of the altar
forming the floor of the temple, which rises to the
height of ninety-nine feet. The building is circular
with a spacious dome, made by a triple roof of azure
tiles, the highest section only covering the centre of
the temple, and is ornamented with rich carving

Temple of Heaven.

and painting. As the round windows are shaded by
venetians of blue glass rods strung together, the light
of the sun within becomes an ethereal blue. This edifice,
with the rare symmetry of its proportions, resting on
the marble eminence, is the most remarkable and imposing structure in the capital. Its dome, the colour of
the aerial vault, and in the shape of the visible heavens—

which the architecture of the earthly temple is intended to represent, as the Heaven above is here worshipped on the earth beneath, the earthly being a symbol of the heavenly—is, in its silent majesty, the sacred rotunda of the East.

The Altar of Heaven.—The Altar of Heaven is in

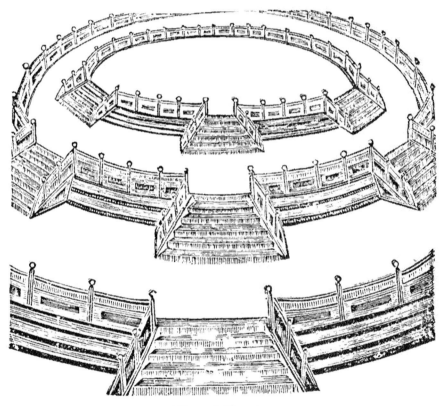

Altar of Heaven.

the southern part of the park, enclosed by a square wall without and a circular wall within, each with marble gateways, and in its rear is the temple of Imperial Expanse, in which are kept the tablets of Heaven and of deceased emperors. When we speak of an altar let not the reader imagine a Jewish or Grecian altar, for this

is a polygonal pyramid of white marble, twenty-seven
feet in height, consisting of three terraces, two hundred
and ten, one hundred and fifty, and ninety feet in
diameter, with richly-carved white marble balustrades,
and four flights of twenty-seven steps each, coincident
with the four points of the compass. The top is paved
with marble stones placed in concentric circles, the inner
circle of nine stones enclosing a round central stone, on
which the Emperor stands; around this runs each succeeding layer, consisting of a successive multiple of nine,
until the square of nine is reached in the outermost row.

There are five marble stands for the incense urns,
the candlesticks, and the vases for flowers. A table is
placed at the side for the reader of the prayers; a master
of ceremonies directs the whole, and at his call the
Emperor kneels and offers incense. Tents are erected
and lofty poles, from which hang lanterns.

Near the altar is a furnace built of green tiles, nine
feet high and seven feet wide; ascended by flights of
steps on the outside, so that a whole victim may be
taken to the top and let down upon the bars of iron and
the wood within.

The Procession.—As the winter solstice approaches,
within the Forbidden City preparations are being made
for the great day. The mortal eyes of men cannot
behold the Son of Heaven who sits on the dragon
throne of ivory; but on the evening preceding the
sacrifice he leaves his palace, going part of the way in
his chariot drawn by an elephant taken from the
Imperial stables, and part of the way in his sedan,
borne on the shoulders of thirty-two coolies. He is

preceded by the National Guard of bannermen, and by a company of two hundred and thirty-four musicians. Then on horseback, the princes of blood in vestments of royalty, the nobles with insignia betokening their rank, the statesmen in court dress, the mandarins in embroidered robes, the high officials, both civic and military, to the number of 2,000, quit the forbidden city, and pass along the silent street, its shops all closed, to the solemn sacrifice; the Imperial palaces pouring forth their princely legions on this grand occasion.

After the inspection of the grounds and halls, the Emperor repairs to the Palace of Fasting, where he prepares himself by quiet thought and lonely meditation for his high service; "for the idea is, if there be not pious thoughts in his mind, the spirits will not come to the sacrifice." The preparations go on. The tablets of Heaven and the deceased emperors, which are pieces of board eight inches wide and two-and-a-half feet high, beautifully carved, are placed on the altar; the tablets of the sun, the five planets, and twenty-eight constellations are put on the second terrace; the round blue jade-stone, the symbol of Heaven, is carried to the altar on an elegantly-carved and gilded chair; and, as the Chinese idea of worship is in part that of a feast, twenty-seven dishes with meats, fruits, and flowers are placed before the tablets—the offerings are made to Heaven, the spirits of the emperors being present as guests.

The Sacrifice.—An officer summons the Emperor, who repairs to the robing-tent and dons his sacerdotal dress, and no priestly vestments that Aaron ever wore exceeded in richness of gold and beauty of design those which are embroidered for the occasion in our city of Soochow. As he ascends the altar the regal choir of two hundred and thirty-four musicians—with voice, and stringed instrument, and soft-sounding cymbal—make the stillness of the night air resound with the song of " universal peace," while on the other side an equal number of posture-makers join in the ceremonies. The Emperor makes prostrations before the tablets, presents the viands, and lights the incense, when the songs of "harmonious peace" and "excellent peace" are sung by the choir. His Majesty then listens to an officer read the prayer to " Imperial Heaven, Supreme Ruler," and a single voice amidst the silence is heard, "Give the cup of blessing and the meat of happiness ; " the Emperor tastes thereof, and bows upon the altar before Heaven in token of his thankful reception, and then listens to the song of " glorious peace."

A shrill voice is heard, " Look at the burning," when the bullock, entire and without blemish, " no garlands having been put on the victim when its life was taken and no blood sprinkled," is placed in the furnace, and the smoke ascends.

Ecce Homo! The only man of the 400,000,000 who can perform this rite of the established religion. The Pontifex Maximus of this mighty empire, in behalf of his people, offers sacrifice ; the patriarch of the nation, at once their chief magistrate and high-priest. " The Emperor for himself, and his line, standing forth in his own dignity and glory, and that of his ancestors, and representing the millions of his subjects, presides at the highest services as a minister of religion, giving expression to the loftiest ideas of worship that have been the inheritance of his nation for several millenniums, and, as the parent and representative of his people, offers up prayers and a whole burnt-offering that the smoke may ascend to Heaven in a cloud of incense."

" The scene is one of imposing grandeur." The high-priest stands in solemn majesty while the legion of statesmen, nobles, and mandarins are prostrate on the second and third terraces in profound reverence and adoration. The worship is after midnight, and "as the pale light is shed abroad upon this princely assemblage, so richly dressed, from the high suspended lanterns, and the lurid flame from the sacrificial furnace ascends and casts its glare over the marble terraces, and the fragrance of incense and the peals of music fill the air under the open vault of Heaven in the early morning, the scene presents all the elements of imposing solemnity," and is a splendid and wonderful pageant. " This mountain top still stands above the waves of corruption, and on this primeval altar there still rests a faint ray of the primeval faith."

The worship of Nature in Nineveh, Babylon, and Egypt presents many striking points of comparison, but the fact is, that the religious systems of these have passed away, while the concentric circles of the great oak of the Established Church of China have widened till the diameter of the oak equals that of the marble altar; the roots going down deeper and deeper into the ground, coiling the clods of earth in its earth-worship, just as the branches of the tree extending upwards point to every part of the physical heavens in its worship of Heaven.

" The high-priests of China love power and adulation too much to share this worship with their subjects," so the State has appropriated this service, and the people are not permitted to worship " Imperial Heaven, Supreme Ruler," and as a matter of fact they are in blissful ignorance of the whole affair.

CHAPTER V.

THE ADORATION OF NATURE.

IT is not held that most of the worship described in this chapter is a worship of nature pure and simple, for it is impossible for any polytheistic system to retain its purity, yet no doubt originally it was simply an adoration of natural objects, first personified and then worshipped, and afterwards deified beings were enthroned upon them, and substituted in their places.

Its Antiquity.—The book of history informs us that the Emperor Shun, 4,100 years ago, "sacrificed specially, but with the ordinary forms, to Shangte; sacrificed purely to the six objects of honour; offered their appropriate sacrifices to the hills and rivers, and extended his worship to the host of spirits." A writer remarks: "When he sacrificed to the hills and rivers, he did so to the spirits supposed to preside over the hills and rivers of note in all the kingdom, and thereby exercised his royal prerogative, for in subsequent ages each feudal lord sacrificed to the hills and rivers in his State, while the worship of the sovereign embraced all such objects 'under the sky.'"

Ming Dynasty.—During the sixteenth century, in the solstitial prayer to Shangte, the Emperor says, "I, the Emperor of the great illustrious dynasty, have respectfully

5

prepared this paper to inform the spirit of the sun, the spirit of the moon, the spirits of the five planets, of the constellations of the zodiac, and of all the stars in all the sky, the spirits of the clouds, the rain, wind, and thunder, the spirits which have duties assigned to them throughout the whole heavens, the spirits of the five grand mountains, the spirits of the five guardian hills, the spirits of the four seas, the spirits of the four great rivers, the intelligences which have duties assigned to them on the earth, all the celestial spirits under heaven, the terrestrial spirits under heaven, the spirit presiding over the present year, the spirit ruling over the tenth month, and those over every day; and the spirit in charge of the ground about the border altar,"—thus summoning the pantheon of nature.

Pantheism —It is said that " Pantheism finds a god in everything.' It is " the spirit, soul, or animating principle of the universe," and is " essentially the doctrine of an all-pervading impersonal essence, breath, or spirit, which is called god." " The educated classes in China are pantheists, and have been for two thousand years. Their writings are full of it, and it has, as it were, saturated the language and literature of the whole country." A Chinese commentator says: " The evolution and transformation of heaven and earth, the maturity and decay of the vital powers of living men, the blooming and withering of plants and trees, with the life and death of all classes of things, is nothing but the action of the divine spirit." No wonder that thinking minds, without a knowledge of the Creator, should deify nature, and worship the soul of nature, instead of looking from nature to nature's God.

Heaven and Earth.—The ethical literature of this land is vast, books abound " exhorting men to be virtuous." The opening sentence of each volume is a solemn charge " to worship heaven and earth." At the Old Year's feast, during the New Year's holidays, and on the wedding day, heaven and earth are worshipped. During the 1st Moon, the 9th day is heaven's birthday, and the 10th day is earth's birthday, when incense is burned towards heaven in the

Worship of Heaven and Earth at New Year.

open courts of the houses. The two great thoughts engraved on the Chinese mind are the duties of honouring the father and mother who care for us in childhood, and of worshipping heaven and earth, the great father and mother of the universe; and so ineradicable are these first truths, that when a man listens to a preacher whom he accredits as a teacher of morality, though the assertion is repeatedly made that we must not worship heaven and earth, yet the hearer walks out of the chapel saying,

" Oh yes! worship heaven and earth;" "Heaven and earth are of most importance." The only possible way is by some startling illustration, as by a shock from an electric battery, to show the terrible sin of adoring heaven and earth, for around this pivot the whole of their religious thought revolves.

Earth.—The Emperor at Peking worships " mother earth " upon the altar of earth, which consists of two terraces of sixty and one hundred feet square each; the tiles of the wall are yellow, as is also the symbol of earth, the square yellow gem; and at this time also sacrifices are offered to the seas, the mountains, and the rivers. At the altar of heaven, the written prayer and the rolls of silk used as an offering are burned; at the altar of earth they are buried.

In South China the earth-worship has been noticed as performed by the peasantry; a clod of earth is set up in the field, and incense is lit in front of it, by way of giving thanks for an abundant harvest.

The Sun.—Tecumseh, the Indian chief, said to General Harrison, " Yonder sun is my father and the earth is my mother," so Confucianism " presents nature veiled in a more transparent personification." The worship of the sun is a part of the State religion, and the mandarins make their offerings to the sun tablet. "Turn thee yet again, and thou shalt see greater abominations than these. . . . There were five-and-twenty men, with their faces toward the east; and they worshipped the sun towards the east." Thus Ezekiel's vision is seen in China.

Moon god.—The queen of night, her light so soft and silvery, attracts the pagan worshipper, and at the full harvest moon in the 8th month a nation bows before the heavenly luminary, and each family lights incense made into a vase with gift flowers as an offering. The picture represents the moon-palace; the hare pestling medicine in a mortar, Mrs. Changngo, who stole the drug of immortality and fled to the moon, and the fragrant tree which one of the genii tries to cut down. The legend affirms

Palace of the Moon.

that Mrs. Changngo "became changed into a frog, whose outline is traced by the Chinese on the moon's surface." The following written prayer is seldom used: "Thy nature is effulgent, transparent without spot; thou, the icy-wheel in the milky way along the heavenly street, a mirror always bright; 100,000 classes all receive thy blessings."

Eclipse.—The Chinese do not differ from other heathen
nations in the terror they manifest at an eclipse, when
the "wild sun eats the real sun," and in the means they
use to appease the heavenly deities. In Africa they say,
"The eclipse monster has eaten the sun." The South
American Indians "thought the moon was hunted across

Save the Sun !

the sky by huge dogs." The Caribs "would dance and
howl all night long to scare the demon away." The
Peruvians "raised a frightful din when the moon was
eclipsed, shouting, sounding the musical instruments, and
beating the dogs to join their howls in the hideous
chorus." The noble Romans "flung firebrands in the air,
blew trumpets, and clanged brazen pots and pans."

In China, during an eclipse, in every direction fire-crackers explode, men knock the covers of brazen foot-stoves, and boys bang tin pans, so that the clangour and din fills the city. The picture represents the mandarin in the act of worship, which is a part of the prescribed rites. As he bows before the dark tablet placed on high on the table, the Buddhist priests clang their cymbals, and the soldiers fire volleys of musketry and fire-crackers. The priests chant, "The sun-palace hidden, the sun's virtue broken to pieces, we pray that the shadows of the darkness may scatter, the brightness of the sun return, and the myriad of things be enlightened," or "Palace of the moon, virtue of water, controlling all of the darkness; suddenly meeting with calamity and darkness, as if affliction were near, we pray thy grace may descend and thy light may return."

Gods of the Four Seas.—The Ruler of the East Sea is Wuming; of the West Sea, Chohliang; of the South Sea, Kyüshin; of the North Sea, Yuchiang; these four manage the affairs of the mighty deep.

The water-god.—The water-god has a tiger's body, a man's face of green and yellow colour, eight hands, eight feet, and eight tails.

One of the emperors saw another of the water-gods near Tsingki'angpu, where the Grand Canal crosses the old bed of the Yellow River. In the time of a flood he came floating down like a log of wood; he was ten feet long, and with a sounding voice; in colour he was black, with the appearance of a monkey; in strength equal to nine elephants: all who gazed at him became blind. The Emperor called to his aid one of the *ting* gods, who caught him, and confined him in a cave at the source of the river, with a great stone resting upon him, so that the waters could not again come with a great flood.

The river-gods.—One of them, named Pingee, ate eight stones, and this light diet made him so light in weight, that he could walk on the water. His character and associates were so bad that he had to flee beyond the Yellow Sea. Shangte made him the river-god.

Another is a young lady named Kissiang, who stole the Imperial pearl, and was transformed into a river-god. Another was Kuihping, who was drowned in the Mihlo River.

Gods of the Mountains.—There are a million gods of the mountains; for every mountain, hill, peak, knoll, and headland has its presiding divinity; the greatest among these being the north, south, east, west, and central peaks. The first mountain-god was seen in the days of the Emperor Yao, when the prime minister Pihling separated the peaks of the Szechuen province, and met the god of the mountains.

Gods of Time.—The god of the year is Leeping; of the month, Hwang Chenyih; of the day, Chenten; of the hour, Lienhung.

Gods of the Four Seasons.—The god of spring is the Green Ruler; of summer, the Fire Ruler; of autumn, the White Ruler; and of winter, the Black Ruler.

Gods of the Five Elements.—The name of the water-god is Pingee; of fire, Chohyung; of wood, Yuenming; of the earth, Yinsen; of gold, Keufang.

Wind, Thunder, Rain, and Lightning.—The mandarins worship tablets in honour of these, and light candles and incense on the 1st and 15th of the Moon. They are not considered to worship the common gods who rule over these departments; these *dei minores* are for the vulgar populace.

Earl Wind.—He gives the gentle zephyr, and sends the angry tempest.

Rain-master.—"A divinity identified by the ancient cosmogonists with a son of Kungkung, bearing the name of 'sombre dark,' and sacrifices by burnt offerings were

Thunder-god.

offered to him in accordance with the ritual of the Chow dynasty." He holds a bowl of water, and if he lets fall only a drop, there is a rainfall of one foot. The Master of Rain rides a white horse over the western sea, followed by twelve boys, and wherever he goes there is rain.

Thunder and Lightning.—The gods in this department are so numerous as to constitute a distinct Board, called "The Board of Thunder." The majesty and wrath of the gods are summed up in these tokens of Heaven's displeasure, and the thunder's roar and lightning's flash are witnesses to the people that there are gods above the sky. "Jupiter tonans."

The principal god of thunder is Went'aisze, a minister of the Emperor Show, who was killed by General Kiang. We sometimes ask the people, Who was it that governed

Mr. and Mrs. Thunder.

thunder before his day? This has never seemed to occur to them. His birthday is on the 24th of the 6th Moon, at which time all the country people flock to his temple. They observe a fast in his honour from the 1st to the 24th of the 6th Moon. He has three eyes,—one in his forehead,—and rides upon a tiger.

Another pair of gods are Mr. and Mrs. Thunder, who

control the artillery of Heaven, and flash the vivid lightning.

Madam Lightning is also a dread deity, who holds the lightning in her hand. She has 10,000 golden snakes, who flash electricity throughout the universe. The purple lightning kills, the red lightning lessens heat, and the white lightning diminishes wind and rain. Her chief assistant is called Teihlin, and her charioteer Ah-hyiang.

The snow-god.—His name is Tunluh. A prince fond of hunting goes to the forest for game. A giant asks the beasts, " Would you prefer to die by the knife or by an arrow ?" An aged deer begs the giant to save him from the prince, and he is directed to pray to Tunluh for snow, so that hunters cannot " go out for game."

The frost goddess.—The spring is thought to rule birth and the autumn death. On the 3rd of the 9th Moon the Green Maiden sends frost. She is worshipped by military mandarins.

God of Caverns.—Every cave, whether on the mountain side or in the depths of the sea, has its presiding divinity.

Tree-god.—The god of trees is only worshipped when an oak of the forest is to be felled with the woodman's axe. Notice is duly served throughout the neighbourhood, announcing at what time the tree is to be cut down, so that those who live near may remain indoors, as the tree-god is to be robbed of his roost, and may avenge himself upon the neighbours. Every tree has its separate individual deity. Oh, polytheism of the forest !

God of the Willow.—Twigs of the weeping willow

are favourite emblems in the hands of gods and goddesses. A Mr. Lee, walking through a willow-grove, was accosted by the willow-god, who told him to dye his clothing blue, as he would soon be the highest scholar in the empire. The prophecy was fulfilled by his appointment as Senior Wrangler at the Hanlin College, Peking.

Gods and goddesses of Flowers.—They are worshipped by florists on the 12th of the 2nd Moon, with music, refreshments, and floral decorations. There are twelve of these gods and goddesses, one for each month, whose biographies, though full of romance, are scarcely worth special notice.

The wheat-goddess.—A merchant of North China in 1873 met a fair maiden with twin stalks of wheat growing from one grain, which he told her was an auspicious omen. She replied that she was going to the city of Tungchow to order the harvest. The merchant, reporting the fact to the prefect, the latter had an image of the wheat-goddess made like this maiden with the twin stalks in her hand, and at the wheat harvest there are annual theatricals in her honour.

CHAPTER VI.

ANCESTRAL IDOLATRY.

IN a preceding chapter the attention of the reader was called to the magnificent marble altar and to the splendour of the Imperial worship. There the national altar was one and the worshipper a single individual; here, the ancestral altars are 70,000,000, and the worshippers 350,000,000. This is *the religion* of China in the sense that it is universal; "the *real* religion of the Chinese, that in which more than anything else they trust, and to which they look for consolation and reward." The Emperor worships his ancestor, and the peasant his. In the worship of Heaven the Emperor alone is the mediator; in the worship of Confucius the scholars take a part; the worship of idols is largely confined to the middle classes, especially the old women; but in ancestral worship high and low, rich and poor, alike do honour to parents once human, but now divine.

Filial Piety.—Ancestral worship is the extension of filial piety beyond the grave, and the amplification of the central tenet of their system of ethics, which the sages teach, the books record, the scholars enjoin, and the people follow. "The chief end of man," as well as "the whole duty of man," is in obeying and serving father and mother. As their interpretation inculcates respect for all superiors, inspiration has nothing to add to their doctrine save the promise ; and though the books do not record that promise yet China has its fulfilment, for this great empire of four times the age of Methuselah testifies to the faithfulness of Jehovah. Over the mountains of their idolatry and the hills of their superstition has the Most High passed, and remembered their reverence to parents. "The fact is, that filial piety in this system has exceeded the limit set by God in His word."

An Ancient Cultus.—We revere the hoary head, so standing in the presence of this ancient cult, which the people believe in their hearts and practise in their lives, we must respect even if we reject it. In the book of history there are clear intimations that the worship of ancestors was observed during the reign of Shun, B.C. 2250. His coronation took place in the temple of the " Accomplished Ancestor," and his successor, Yu, in the same holy place received the reins of government. The minister of religion was designated the " Arranger of the Ancestral Temple." It is said of Shun, when he returned from his tours of inspection, that " he went to the temple of the Cultivated Ancestor, and offered a single bullock."

In an ode which was written about the time of Samuel, the ancestors respond—

> " What shall the ceaseless blessings be ?
> That in your palace high,
> For myriad years you dwell in peace,
> Rich in posterity."

Confucius.—The sage, finding this ancient worship in existence, gave it his most emphatic sanction, and with him "the worship of parents was part of the duty of filial piety." He says : "The services of love and reverence to them when alive, and those of grief and sorrow for them when dead,—these completely discharge the fundamental duty of living men." One of the five characteristics of the model son is, " in sacrificing to them he displays the utmost solemnity." His millions of followers emulate his example ; " he sacrificed to the dead as if they were present; he sacrificed to the spirits as if they were present." He said, " I consider my not being at the sacrifice as if I did not sacrifice." When asked, " Do the dead have knowledge of our services, or are they without knowledge ? " the reply was, " If I were to say that the dead have such knowledge, I am afraid that filial sons and dutiful grandsons would injure their substance in paying the last offices to the departed ; if I were to say that the dead have not such knowledge, I am afraid lest unfilial sons should leave their parents unburied. You need not wish to know whether the dead have knowledge or not. There is no present urgency about the point. Hereafter you will know it for yourself." Thus he considered the services as of very doubtful benefit to departed ancestors, yet enjoined their devout observance.

A Son.—" Have you a son ? " " How many sons have you ? " are questions often asked. Ancestral worship has been a blessing to China in so far as it has exalted marriage, not so much elevating the relation of husband and wife, as making it a means to the great end of securing an heir. The Chinese well understand the Jewish law of " raising up seed to his brother," only instead of preserving the inheritance, it is perpetuating the worship. To continue the family line a nephew or the son of a friend is adopted, and sometimes concubinage is resorted to. The

Classics say, "The most unfilial is he who has no son."

"The offerings to the dead, to be successful and acceptable, must be presented by a relative of the male line. It is, by inheritance, the right, duty, and privilege of the oldest son or his heir to perform this sacred rite. If he is cut off by death, it is the duty of his brothers to appoint one of their sons to succeed him in his estate and filial duties. This individual—though an infant in the arms of the nurse—is master of ceremonies in ancestral worship. As the virtue of the offerings depends upon the regular line of descent, the priceless value of a son may be imagined, and the great preference of sons over daughters."

Fear, the Chief Motive.—The basis of this cultus is filial piety, but the prompting motive is fear. The Chinese know not of Heaven, where departed spirits hunger no more, neither do they know of the Lamb who leads to the fountain of living waters. The dead are dependent upon the living for food, clothing, and money; the first is presented upon the table, the second is paper-clothing burnt, and the third is tinfoil sent upwards in smoke. If the spirits have these they are contented and happy, but if they are hungry, naked, and penniless, they come back and punish those who neglect them, just as a parent chastises an undutiful child. Sickness and calamity deceased ancestors may bring, so they must be appeased, because those "who are neglected by their living relatives become beggar spirits in the world of darkness, and are forced, in order to secure even a wretched existence, to herd with the spirits of the multitudes who have died in war, at sea, of starvation, or in foreign countries."

Three Souls.—Truly the Chinaman is a compound being; he is not satisfied with soul and body, but must needs possess three souls and six spirits. Where this doctrine of trichotomy came from we cannot tell, but it is the universal faith of the people from the statesman to the farmer. This tripartite division of the soul is, at the outset, a formidable obstacle to the preacher, and it takes more than logic and rhetoric to convince our Mongolian brother that his soul is a unit. The "six spirits," or the animal spirits, go down into the earth at death: of the "three souls" one goes into Hades, and with it the priests deal; the second enters the coffin, and is laid in the grave, but is not satisfied with its dismal abode; the third tarries round about the old homestead: ancestral worship deals with soul number two and soul number three.

The Ancestral Hall.—These buildings are not so conspicuous as the idol temples, but they are very numerous, as any family or clan may have its temple, generally marked by the funereal cedar. Here the "spirit tablets" of departed forefathers are kept, "containing the simple legend of the two ancestral names carved on a board," and "to the child the family tablet is a reality, the abode of a personal being who exerts an influence over him that cannot be evaded, and is far more to him as an individual than any of the popular gods. The gods are to be feared and their wrath deprecated, but ancestors represent love, care, and kindly interest." If the clan do not own an ancestral hall, there is "in every household a shrine, a tablet, an oratory, or a domestic temple, according to the position of the family." It is a grand and solemn occasion when all the males of a tribe in their dress robes gather at the temple, perhaps a great "country seat," of the dead, and the patriarch of the line, as chief priest of the family, offers sacrifice.

Much property is entailed upon these ancestral halls to keep up the worship, but as this expense is not great, all the family have shares in the joint capital, and the head of the clan sometimes comes in for a good living. At baptism converts to the Christian faith renounce their claim to a share in this family estate, because of its idolatrous connections.

In these halls the genealogical tables are kept, and many of the Chinese can trace their ancestry to ten, twenty, thirty, and sometimes even to sixty generations. These registers are kept with great care, and may be considered reliable.

The Grave. - Heathenism often follows in the wake of the natural feelings. Are not the graves of earth, where rest the mortal remains of loved ones, dear to us? In the soft days of spring, do we not carry in our hands the wreath of flowers to decorate the sacred spots? Does not the traveller from distant lands make pilgrimages to the revered tombs of his parents? And where do we retire for meditation and record our solemn vows?

Ah! yes, but we did not worship our dead father and mother, we worshipped God; we did not make our vows before the monument of marble, we recorded them before God; we did not pray to our forefathers, we prayed to God.

In April the people everywhere gather at the family graves to sweep them and put the grounds in repair. If in the country, the family, male and female, old and young, dressed in their richest robes, go in a boat with a load of paper money, their provision baskets, and also lanterns, which are necessary, that the spirits may see. Before the grave, which is a mound, "the master of ceremonies arranges the various offerings" of meats, vegetables, and

Worshipping at the Grave.

fruits; burns the incense and paper sycee, and lights "the candles, for the spirits, being in the dark, need light;" "the straw baskets, filled with tin-foil money, a paper trunk, packed with paper clothing, and a paper sedan chair for the deceased to ride in," are committed to the flames; and "libations of wine are poured on to render the fluid invisible, and consequently available for the spirits." "As the blaze of the burning mass ascends, the master of ceremonies kneels on a red cloth spread before his offerings and bows his head nine times, precisely as the people do in the temples before their deities. His example is followed by all the members of the family present, not excepting even the younger, who are receiving their first lessons in ancestral worship." Thus on the hillside and in the grove, in the beautiful sunlight, they " worship the departed around a festive sacrifice, and go through a variety of ceremonies and prayers."

The following extracts are from a prayer of the Emperor Taokwang, April 1832 : " I presume to come before the grave of my ancestor. . . . Cherishing sentiments of veneration I look up and sweep your tomb. Prostrate, I pray that you will come and be present, and that you will grant to your posterity that they may be prosperous and illustrious. . . . Always grant your safe protection. My trust is in your divine spirit. Reverently I present the five-fold sacrifice."

The Home.—There are six feasts in the year when the Chinese conduct family worship, but the principal one is the last night of the old year, when the son returns from a distant city or even from a foreign land, to be present at the sacrifice, which to him possesses the solemnity the passover had to the pious Israelite. The table is spread. There are three kinds of meat—fish, fowl, and pork ; there are bowls of rice and vegetables, a decanter of wine, and bouquets of flowers ; the viands are offered hot, so that the dead may feast on the " flavour " or steam of the food, which is on the morrow eaten by the living. At the door, on a small table or bench, are placed a few dishes, so that the spirits of the stranger or the beggar may feast, and not intrude into the presence of the ancestral guests. There is every form of solemn worship,—the prostrations of the living, the sacrifice reverently presented, and the prayers offered,—for "one of the strongest motives for this worship arises out of the belief that success in worldly affairs depends on the support given to parental spirits in Hades." Few petitions are

Sacrifice to Ancestors.

offered to the gods in the "forms of men," but many to deified father and mother.

An emperor in the Ming dynasty used the following prayer: "I think of you, my sovereign ancestors, whose glorious souls are in heaven. As from an overflowing fountain run the happy streams, such is the connection between you and your descendants. I, a distant descend-ant, having received the appointment from Heaven, look back and offer this bright sacrifice to you, the honoured ones from age to age, for hundreds of thousands and myriads of years. . . . Now ye front us, O spirits, and now ye pass by us, ascending and descending, unrestricted by conditions of space. Your souls are in heaven; your tablets are in that department. For myriads of years will your descendants think of you with filial thoughts unwearied."

Here is the "Mount Zion" of the devout Chinese; at the feast each one enters the "Holy of Holies," the idol temples being "the outer court of the Gentiles" for the uninitiated multitude. As far as the feelings of a Mongolian are capable of being moved he approaches the sacrifice with "a pure heart, fervently," and thus ancestors become tutelary spirits; they are the household gods, the guardian angels who watch over the home. "There is nothing revolting or cruel connected with it, but everything is orderly, kind, and simple." "Parents and children meet and bow before the tablet, and in their simple cheer contract no associations with temples or idols, monasteries or priests, processions or flags. It is the family, and a stranger intermeddleth not with it; he has his own tablet to look at, and can get no good by worshipping before that bearing the names of another family." "As the children grow up, the worship of the ancestors whom they never saw is exchanged for that of nearer ones, who bore and nurtured, clothed, taught, and cheered them in helpless childhood and hopeful youth, and the whole is thus rendered more personal, vivid, and endearing." These great occasions, especially at the closing hours of the departing year, "are grand family reunions, where the dead and the living meet, eating and drinking together, where the living worship the dead, and the dead bless the living."

The Slavery.—Ancestral worship is one of the paradoxes of heathenism, for it contradicts the accepted beliefs in future rewards and punishments and in transmigration. They worship for three generations, or for five at the furthest, as they consider the state of the soul to be at that time the equivalent of annihilation.

"The Classics do not chronicle the changes, innovations, and additions which have been made in this worship during two thousand years," but the "teachings of the sages have been the means of perpetuating, if not inaugurating, a system that has, during successive dynasties, fastened upon the millions of China a most degrading slavery,— the slavery of the living to the dead."

Magistrates, "before passing sentence, usually ask if the father or mother are living, or if there are other brothers, for he shrinks from the responsibility of placing a man, whose duty it is to sacrifice to the dead, in a position where he would be forced to neglect these sacred offices."

The Emperor Tungchi, in 1874, died at nineteen without an heir. There were many distinguished statesmen among the princes of blood, but to satisfy the *manes* of his Imperial ancestors, the successor must be of a generation below, and so a child of five years was chosen, and the interests of 350,000,000 were committed for many years to a regency, rather than interfere with ancestral rites.

"As a system ancestral worship is tenfold more potent for keeping the people in darkness than all the idols in the land." "By its deadening influences the nation has been kept, for ages, looking backward and downward instead of forward and upward." The people oppose progress "because it would disturb the *status* between men and spirits, and thus prove fatal to the repose of the dead and the safety of the living."

"Should a man become a Christian and repudiate ancestral worship, all his ancestors would by that act be consigned to a state of perpetual beggary. Imagine, too, the moral courage required for an only or the eldest son to become a Christian, and call down upon himself the anathemas not only of his own family and friends, but of the spirits of all his ancestors."

When we preach against this form of paganism it seems as *heathenish* to the Chinese, as if at home we taught a child to disobey his father and despise his mother. "It forms one of the subtlest phases of idolatry—essentially evil with the guise of goodness—ever established among men."

CHAPTER VII.

CONFUCIUS : HIS CHARACTER AND INFLUENCE.

IT is not easy in our own minds to form a just estimate of the character of a man with whom we are intimately acquainted, and it is still more difficult to speak of him to others in such a way that they may judge correctly of his virtues and defects. What shall be said of the task of formulating the life and history of the Chinese sage, who lived when the Jews returned from Babylon, when Greece was invaded by Xerxes, and Egypt conquered by the Persians? Light passing through the vista of twenty-five centuries is at best dim; is it right to subject the master to the tests of this "enlightened nineteenth"? Or shall it be said of us, that "we weigh Confucius in the balance of the sanctuary"? We discuss the sages of Greece,—men whose thought lies embodied in the development of truth in after centuries,—now we present the living philosopher, "who, like a skilful engineer, excavated a channel of thought for future ages," and who projected his teachings upon such a plane, that, without addition or change, they have held despotic sway over an empire of intellect for eighty generations, perhaps the greatest mental wonder in the world.

Ancestry.—Pride of blood is universal. If any family

can with cause boast of lofty ancestry, it is the descendants of Confucius, who, during the reign of the Emperor
K'anghe, 2,200 years after the time of the sage, numbered
11,000 males, as shown by their genealogical tables so
carefully preserved in ancestral halls. They claim to
trace their line to the sovereigns of the Shang dynasty,

Confucius.

centuries before Confucius. "His father, known to us by
the name of Leangho, an officer remarkable for his
strength, bravery, and skill, won distinction at the siege
of Pihyang. A number of his comrades had entered the
city by a gate purposely left open, when the enemy
attempted to shut them in by letting down the drop-

gate, but Leangho stood below, and held up the massive structure till his friends could escape.

His Birth.—Leangho, near threescore and ten, without a son, sought a second wife of the Yen family. The father, pleased that the county governor should seek an alliance with his house, summoned his daughters, and telling them of the application for a hand and a heart, asked which of them was willing to be "the old man's darling." Miss Chingtsae, the youngest, said, "Father, why ask us? It is for you to decide." "You will go, my daughter." She was the mother of Confucius B.C. 551.

This mother prayed for a son at Mount Nee, and when he was born his head was shaped like this mountain. Two dragons appeared above the roof of the cottage as the guardians of the infant sage, and five venerable men came from afar to pay their respects. Within the chamber the young mother heard music, and a voice saying, "Heaven is moved at the birth of thy holy son, and sends down harmonious sounds." On his body were forty-nine marks, and the words, "He will originate principles and settle the affairs of men." Tradition asserts that the child was bathed in a stream which bubbled up from the floor, and thus a fanciful claim was given to the appellation, "Son of the essence of water." A unicorn came to his mother and presented her with the tablet he brought in his mouth, on which was inscribed, "The son of the essence of water shall succeed to the withering Chow, and be a *throneless king.*" She tied some red silk to his horn; he tarried a night and departed. The purport of the language taken to be prophetic was, "A child of perfect purity shall be born on the decline of the Chow dynasty, and reign without the insignia of royalty." "The dignified title of *throneless king* is the earliest declaration of the royalty of intellect, an idea which has appeared in subsequent ages in languages of which Confucius never dreamed."

Dragons and Wise Men.

His Youth.—The aged soldier left the son of his old age, an orphan of three years, to the care of his mother, who, though not so celebrated as the mother of Mencius, yet carefully watched over his education and moral training. As a boy, it is recorded, "he used to play at the arrangement of sacrificial vessels and at postures of

ceremony." At the age of seven he goes to a free
school, and "he differed from other children in that his
knowledge was not acquired but intuitive." In the
Analects Confucius tells us that "at fifteen he bent his
mind to learning." His biographer mentions an occasion
when, visiting an ancestral temple, and making minute
inquiries about the sacrifices, it is said in derision, "Why
does the district magistrate's son want to know these
things?" Confucius, hearing the sneer, replied, "This
is *ceremony.*"

The mother struggled with poverty, but in after years
the sage looked back on a youth of penury as directly
promoting intellectual vigour. "When I was young my
condition was low, and *therefore* I acquired my ability in
many things." With no books—only a few odes, frag-
mentary documents of history, and scattered manuscripts
—he made antiquity his study, and there sought for ideal
perfection.

The Age.—The sixth century before Christ was rendered illustrious by great sages, who exercised a mighty
influence on the minds and religions of men. In Greece
rose Pythagoras, Shakyamuni lived in India, Zoroaster
in Persia, and in China Confucius. To appreciate the
superiority of the sage, we must look at the darkness of
the age. "The state of China in the time of Confucius
was analogous to one of the European kingdoms during
the feudal system. There were thirteen principalities
of greater note and a large number of smaller dependencies.
The chiefs quarrelled and warred among themselves, and
a similar condition of things prevailed in each State, the
hereditary families encroaching on the authority of their

rulers, and these families being frequently hard pressed by their inferior officers." The wilderness of ancient China was an unpromising field for a philosopher, but he accomplished for his people what conquered Greece did for her conquering Roman foe.

Marriage.—He was married at the age of nineteen. It is thought he was divorced from his wife, but the interpretation of the passage on which the fact is based is uncertain. At the birth of his son the prince sent him a congratulatory present of fish, whereupon, in compliment to his friend, he called his boy " Uncle Fish." The records of the philosopher's life show no play of parental affection, and he seems to have maintained a distant reserve in the treatment of his son. " Have you heard any lessons of your father different from what we have learned ? " asked a disciple of " Uncle Fish." He replied, " He was standing alone, and as I passed by he asked, ' Have you read the odes ? ' and on my saying ' Not yet,' he remarked, ' If you do not learn the odes, you will not be fit to converse with.' Another day he asked, ' Have you read the book of propriety ? ' ' Not yet.' ' If you do not learn the book of propriety your character cannot be established.' I have heard only these two things from my father." The disciple was delighted, and said, " I have got three things. I have heard about the odes, the rules of propriety, and that a superior man maintains a distant reserve towards his son."

Public Teacher.—In his twenty-second year Confucius became a public teacher, and soon after his house was a resort, " not for schoolboys, but for young and inquiring spirits, who wished to increase their knowledge of the history and the doctrines of the past." However small the fee the pupil might bring, provided there was a thirst for knowledge, he was welcome in his academy. " From the man bringing his bundle of dried flesh for my wages, I have never refused instruction to any one." His object was not simply to impart knowledge ; it was to teach men to think for themselves. The sage thus aptly describes the art of teaching : " I do not open the truth to one who is not eager to get knowledge, nor help out one who is not anxious to explain himself. When I have presented one corner of a subject to any one, and he cannot from it learn the other three, I do not repeat my lesson."

When Confucius was thirty-five years old, the prime minister of the State of Loo, upon his death-bed, directed that his son "should enter the Confucian school," as its teacher was one thoroughly conversant with the teachings of antiquity. The patronage of this family gave quite a turn to the sage's fortunes. " The same year he was able to visit the capital, and make fuller inquiries into the ceremonies and rules of the founder of the Chow dynasty." At times his disciples numbered three thousand, probably many of them poor men, who had left their proper avocations, and came to the master from all parts of the country to ask special counsel ; and as for a half century he had fame as a political reformer and moral philosopher, public opinion began to be regulated by his opinions. " The influence he exercised as the recognised authority upon all questions relating to the early history of the empire, and as the eloquent expounder of those great moral principles which his historical studies had convinced him should form the basis of legislation," was felt throughout the thirteen states.

Devotion of His Pupils.—The sage, possessed of a personal magnetism, "moved amid a company of admiring followers." His family and his friends, who watched every movement, recorded everything said or done, and drank from the fount of his practical wisdom. His generosity was unbounded. A prince gives him a present of 6,400 piculs of grain; he gives it to his poor disciples, and says, "The prince gave it to me because he loved me; it is much better to love many than to love one." In his peripatetic school, with his students he is unrestrained, and conducts himself with simple and genial frankness, and their "devotion is a proof of his extraordinary force of character and of the moral excellence of his life." "The pupils walk with him, and ask questions on all conceivable subjects; on literature, music, costume, court etiquette, war, taxation, statesmanship."

One day, seeing a bucket in a temple with the handles attached halfway down the sides, so suspended that when empty it swung crooked, when partly filled it hung straight, and when full it turned over, Confucius moralised on humility, to the effect that a man with no knowledge will be deflected from the right line, a conceited man will turn a somersault, while a moderate estimate of one's powers is best. He told his students that it "was impossible to have too much knowledge, but we must beware of having too much riches, pride, and power." "*Aimless living* was one of the things he hated." On one occasion, walking beside a stream, he said, "I was making a comparison in my own mind between the running of water and of doctrine. The water runs unceasingly by day and by night. Since the days of Yao and Shun the pure doctrine has uninterruptedly descended to us. Let us in our turn transmit it to those who come after us, that they, from our example, may give it to their descendants to the end of time."

The prominent causes of the influence of Confucius were, first, "his books became the standard of religious, moral, and political wisdom;" second, he organised the *literati* into a host of well-disciplined minds; third, the power he exercised over his personal disciples; and lastly, their enthusiastic admiration. "They began the pæan which has since resounded through all the intervening ages," speaking the praises of him who was as far above his fellows as Mount T'ai—the highest peak in China, and around which the sage passed and repassed many times— is above the hills of Shantung. "There can be no doubt that he exerted a greater influence on the destinies of the empire than he could have done had he been seated on the Imperial throne."

The recorded testimonies of his disciples would fill pages. "The talents and virtues of other men are as mounds and hillocks which may be stepped over ; Confucius is the sun and moon, which cannot possibly be stepped over." " Our master cannot be attained to, just in the same way the heavens cannot be gone up to by the steps of a stair." " From the birth of mankind till now there has never been one so complete as Confucius." The author of the " Doctrine of the Mean " says, " Wherever the sky overarches and the earth sustains, and sun and moon shine, and frosts and dews fall, all that have blood and breath unfeignedly honour and love him. Hence he is called the companion of Heaven." Heaven, earth, and Confucius are the trinity of the scholars.

A Mandarin.—At the age of twenty he had so gained the respect of his townsmen for his "grave demeanour and knowledge of ancient learning," that he received an appointment in the revenue office, and succeeded in fixing the standard for weights and measures (which has, unfortunately, been lost), and in the year following he was made supervisor of the fields, herds, and parks, and his district became famous for its fine stock. At the death of his mother, "in conformity with an ancient usage which had then fallen into disuse, he immediately resigned all his employments to mourn for three years, during which time he devoted himself to study (retiring to his home as Paul did to Arabia), and examined everything past and present with the closest scrutiny.' When near fifty years of age he was appointed governor of the city of Chungtu, and afterwards was Minister of Crime in the kingdom of Loo. His principle of government was *centralisation*; and he succeeded in "dismantling the fortified cities held by the great clans, which served the same purpose as the castles owned by the barons of Europe in the feudal ages." Among the beneficial effects of his administration were these—that old and young ate apart, men and women walked apart, a parcel might in safety be dropped along the road, honest prices were asked for goods, and coffins were four inches thick. His eulogists say, "A transforming government went abroad. Dishonesty and dissoluteness were ashamed, and hid their heads. Loyalty and good faith became the characteristics of the men, and chastity and docility those of the women. Confucius became the idol of the people, and flew in songs through their mouths."

The wise administration of Confucius, during the time he figured as a politician, was raising the kingdom of Loo to a pre-eminence over the rival states. The duke or governor of Che, seeing Loo becoming the resort of the learned, thought it was becoming a dangerous neighbour, and he resolved to alienate the sovereign from his minister, and "drive the obnoxious cynic from his counsels." His artifice succeeded. Eighty beautiful women, skilled in music and the dance, with one hundred and twenty "blooded" steeds, were sent as a present to the throne. The king abandoned himself to the pursuit of pleasure, and the presence of the sage became irksome to the ruler. The court was no place for the patriot. The great sacrifice to Heaven, by which Confucius hoped the prince might be brought to his right mind, was neglected, so he "regretfully took his departure, going away slowly and by easy stages. He would have welcomed a messenger of recall. The sovereign, however, continued in his abandonment," and the sage left his office, his home, and his country.

A Wanderer.—"For thirteen years he travelled from one feudal state to another, seeking rest and finding none, always hoping to meet with a ruler who would adopt his counsel, and always disappointed." Confucius saw "the application of his theory of government was a great success, and amidst these troublous times of semi-barbarous, warring kingdoms, the heart of the statesman was filled with sadness." He said, " But what matters the ingratitude of men? They cannot hinder me from doing all the good that has been appointed me. If my precepts are disregarded. I have the consolation of knowing in my own breast that I have faithfully performed my duty." "His fame had gone before him, and most of the princes whom he visited received him with distinction, and would gladly have given him office and

The Sage's Chariot.

retained him at their courts; but no one was prepared to accept his principles and act them out."

A duke, pleased with having his domains honoured by the presence of so great a man, but who did not wish to follow his rigid system of honest government, proposed to give the sage the revenues of the town of Linkew. Confucius declined the offer, and said to his followers: "A superior man will only receive reward for services which he has done. I have given advice to the duke, and he has not yet obeyed it, and now he would endow me with this place. Very far is he from understanding me." His motto was office and principle, or poverty and honour. He said, " *With coarse rice to eat, with water to drink, and my bended arm for a pillow, I have still joy in these things. Riches and honours acquired by un-righteousness are to me as a floating cloud.*" Just as no one mourns over the results of the prison life of Bunyan, we can be glad that Confucius' years were not taken up with the busy details of an official career, but that he had time to study and to reflect, to teach and to write.

Called of Heaven.—During all the hardships which fell to the lot of the sage, who truly, in an earthly sense, was a " pilgrim and a stranger," "with no abiding city," his soul seemed profoundly impressed with the thought that he was appointed to this high task by Heaven. He said, " But there is Heaven; it knows me." Again, " I am a man who belongs equally to the north and the south, the east and the west." He had a presentiment of the future of his school. " He would travel, and his way might be directed to some wise ruler, whom his counsels would conduct to a beneficent sway that would break forth on every side till it transformed the empire."

Often in passing from place to place his life was in great danger, and once, when an attack was made upon his company, he sat quietly teaching his chosen pupils in a forest while armed banditti stood guard around the undaunted sage, who said, "After the death of King Wan, was not the cause of truth lodged in me? If Heaven had wished to let this cause of truth perish, then I, a future mortal, should not have such a relation to it." At one time a malicious chieftain sent a band to assassinate the philosopher. He observed to his disciples: "Heaven has produced the virtue that is in me; what can Hwantuy do to me?" "He claimed no Divine

The Sage and the Banditti.

commission or Messianic destiny," but simply that he was a teacher sent to help mankind.

A Man of the Past.—The sage constantly referred to the golden age of the past; antiquity was his theme in school, antiquity his example in court, antiquity the lamp to guide the nation, antiquity the goal to which China was to be carried in the backward flight of time, antiquity "the perfect type of society and manhood."

His watchword was not Advance! but Return! for "he came not to fulfil but to restore." "The book of Confucius is a Bible with a paradise lost, but no apocalyptic vision of a paradise to be regained." He stated, "I am not one who was born in the possession of knowledge; I am one who is fond of antiquity, and earnest in seeking it there." Confucius pretended to no originality in his teachings. "I am an editor, and not an author." He

The Musician.

did not introduce a new system of ethics or political philosophy, but, satisfied with the state of perfection to which, in his imagination, the aborigines attained, he sought only to *transmit* the lessons of morals and government which they had inculcated, not to be the *maker* of a new code or the founder of a new school. He says, "A transmitter and not a maker, believing in and loving the ancients, I venture to compare myself with our old Pang."

The Musician.—The pictorial life of Confucius, which is engraved in stone upon the walls of the temple in his native town, continually represents the sage as playing upon his harp, and this love of soft sounds gave a mellowness to a character naturally so rigid and inflexible. "His enthusiasm for peculiar forms of ancient music, which he describes as both beautiful and good, was so great, that it made him forget the taste of food for days." In learning music he took King Wan as his model, a man he describes as "black, tall, and with a sea-eye."

Humility.—Confucius was conscious of his personal defects, and spoke humbly of himself. "The sage and the man of perfect virtue, how dare I rank myself with them?" "In letters I am perhaps equal to other men, but the character of the superior man, carrying out in his conduct what he professes, is what I have not yet attained to." "The leaving virtue without proper cultivation, the not thoroughly discussing what is learned, not being able to move towards righteousness, of which a knowledge is gained, and not being able to change what is not good,—these are the things which occasion me solicitude."

Sinless.—The sayings of the Gentile sage forcibly remind one of the words of the Apostle to the Gentiles: "Not as though I had already attained or were already perfect." The Chinese now say of the repeated attestations of his shortcomings, "Oh, these are only polite euphemisms!" They consider that Confucius was immaculate. He was without sin; he never sinned; he could not sin. They lay claim for him to infallibility. The

Confucianist makes the *sinless perfection* of the sage as absolute as the Christian does for his Lord. This makes it necessary for us to speak on the subject clearly and firmly, yet gently, for it is not in good taste for the Western teacher " to drive his carriage roughly over the master's grave."

Ritualism.—The combination of the great and small in the character of Confucius makes the delineation of his character difficult, as it is a combination of the telescope of the philosopher and the microscope of the ritualist. Ethics and etiquette are twin sisters in Confucianism. The sage who was the founder of ritualism was a " Chinese of the Chinese, and stamped his image upon the nation ; " apes, who make mock at celestial mummery, should come to the Middle Kingdom, and take lessons from mandarins and posture-makers in " genuflections, bows, and facial movements." " In every country but China fashion is the synonym for change, but Confucius fettered this Proteus and arrested this revolving wheel." " A whole book in the Analects is occupied with his deportment, eating, and dress." His was true politeness ; " he bowed down to the cross-bar of his cart on passing a mourner." " When the prince called Confucius to employ him in the reception of a visitor, his countenance appeared to change and his legs to bend beneath him," so we have " the comical figure of a great sage trembling in the legs when officially receiving a public guest." Going to the palace, " He bowed to the other officers among whom he stood, moving his left arm or his right, but keeping the skirts of his robe before and behind evenly adjusted. He hastened forward with his arms like the wings of a bird. He ascended the platform holding up his robe with both hands, and his body bent, holding in his breath also, as if he dare not breathe. When he came out from the audience, and had descended one step, he began to relax his countenance, and had a satisfied look." " If his mat was not straight he did not sit on it." He was nice in his diet, " not disliking to have his rice dressed fine, nor to have his meat cut small. There must always be ginger on the table, and when eating he did not converse."

To Confucius *man-millinery* was all important. " His dress, which has not a speck of red about it, consists of silk and furs. If he wears lamb's fur, his garment is black; if fawn's fur, white; if fox's fur, yellow. His right sleeve is shorter than his left." In bed he was not unmindful of posture. " He did not lie like a corpse, and he did not speak. He required his sleeping dress to be half as long again as his body."

This is the original portrait; the number of copies has been prodigious. As you pass along the street and see through the open door a feast in the great hall of a mansion, and the guests with long bonnets, top boots, and robes of blue, green, or black silk and satin, all stepping about and parading around, interchanging bows and compliments, with nothing to talk about, you can think of no other emblem of the model literary Chinaman than the *strutting pigeon.*

On the other hand, looking at this empire of Confucian formalists, where from " throneless king " and sceptred monarch, through all ranks and classes, it is nothing " save ceremony, general ceremony," we cannot but feel there is an element of *stability* in forms, etiquette, and ritual in giving uniqueness and symmetry to the mass, though it deadens the sensibilities of the heart, fetters intellectual activity, and merges individuality into the rank and file of uniformity, so that "religion in China is rather a body of ceremonies than a system of doctrine."

The Silver Rule.—The Confucian philosophy is eminently practical, dealing with man in his relation to his fellow-man, and teaching him "to do justly and love mercy," but with no searching into the workings of the immortal mind, as in the Grecian schools, no lofty reasoning; not metaphysical in any sense. Five hundred years before the days of our Saviour the sage enunciated the silver rule,—the golden rule in a negative form. It is recorded twice, "What I do not wish men to do to me, I also wish not to do to men;" "What you do not want done to yourself, do not do to others." Our Lord commands men to do what they judge is right and good; Confucius forbids doing what we esteem wrong and hurtful; yet the silver and the gold are both precious metals. If Locke could speak of the one as "the most unshaken rule of morality and foundation of all social virtue," the other might be considered the keystone in the arch of Chinese ethics, and to have enunciated such a rule proves the sage to have been both good and great.

For Confucius' views about ancestors, see Chapter VI.

The Marvellous.—The facts in the next two pages are taken from the stone-engraved pictorial life of the sage, which adorns the walls of the temple near his grave. They are given just as they are there stated.

A vertebra as large as the wheel of a wheelbarrow having been found, a messenger from the duke asks Con-

fucius, "Who of the ancients had such a big bone?"
He answered, "When the Emperor Yu assembled the
host of gods at Mount Weikee, Pangfung came last, and
Yu cut off his head. His bones were as big as the wheel
of a barrow."

A large red bird brings to the king an inscription on

Weeping for the Unicorn.

bamboo, and places it at the palace door. He inquires of
the sage the interpretation, who says, "that a king of the
Hea dynasty had a 'precious efficacious prescription,' and
that he left it on a mountain in a casket, and now the
bird brings it to him as a gift from Heaven."

Confucius, with one of his disciples, went to the summit

of Mount T'ai, and the latter asked, " If that white thing outside of the Chang Gate at Soochow (600 miles) was a bolt of white cloth?" Confucius said, " No, it is a white horse." " The eye of the sage is god-like," says his biographer.

Prophetic.—Confucius on one occasion told his disciples to take their umbrellas and rain-shoes. There was afterwards a big rain, though the sky was clear when they set out. They asked how he came to be a weather-cock. He answered, " Last night I saw the moon and Taurus in conjunction."

A one-footed bird, flying into the court of the palace of Shang, stretched out its wings and hopped. The king sends to inquire of the master the meaning of its appearance, who replies that it had been lamed by a little child, who said, " Wherever you fly to there will be a flood." The philosopher says, " It portends a flood, let the people build their dykes and open the sluices." The other States were flooded, but the State of Shang escaped the devastations.

Superstitious.—A man digging a well finds a little animal like a rat. When it was brought to Confucius he examined it very carefully, and said, " There are many kinds of goblins; this is the earth-goblin, and is called a sheep-sprite."

We noted the great event of the appearance of the unicorn at the birth of the sage. In the latter days of his life, Confucius, hearing that some countrymen had killed a unicorn, left off the compilation of the " Spring and Autumn," and hastened to the spot. When he beheld the dead animal he wept, and cried " O unicorn!

O unicorn! King among the beasts, since you are dead, my doctrine can make no progress."

Want of Truth.—It seems unfair to take one or two incidents in a long life, and make general deductions as to character; on the other hand, it is not required that we should be silent, for one of the things which Confucius proposed to teach was *truthfulness.* Let us see how his practice corresponded with his theory. An instance is given in his history of a brave officer bringing up gallantly the rear, who modestly said his horse would not go faster. Confucius praised the man for attributing it to another than the right cause.

Again, a man called whom the sage did not wish to see, and he feigned sickness (as now is done in fashionable circles); but as he wished him to know he intended disrespect, when the visitor departed he took his harpsichord, sat in the door, and played. This is a celebrated event in Chinese books and pictures. As it is an axiom that Confucius was sinless, the only way of escape for the commentator is that *deception is not a lie,* so the above instance is the dead fly in their moral ointment.

Confucius once journeyed southward near the Yangtse River. He was stopped on his journey by a prince, and promised to go no further. He went on notwithstanding, and when questioned by a disciple said, "It was a forced oath; the gods do not hear such." Well doth the prophet Esaias say, "O my people, they which lead thee cause thee to err and destroy the way of thy paths."

The Historian.—The "Spring and Autumn" is a brief history of the State of Loo, written by the pen of the sage, and of it he says: "It is the Spring and

Autumn which will make men know me, and it is the
Spring and Autumn which will make men condemn me."
The work is a table of events, from five to eight per
annum, chronicled in about as many words. " We find
a congeries of the briefest possible intimations of matters
in which the court and State of Loo were concerned,
without the slightest tincture of literary ability in the
composition. Whether the fact be a display of virtue
or a deed of atrocity, there is nothing in the language
to convey the shadow of an idea of the author's feelings
about it. A base murder and a shining act of heroism
are chronicled just as the eclipses of the sun." In
Greece it was an age of distinguished writers, and from
ancient times the position of the historiographer in
China has been an exalted one. There are several
passages in the " Spring and Autumn " to show that
Confucius not only conceals the truth, but also mis-
represents. His great translator thus speaks: "(1) He
had no reverence for truth in history, I might say no
reverence for truth without any modification. (2) He
shrank from looking truth squarely in the face. (3) He
had more sympathy with power than with weakness, and
would overlook wickedness and oppression in authority."

His Influence.—The influence of the master in China
for good has been marvellous. The simple fact that the
Confucian Classics constitute the entire curriculum of the
schools proves his power in the domain of mind, and the
people, without considering the fact that there were books
in his day, universally ascribe to him the invention of
letters. His defects were like the spots on the sun's disc,
that do not "obscure the splendour of those rays" which

sent many a beam of light across "the unpoetic life of China." "We must admire his purity of life and nobility of spirit." "He possessed a stoical reliance on the dignity of human nature; he appealed to humanity; his response is the veneration of millions; a tribute not to miraculous power, but to pure force of character." The light of nature, as it shines in the life of Sinim's philosopher, proves that "when the Gentiles, having not the law, do by nature the things contained in the law; these, having not the law, are a law unto themselves." The moral law of China was written on the Mount of Conscience.

The entrance of foreign civilisation, the introduction of Western science, the displacement of the "Five Classics and Four Books" in the schools, and most of all the foolishness of preaching, will cause the sun of Confucius, which reached its zenith ages ago, to turn on its westward decline. "Where is the wise? Where is the scribe?"

The Books and the Altar.—It is said that the concluding act of his life was the solemn dedication of his literary labours to Heaven. "He assembled all his disciples, and led them out of the town to one of the hills, where sacrifices had usually been offered up for many years. Here he erected an altar, upon which he placed the books; and then, turning his face to the north, adored Heaven, and returned thanks upon his knees in a humble manner, for having had life and strength granted him to accomplish this laborious undertaking; he implored Heaven to grant that the benefit to his countrymen might not be small. He had prepared himself for this ceremony by privacy, fasting, and prayer." The stone engraving represents the sage in the attitude of supplication, while a beam of light descends from the sky.

Death.—Confucius "died lamenting that the edifice he had laboured so long to erect was crumbling to ruin." His biographer tells us that early one morning he got up,

The Books and the Altar.

and, with his hands behind his back, dragging his staff, he moved about the door, saying—

"The great mountain must crumble ;
    The strong beam must break ;
    And the wise man wither away like a plant."

He called his disciples, and, referring to ancestral worship, said : "According to ancient statues the corpse was dressed, treating the dead as if he were still the host. Under the Yin dynasty the ceremony was performed between the two pillars of the main hall, as if the dead were both host and guest. I am a man of Yin, and last night I dreamt that I was sitting with offerings before me between the two pillars. No intelligent monarch arises; there is not one in the empire that will make me his master. My time has come to die." In seven days he expired.

"Such is the account of the last hours of the great philosopher of China. His end was melancholy. The rulers had not received his teachings. No wife or child was near. Nor were the expectations of another life present with him as he passed through the dark valley. He uttered no prayer, and he betrayed no apprehensions. Deep treasured in his own heart may have been the thought that he had endeavoured to serve his generation, but he gave no sign." As Job hath said, "The mountain falling cometh to naught, and the rock is removed out of his place."

CHAPTER VIII.

THE CONFUCIAN SACRIFICES.

THOUGH while he lived no sovereign received him as a counsellor, accepted him as a legislator, or placed him in permanent office, yet no sooner did he rest in his tomb than the name Confucius was sounded through the six kingdoms. Many titles were conferred by emperors in after ages; "Confucius, the ancient teacher, accomplished and illustrious, all-complete, the perfect sage." Afterwards it was abbreviated, "Confucius, the ancient teacher, the perfect sage." Just after his death one of the kings caused a temple to be erected, and ordered that sacrifices should be offered at the four seasons of the year.

The Temple and the Grave.—The most famous temple in the empire is that of Confucius in his native city of Kewfoo, in the province of Shantung, about one hundred miles south of Chenanfoo. Within this sacred enclosure is the stump of the old tree the sage planted with his own hand, the well from which he drank, and a pavilion on the spot where his school-house stood, where were educated the philosophers of China. In front is a grove of trees with the library building and a number of monumental slabs. By the side is the palace of the duke of the Confucian clan, and within are buildings, one of which contains a statue of Confucius' father and a tablet to his mother, a pavilion with the dragon throne on which the Emperor sits, and a little room containing the pictorial life of the sage, engraved on stone. The main building has a large gilded image of

Avenue to Grave of Confucius.

Confucius, and near him the images of his twelve most celebrated disciples (Mencius is here as one of the twelve), and a little more remote are the images of his two-and-seventy disciples.

The grave is a mile from the city, and the broad paved avenue has rows of magnificent trees on each side. The

cemetery is a dense oak forest of a mile square, surrounded
by a city-like wall, and contains the mortal remains of
the long line of the descendants of the sage, the mounds
to the dukes being larger than the others. There is a
pavilion or tent of reflection for the pilgrims who visit
the holy tomb. A small enclosure contains the grave of

Grave of Confucius.

Confucius, which is a mound twelve feet high and thirty
in diameter. There is a row of stone men and stone
lions in front and a monument, which styles him "king;"
and what earthly potentate is his equal? Near the grave
is a pavilion marking the spot where T·ze Kung mourned
six long years, for after his decease many of his disciples remained to weep.

Kings adore.—The founder of the Han dynasty, B.C. 194, visited his tomb and offered an ox in sacrifice, and the clothes and hat, as seen in the picture, being still preserved, were placed before the altar. His grave is the Mecca of China, and emperors have made frequent

Emperor offering Sacrifice.

pilgrimages to the spot. K'anghe, the most illustrious of this dynasty, two hundred years ago, "set the example of kneeling thrice, and bowing his forehead in the dust before the image of the sage." In Peking the Emperor twice a year repairs to the capital temple, and worships Confucius just as he does Heaven.* "The worship is performed with peculiar solemnity. At the Imperial College the Emperor himself is required to attend in state," and conducts the services. "After the many preliminary arrangements have been made, and the Emperor has knelt twice, and six times bowed his head to the earth, the presence of Confucius' spirit is invoked." It is not honour given to a sage, it is homage to a god. Listen to the pæan: "We praise thee, O Confucius, surpassing in thy perfections, profound in thy knowledge, able to comprehend both heaven and earth. Thou priest of universal nature, whose advent was heralded by a unicorn, we celebrate upon the golden lyre thy light that floods the world; . . . we come to offer thee perpetual oblations, oh! thou unequalled by any being. . . . oh! thou most holy one, who, being in accord with the mind of the gods, arouses the people to duty. . . . From thee proceeds profound instruction to guide our feet along the path. Thou civiliser of the populace, thou teacher of the student, with all ceremony we worship thee. Most great one, thy virtue was greater than a thousand saints, thy teachings better than a hundred kings. Like the sun and moon they enlighten men. We would venerate thee, O founder of learning. Deign to be present, and accept the fragrance of our offerings, which with grateful strains we present in token of our sincere admiration."

His Manhood. —In the tenth book of the Confucian

---

* A remnant of high antiquity is found in the Peking temple ; ten stone drums or irregularly-shaped pillars, from one and a half to three feet high, and two feet across, commemorating a great hunt B.C. 827.

Analects his disciples describe him so naturally, that it is impossible to ascribe the supernatural to him. The Chinese look upon him as the model man, the perfect sage. As is remarked, " No character in history is less mythological than Confucius. He is no demi-god, whose biography consists chiefly of fable, but a real person. The facts of his life, the personal aspect of the man, the places where he lived, the petty kings under whom he served, are all known." Not only do they fail in ascribing the supernatural to him, but the people make a distinction between *holy* and *divine*. He is simply *holy*, with no attribute of divinity. Here, then, is a marvel in Chinese religion, that a man, merely a man, and nothing more, is worshipped as a god.

The god of Office.—The worship of the Chinese in all its departments is not so much with the view of adoring the deity as of obtaining personal benefit. Literature is the basis of official promotion, and they rise to office by a system of competitive examinations, which are attended with as great excitement as a national election ; for example, when 23,000 enter the examination hall at Nanking, and 140 receive the degree of A.M., they worship Confucius with the hope of getting office, which in native works on ethics occupies the same relative position as paradise in our Bible. Office to the Chinese is as heaven to us. The man who bows down before the tablet of the sage has one thought for Confucius and two for himself. When the degrees of A.B., A.M., or LL.D. are conferred the recipients go in state to the Confucian temple, bow the knee, and prostrate the body in token of the distinction they receive.

Literary Temples.—In the empire there are 1,560 Confucian temples, one for each province, department, and county. The provincial temple in Soochow is in a small park one-third of a mile in length; in front is a grove of small cedars, and the grounds are ornamented by numbers of stone monuments firmly fixed in the backs of tortoises; then there are large halls with astronomical diagrams, and a map of the city on stone a thousand years old, and also side-rooms for the tablets of the 500 sages. The main hall is fifty by seventy feet, the massive roof supported by wooden posts. The temples of the Shantung province have large images of the sage, with the shrine and paraphernalia of the Buddhists, but here there is the simple tablet which reads, "Most Holy First Teacher, Confucius' spirit tablet." The visitor, hearing the buzz of wings and chirp of voices overhead, notes the thousands of swallows which here homeward fly, and takes care to stand just without the sacred portals; so superstitious are the scholars, that they will not suffer one of these living birds to be driven away, lest it be ominous of evil, and they speak of them as "the ten thousand happinesses come to court." The premises, the finest in the city, are overgrown with thistles and weeds, and are never put in order save at the vernal and autumnal sacrifices.

The Sacrifice.—On the day preceding the sacrifice, in an adjoining temple, several thousand satin-robed scholars go in and bow before the sage's tablet; the music on the long guitars and instruments of steel is of the softest kind, and in front is the company of dancers, flag-bearers, and posture-makers with their bodies bending to the right

and left.   As I stood for a couple of hours watching them
one by one making prostrations before the resting-place
of the philosopher's soul, many near me said, " Foreign
teacher, you worship Jesus ; this is the way *we* worship
Confucius."

The great sacrifice is in the fifth watch of the night.

Sacrifice to Confucius.

One ox, twenty-two sheep, and twenty-two pigs are slain,
and placed, skinned and whole, on the altar, and are
afterwards taken to the yamens and eaten by the
mandarins ; a great tent is spread above the stone daïs
in front of the temple, when the Governor-General, with
a thousand attendant mandarins and scholars, arrives in

state, and, as the chief priest of the *literati*, who are divided according to rank, to chant, to respond, to bear flags, to make postures, and to sing the doxology, he conducts the worship according to the forms of the Book of Rites; and at the call of the master of ceremonies, with pomp and parade they present a feast and pour out libations, the grounds being brilliantly lighted, and the lamps making radiant the richly-dressed congregation of provincial magnates. A grand chorus then joins in singing the soul-stirring doxology—

> "Confucius, Confucius! How great is Confucius!
> Before Confucius there never was a Confucius;
> Since Confucius there never has been a Confucius;
> Confucius, Confucius! How great is Confucius!"

In the Middle Kingdom every year 66,000 animals are offered in sacrifice to the ancient sage. Listen to the Emperor invoking the spirit of Confucius! "Great art thou, O perfect sage! Thy virtue is full; thy doctrine is complete. Among mortal men there has not been thine equal. All kings honour thee. Thy statutes and laws have come gloriously down. Thou art the pattern in this Imperial school. Reverently have the sacrificial vessels been set out. Full of awe we sound our drums and bells." The spirit is supposed to be present, and the Emperor offers the prayer: "I, the Emperor, offer a sacrifice to the philosopher Confucius, the ancient teacher, the perfect sage, and say, O Teacher, in virtue equal to Heaven and earth, whose doctrines embrace the past time and the present. . . . in reverent observance of the old statutes, with victims, silks, spirits, and fruits, I carefully

offer sacrifice to thee. May'st thou enjoy the sacrifice."
Could the homage of a nation be more complete?

The School.—When a boy enters school he prostrates
himself before the tablet of Confucius. On the 1st and
15th of every month little boys are seen going along the
streets with a roll of books in one hand, and candles and
incense in the other. "Little boy, where are you going

School-boy worshipping Confucius.

to?" "I am going to school." "What are you going
to do with the candles and incense?" "Worship Confucius, the Holy Man." And so in every schoolroom by
every one, who, as they say, "reads books," the sage is
adored precisely as they do the temple images. This is

a fearful aspect of Confucianism, that from earliest childhood boys are taught that success in letters depends on serving, worshipping, and glorifying Confucius.

His Rank in the Pantheon.—It has been said, "If the Chinese pay divine honours to any being in heaven, or on earth, or under the earth, it is to Confucius. To him they offer prayers and sacrifices, and him they worship and adore."

The chief god of the Indian religion is Buddha; of Chinese Taoism, the Pearly Emperor; of the Church of the learned, Confucius. Comparing the influence of the three, though the people consider the first two as having more power in the unseen world, yet the head of the literary Church, in the respect of the nation, and in the honours bestowed by the scholars, is beyond all question the chief god of China.

CHAPTER IX.

The god of Literature.—Wenchang, the god of literature, is one of the leading deities of China. A constellation, known as part of the Ursa Major, is called by

Wenchang.

this name, and by some the god of literature is considered as the ruler of this group of six stars; by other authorities he is considered as another god altogether. The wheel of transmigration turned seventeen times the fate of Wenchang. His most distinguished metempsychosis was as a snake which revenged the wrongs done to his ancestors. He then met with Buddha, who forgave his sins, allowed him to throw off the serpent's coil, and return as a man. He is one of a triad with Confucius and the god of war. It is said that Wenchang prevents the vicious, even though learned, from obtaining academic degrees.

Behind Wenchang there stands an old man clothed in red, who nods his head if the essay is worthy of passing. It is said the god's opinion does not pass as law unless he has the assent of the old man in red.

Wenchang's special attendants are two boys, named Heaven-Deaf and Earth-Dumb. In the book of literary decrees the names of successful

Kwéi-sing.

candidates are written, and these two boys, Deaf and Dumb, cannot divulge the secret.

The Star of Literature.— Kwei-sing, the star of literature, holds in his right hand a pen, and in his left a peck measure. He takes a more active part in the competitive examinations than does Wenchang; so literary men, before going to the examination hall, invariably offer sacrifice to the star of literature.

The god of War.—Kwante, the god of war, is the head of the military, as Confucius is of the gentry. He was a general who figured in the time of the Three Kingdoms, just after the commencement of our Christian era, and his bloody sword won for him the unenviable position of god of the battle-field.

He is one of the most popular gods in the Chinese pantheon, and during this generation his fame has been increasing. In 1856 he appeared in the heavens, as Castor and Pollux did to the Romans, and successfully turned the tide of battle in favour of the Imperialists, for which the Emperor raised him to the rank of Confucius. There are 1,600 State temples at which the mandarins worship twice a month, besides the thousands of smaller temples, where sacrifices

God of War.

of sheep and oxen are offered to him. In every camp, in every tent, in every officer's room, there hangs the large portrait of the Chinese Mars. His worship is not confined to the officials and the army, for many trades and professions have selected him as a patron saint, and few pictures are so familiar, as one looks into the homes of the people, as that of the god of war. The executioner's knife is kept within the sacred precincts of his temple, and when the mandarin who superintends the decapitation returns from the execution ground, he stops here to worship, for fear some ghost of the criminal may follow

Three Primordial Sovereigns.

him. He knows the spirit would not dare to go into Kwante's presence, so he takes this means of getting rid of his invisible attendant.

Three Primordial Sovereigns.—After the time of Pankoo there were three kings, whose united reigns aggregated 18,000 years. The people constantly speak of the King of Heaven, the King of Earth, and the King of Men; Heaven, Earth, and Man forming, in their esteem, a kind of trinity.

The Five Planetary - gods.—The Green Ruler, corresponding with Jupiter; the Red Ruler, corresponding with Mars; the Yellow Ruler, corresponding with Saturn; the White Ruler, corresponding with Venus; and the Black Ruler, corresponding with Mercury. .

The Five Emperors.—In the legendary period the Chinese speak of their five emperors, all of whom, save

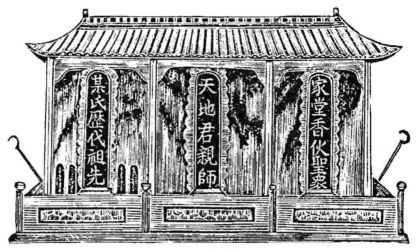

Household Gods.

Yao and Shun, Confucius rejected as being unauthentic. (1) Fuhhe. (2) Shinnung, the divine Husbandman, who taught agriculture to the nation. (3) Hienyuen, who taught medicine, and who also first taught the art of dress. (4) Yao. (5) Shun. These are all worshipped.

Penates, or Household gods.—In every house, except the hovels of the poor, just within the gateway or first entrance-room, and opposite the front door, high up are three pigeon-holes, where reside the family gods. In the middle one, on the tablet, are the words, "Heaven,

Earth, Ruler, Parent, and Teacher;" on the left, inscribed on the tablet, "We burn incense to the holy multitude of family gods;" on the right are the ancestral tablets, placed in order of rank, the oldest in the rear.

Door gods.—In front of the yamens and temples

Door Gods.

on the doors are painted two giant pictures of the door gods; they were ministers of state in the Tang dynasty, by the name of Wei Tsukung and Ching Sohpao.

God of Agriculture.—Mangtseang lived about the thirteenth century, and is popularly believed to be able to keep away the plague of grasshoppers. He was a

beardless young man, and exceedingly fond of children.
The mandarins worship him, his temple is found in
every hamlet, theatricals in his honour are quite
renowned, and his processions go to every village. His
birthday is on the 13th of the 1st Moon, and during
the following week a long table is placed before his
youthful majesty, spread with various kinds of food,
fruits, and artificial flowers; and a retinue of angels
bow towards him.

God of Agriculture.

He is also worshipped by the coolies; they say,
Mangtseang went barefoot, and so do we (with only
straw sandals); so we worship him." He is one of the
chief gods of the nation.

Gods of the Tides.—These two gods were Wuynin,
of the kingdom of Wu, whose capital was Soochow, and
Wenchung, of the kingdom of Yuih, whose capital was
Hangchow; they were enemies during life, but now
exercise joint sovereignty over the tides; perhaps to

account for the ebb and flow the Chinese regard it as necessary to have two opposing gods.

The Golden-dragon King.—There are four of these gods and four ministers, but the people along the Yellow River recognise which one it is. They appear as snakes with square heads and with horns; and when the "river king" comes floating on the flood of turbid waters, when

Tidal-god.

there is a freshet on the Yellow River, "China's sorrow," he is hailed with delight, as immediately the "waters assuage." The governor of the river receives the divine snake in a lacquer waiter, carries him in his sedan to the temple, and the mandarins all worship the heaven-sent messenger. This "golden-dragon king," who comes as a serpent, is very fond of theatricals, so the best actors are invited, a programme is placed before him, and he nods towards the play he wishes performed. After some days the coiling god takes his departure, and the governor of the Yellow River memorialises the throne to assign him rank and erect a tablet. These memorials appear in the *Peking Gazette;* one was sent up by an official, now one of the most distinguished of this province, and another it is said, a few years ago, was sent to the Emperor by the " Bismarck of China." Mandarins who do not countenance idolatry, when they are appointed to the control of the Yellow River, are thoroughly satisfied with the divinity of this snake.

The Five Dragons.—The dragon of the east is called

Golden-dragon King.

Jao-Kwang ; of the south, Jao-Chwen ; of the west, Jao-Ming ; of the north, Jao-Kyih ; and of the middle, Jao-Ping. The governor worships twice a year and the prefect twice a month. In times of drought these dragons are worshipped, and in front of the temples there is a pond from which they draw rain. In the inner temple there is an image of Mrs. Dragon.

Temple of Worthies.— In this city there is a temple – it is only a specimen of what is found elsewhere— which contains several hundred tablets of mandarins who have been the benefactors of their race, and of the widows of mandarins, to whom regular sacrifices are offered by the highest officials.

God of the Classics.—He was named Chen Kongchen, and flourished in the Han dynasty, and was able satisfactorily to expound the most intricate passages in the Classics. He adopted the civil measure of punishing the misdemeanours of his handmaids, by requiring them to memorise the words of Confucius, so his Ahmahs became classical scholars.

The god of Writing.—Ts'ang Hieh " was reputed as the inventor of the art of writing in the mythical period of antiquity. He is said to have elaborated the art of forming written characters by imitating the footprints of birds."

The Written Character.—The reverence for the written character, though highly commendable as a part of the national devotion to learning, is carried too far, and becomes a very specious kind of idolatry ; for printed paper is sacred, the sin first mentioned is its misuse, and its preservation the first among meritorious actions. Men with two mammoth baskets suspended from the ends of a pole across the shoulder go along the streets, tear down placards, empty waste-paper baskets, gather up every scrap of written paper, take it to their employers, who pay sixty cents per hundredweight. carry it to the " Pity Character" furnace and burn it. The ashes are sent to the port and carried out to sea, to be thrown overboard in a storm, so as to cause the waves to be stilled. These furnaces or altars are often connected with temples, and large sums of money are thus expended. It is considered an offering to letters, to Confucius, and to the god of literature.

Mencius.—In considering the character of this great

philosopher, the question arises, How can a man become a god in China?   I answer, By the erection of a temple and the offering of sacrifices.   The only temple Mencius has is near his grave in the province of Shantung, where sheep and pigs, by Imperial order, are placed on the altar, but he is not deified in the estimation of the people.   His descendants of the seventieth and seventy-second genera-

Mencius.

tions are now living.   He was born B.C. 371, and died at the advanced age of eighty-four, a contemporary of Plato, Aristotle, Zeno, Epicurus, and Demosthenes.

"The mother of Mencius" is perhaps the most celebrated woman in Chinese annals.   As a widow, she chose her residence near a school, and said, "This is the proper place for my son."   Finding that he was neglecting his lessons she took a knife and cut through the web she was weaving, and when he, astonished, asked the reason, she told him " that her cutting through the web was like his neglecting his lessons." The maternal admonition laid the foundation of his future greatness. In after years, wishing to leave the kingdom of Tse because his doctrines were not practised, he said to his mother, " I wish to leave my position and salary, but I think of your old age, and am anxious." She replied, " You are a man in your full maturity, and I am old. Do you act as your conviction of righteousness tells you you ought to do? Why should you be anxious about me?"

The writings of Mencius form one of the " Four Books," and are memorised by all school boys; the study of most of the contents is like "chewing dry corn stalks," but passages in his works are the brightest, most inspiring discussions to be found in Chinese literature. Confucius was a plain, practical philosopher, who spoke of duty, while Mencius was metaphysical, and reasoned about man's nature. The honour conferred on Mencius is not one ten-thousandth of what the sage receives, and he is spoken of as " A number two saint."

He was in his day "a great professor of morals and learning, who taught the principles of virtue and society." He says, " The way of truth is like a great road. It is not difficult to know it. The evil is that men will not seek it. Do you go home and search for it, and you will have abundance of teachers." Much of his time was spent in the palaces of kings, but Mencius bore himself " loftily," as if a royal teacher.

Under a despotic government he was a bold and brave

man to raise the standard of liberty, and exclaim, "The people are the most important element in a nation, and the sovereign is the lightest." His two principal elements in a successful rule are, "to make the people prosperous, and to educate them." In urging the necessity of educated officials, he says, "Some men labour with their minds and some with their strength. Those who labour with their minds govern others, those who labour with their strength are governed by others."

Mencius' celebrated teachings about human nature are discussed in Chapter II.

Perhaps the nearest approach of a pagan philosopher to the simplicity of Christianity is where he says, "The great man is he who does not lose his child's heart," reminding one of "Except ye be converted and become as little children;" the difference being, "Christ speaks of the child's heart as a thing to be regained; Mencius speaks of it as a thing not to be lost."

The Disciples of Confucius.—The tablets of the five hundred disciples are in the Confucian temples, and have sticks of incense burning before them. Scattered throughout the empire are temples erected near the homes of those students who sat at the master's feet, and thither the local governors repair, offering sheep, pigs, and oxen in sacrifice. If the men who were styled "Jupiter" and "Mercurius" at Lystra rent their clothes when the people cried out, "The gods are come down to us in the likeness of men," and the priest "brought oxen and garlands unto the gates, and would have done sacrifice with the people," surely these temples and animal sacrifices are not simply funereal, but are also idolatrous.

The Eight gods.—In ancient times the Emperor sacrificed to the " eight gods." (1) The Lord of Heaven. (2) The Lord of Earth. (3) The Lord of War. (4) The Lord of the Male Principle of Nature. (5) The Lord of the Female Principle of Nature. (6) The Lord of the Sun. (7) The Lord of the Moon. (8) The Lord of the Four Seasons of the Year.

The Divine Husbandman.—" This title was attributed to Shin Nung, the successor of the great Fuhhe, B.C. 2737." " He first fashioned timber into ploughs, and taught the people the art of husbandry. He discovered the curative virtues of plants, and instituted the practice of holding markets for the exchange of commodities."

Spirits of the Land and Grain.—" The deified being Kow Lung is the universal tutelary genius of the land," and with him is associated Kih Yien, and these two " are the chief presiding influences governing the well-being of the empire." These are worshipped with sacrifices by the highest officials on the open altars, " in the first month of spring, in conformity with traditions of the highest antiquity."

Gods of the Precincts.—Each of the sixteen hundred counties in the empire is divided into a number of districts corresponding to the wards in a city or the precincts in the country, and each of these neighbourhoods has its own special protecting god, besides innumerable sub-divisions of territory, so that there are many hundred thousand, if not one or two millions, of these *t'u-dee* or local gods. Generals, statesmen, crownprinces dying in boyhood, mandarins, doctors, and benevolent men are the tutelary deities of the precincts and wards, and are constantly worshipped.

The god-constables.—Among the class mentioned above, within every yamen, there is a temple to the *t'u-dee* or constable of the district, who acts as chief of police for all the official secretaries and runners. If anything goes wrong in the precinct or ward, a theft or

Granary King.

a riot, the mandarin bamboos the constable, the protector of the public peace; so if in Tartarus the spirits get into a row, the god-constable must answer for it, and the city-god of Hades may have him beaten with one hundred or six hundred strokes, as his divinity thinks proper.

The Prison-god. In the Han dynasty the Emperor directed Siao-Wu to revise the criminal statutes, and at death he was made god of the gaol, by the name of Siao Wang. He is worshipped by the Board of Punishments, the criminal judges, the gaolers, and the prisoners. The latter hope that the gaol-god will keep their guilty consciences at ease, and may open a way to escape. Before execution criminals are dragged into his presence as they are taken from prison, and made to bow to the gaoler of Tartarus.

God of the City Wall. — Called "The Eighth Minister." He rules the city wall, and directs the military operations in case of a siege; he is worshipped by the Board of Public Works.

The Guardian Temples.—There is always a chief guardian of the heir-apparent called the *T'ai Pao ;* his temples are numerous throughout the land, and the highest mandarins offer sacrifice. The *T'ai Pao* is now considered an official title. The Soochow temple is in honour of a crown prince of the Chow dynasty, who, disowned by his father, fled to this city; his temple was rebuilt a few years since by Goo Wu.

Eighth Great King.

The Granary King.—His image is a large one, and he has three eyes. He is worshipped by the landed gentry about the time they collect their "rent rice."

Every granary, or storehouse, has a tablet of this deity.

The Eighth Great King.—The Manchus have a special mandarin to attend to their lawsuits, and "The Eighth Great King" is his counterpart in the other world. He was the "Eighth Prince," an uncle of the last of the Ming Emperors, and cast in his allegiance with the new Manchu ruler. He advised the Soochow people to submit; they, however, stoned him to death, and sunk his boat.

CHAPTER X.

SHAKYAMUNI GAUTAMA BUDDHA, the founder of the religion that bears his name, of royal descent, was born probably about 624 B.C., in Kapilavastu, a city to the north of Benares, the headquarters of the Buddhist faith in India. This was not his first appearance upon the earth, for it is said five hundred and fifty times had he come as vegetable, animal, or man, till now he appears a Buddha. Very convenient it is for the historians of this faith to locate their characters several million years ago, as thus critics have not the opportunity of examining the authenticity of the narrative. In this present kalpa there have been seven Buddhas, all fictitious, one of whom, Janteng, the Lamp-light Buddha, was the celebrated preceptor of our hero in a previous existence.

If name gives fame he was fortunate. His princely name was Siddartha, " All-prospering ; " Buddha means " The Awakener," and was his official title ; Gautama was the sacerdotal appellation of his clan ; among the Celestials he is known as Shakyamuni, "the sage of the Shakya tribe," or, from its significance, Shakya, "the lion,"—as the lion is king of the forest, so by his moral pre-eminence Buddha rules among men.

The Buddhistic legends of this wonderful person are full of romance, and the outlines of the portrait, as seen by the Chinese, here presented, are mostly taken from his "Pictorial Life" in four volumes, published in Hangchow. The legends from the Indian Ocean deal more in the marvellous than the story as told in this biography. Kind reader, do not ask "Is this authentic?"

Ancestry.—Of his remote ancestry we have some information. A teacher of one of the ancient Buddhas took two lumps of clay mixed with blood, and put them in jars, trusting to a vow that they would become men. After ten months there emerged from these jars two human beings, one a man and the other a woman, who became the rulers of India, and the ancestors of a line of rajas, one of whom begat four sons; the eldest was Suddhodana, the father of Shakyamuni. As Buddha was to appear among men, at the arrival of the due time he sought the most prosperous kingdom and the family under the luckiest star. He considered the merits of several countries, and found that they lacked in one particular or another of being the "model state;" but, with the assistance of the Devas "going through the court almanac of Indian princes and princesses," at last selected Kapilavastu, seated in the very centre of the earth, and King Suddhodana and his bride as the elect parents.

His Birth.—In a dream Queen Maya sees the heavenly Buddha riding upon a white elephant with six tusks, and entering her right side her body became transparent as glass. The seer gave an answer to the inquiring king that a sage was to be born who should glorify the Indian faith. Heaven supplied Maya with food. In the palace garden, under a Palasa tree, which bent down its branches around Her Majesty, was the young prince born, a Buddha,—not as a man, for out of the side came he forth, the four regents of the skies presenting him to his happy mother. A light illumined the heavens, a rainbow stretched athwart the sky, a multitude in the air sang,

Buddha.

there was a shower of roses, and nine dragons spouted water, for him to bathe in fountains both cold and hot. The babe walked seven steps to the four points of the compass, and with an expressive wave of his tiny hand said, "Above heaven and under heaven, I alone am great."

When the tidings reached the palace the king thought, What carriage is suitable to bring him in? A chariot is sent from Heaven, and the gods walk with men, and push it along in the triumphal procession, while maidens from Mount Sumaru went before with singing. The aged Asita comes in, takes the babe in his arms, points out his thirty-two marks and eighty symbols, the tattoo of the Devas, the signs of destiny, foretells his future as a teacher, and weeps because at fourscore he could not see the mighty things about to come to pass.

The Infant Buddha.

Suddhodana ordered a release of criminals, the liberation of animals, and 3,200 priests to chant prayers. Princes and nobles, merchants and peasants rejoiced, and the brute creation showed their joy; it is recorded that at that time cows gave ten quarts of milk.

His Boyhood. — The young mother left him an orphan of seven days. His aunt tenderly cared for him with thirty-two nurses, eight to carry him, eight to bathe, eight to feed, and eight to play with him. He grew in stature day by day, as the moon increases night by night from the crescent to the full orb. One day, carried in the arms to the temple, the idols rise and bow to him, owning his sovereignty, the worshipped taking their place as worshippers. During eight years he played in the palace garden; it is said that his dear aunt made him a golden saddle to ride a goat. Of his differing from other children it is recorded that he did not cry, nor frown, nor pout, that he kept his clothes unsoiled, and his nose clean.

The king chose the most renowned teacher the realm afforded for the prince, who walked into the schoolroom and asked, " Will you teach me Sanscrit and the sixty-four books of the Immortals ? " The preceptor listened with amazement to his skill in numbers, as he ran through a trigonometrical table.

" At fifteen years of age he was, in an assembly of nobles and Brahmans, formally invested with the rank of heir-apparent." The lords presented to his royal father basins of water brought on their heads from the four seas, which, mingled with oil, was sprinkled on Siddartha's head, after which he was saluted as Crown-Prince, and received the seal of the seven precious things. He grew up with princely mien, yet gentle and wise, a handsome and thoughtful youth, with a serious face and sad countenance; an old head on young shoulders. " His father, however, became displeased at the religious and melancholy tone which pervaded the prince's life, and tried to educate him in the arts and accomplishments suited to the future occupant of a great throne." As was wont with the Shakya princes, he was trained in gymnastics, and excelled all in archery, wrestling, and other manly exercises. Soon he had occasion to use his skill.

Love at First Sight.—The king issued a proclamation : " The Prince Royal desires the fair ladies of the Shakya clan to assemble at the court, when he will distribute precious ornaments." Accordingly there came to the festival a lovely and charming company, " all excel-

ling in beauty, decked with costly jewellery, and arrayed
in finest robes," as competitors in grace and loveliness.
The umpire was no other than Siddartha, who, placed
upon a rural throne, gave gifts to each,—gems, and
pearls, and costly toys.—as one by one the flowers of
Kapilavastu's capital filed before His Highness. Each
one, because of the grace of the prince's demeanour, could
not look him in the face, but, passing by and bowing,
took her gift and departed, the tender-hearted king, with
the assembled throng, watching his countenance to see
on whom his eyes would fasten ; but the "playful smiles,
arch looks, and tender blushes" were all lost on the
youthful and solemn face.   Just then the prince was seen
to start, as the beautiful Yasodhara, a dark-eyed Indian
maiden, claimed her prize, and " love looked love to eyes,"
as upon her he bestowed his signet ring and necklace of
pearls.   She was asked in marriage, but the father said
other suitors claimed her hand, so let the contestants
" engage in feats of manliness," " the victor's crown to be
Yasodhara," who now in her turn sits upon a dais to watch
the exploits of youthful warriors.   Siddartha called for
the ancestral bow, which only Sinhahanu could use, and
as he thumbed the string the people with trepidation
asked, " What sound is that ? "   He then sent the arrow
which pierced seven iron drums and seven iron pigs.
Mounted on Kantaka, his noble steed, none could equal
him in equestrian sports.   The result was that the Prince
Imperial " selected a lucky day, and led home to his
palace the beautiful Yasodhara, adorned with gems and
jewels, and attended by five hundred bridesmaids."

The Indian Paradise.—Suddhodana built for them

a marble palace in the royal park, surrounded by a high wall with a gate guarded by helmeted warriors, and provided three thousand nautch girls, in three gay bands by day and by night, to play and to dance.

> "Thus passed ten years,
> With lovely sights were gentle faces found,
> Soft speech and willing service, each one glad
> To gladden, pleased at pleasure, proud to obey ;
> Till life glided beguiled like a smooth stream
> Banked by perpetual flowers, Yasodhara
> Queen of the enchanting court."

The measures his father adopted were ineffectual in averting the dread fate so early announced by Indian seers. " He, the most learned and the most powerful of men, came to sad grief through women. All Buddhistic traditions agree in stating that it was the experiences with the ladies of his harem which disgusted him with the whole world, and put him in a misanthropic mood." He lived in a false world of music and tinsel, and sighed to learn of men and things as they actually existed. His father assented to his request, and issued a mandate, that the streets of Kapilavastu be swept and sprinkled with scented water, the ground carpeted with flowers, and that the people array themselves in holiday attire to welcome their future king as he rides forth in his chariot.

Age, Sickness, and Death.—Amidst the greetings of the happy multitudes, his eyes, which had only beheld youth and beauty, were fastened upon an old decrepid man, bent down with years and infirmity, a staff supporting his tottering limbs. " Charioteer, what is this?" "Great Prince, this man is old." "And what does *old* mean?" "The body wastes away, the limbs grow feeble; mind and memory gone." "And my body, —must I grow old?" "Even so, holy prince, rich and poor share this common lot."

Again he essayed beyond the gates of the city, when there appeared before Siddartha a sick and pain-worn man, lean and yellow, upon whom the plague had seized, as anon with his writhings, almost expiring, he rolled in the dust, crying, "Alas! Alas! pity, master, pity." "Who is this unhappy being?" The coachman answered, "It is a sick man." "And what is sickness?" "This man's body is unsound, and his limbs helpless; he endures pain without remedy." Again the prince inquired, "Is sickness common to man generally?" to which Channa replies, "Gods and men alike are unable to avoid this misery." "And must I some day be sick?"

The next time he sallies forth he beholds a corpse. "Who is this lying on his bed, with people following him, lamenting as he is carried onwards?" "Most holy prince, this is a dead body." "And what is death?" The garrulous Channa, who drives him, answers, and the prince asks, "Must I also die?" "Neither gods nor men can escape this inevitable fate."

The Flight.—At night he listens to voices in the air, the Devas calling him to abandon sensual pleasure and seek for rest. He arises from his bed, and passing through the hall, the lamps untrimmed, smoky and defiled with oil, the women asleep in every unseemly position, uneasily moving and muttering, some with eyes half-closed, others dribbling from their mouths, grinding with their teeth, and snoring through their noses, he exclaims, "Where is beauty when the decorations are taken away, the jewels removed, and the gaudy dress laid aside? I will go; the time has come."

Returning to his wife's chamber, built of white marble, with soft light falling on the royal couch from perfumed lamps, he gazed a long farewell, and "once for all forsook his home, his kindred, and his kingdom."

He calls for his noble steed Kantaka, strokes his mane, mounts the saddle, and bids him fly on the wings of the wind. The Devas cause a deep sleep to fall on all within the palace walls, the clanging hoofs on the stones are not heard, the sentinels awake not, and, the gate which takes five hundred men to open, and whose creak may be heard for many yojanas, flies open, and the prince flees. Reaching the forest, he sends back horse and groom, saying to the latter, "I to-day have left my kingdom, with only you to follow me; you follow me both in heart and in body. Tell my father I am not angry or unfilial, but all creatures are deceived, and not on the true road, and I wish to save them. Take this royal mantle and circlet of pearls to my wife, and say, "Love must have separations. I wish to mitigate suffering."

The Great Renunciation.—Siddartha no more, prince no longer, Shakyamuni "made his great renunciation complete by cutting off with his sword the long locks of the warrior" and putting on the yellow robe. By all the severe tortures of Brahminism he seeks "the path," he dwells in the jungles far away from the haunts of men, with shaven pate and soiled garments, in squalor and discomfort. From that day, as "the author of a religion, his name has become a household word of reverence among millions of people. Yet the glory which has gathered around the name of this historical individual has utterly dazzled the eyes of his followers, and made them forget the real man in order to grasp at a fictitious deity."

The Hermit.—He dwelt among the immortals who lived on weeds, fruits, and flowers,—some with one meal a day, some one in two days, and some one in three days. He took his seat, tailor-fashion, with eyes fixed on the end of his nose, and counted his breathings to keep from thinking, with daily one head of wheat and one of hemp for his diet during the four seasons of six long years; he did not arise to attend to the necessities of the body, with no difference in his position, without moving to one side or the other, without leaning to either side or on anything, with nothing to protect his head from the wind or rain, insensible even to the droppings of the birds; his eyes did not look aside, and his heart was without fear.

After six years of penance he was so lean he could scarcely move, and his body was like a dried tree, when two kind milkmaids brought him milk and he was strengthened. His clothes all rotten, he spied old raiment under a tree. His biographer states that the fame of his mortification "spread abroad like the sound of a great bell hung in the canopy of the skies."

At this time, there arrives a delegation of nobles sent by his father to invite him back to his palace, and urge upon him to receive the kingdom, which offer he declines.

Mara and his Temptations.—Then comes the time when the tempter tries his power. Shakyamuni advances to the Bodhi-tree, when a delegation of women from

Onset of Devils.

the harem of Hades try their seductive arts, but fail to tempt him to leave the "lion's throne," a cushion of grass prepared by heavenly hands.

He then fell into the agony of a mental conflict, which the legends portray by more than a Miltonic picture of a battle between Buddha and Mara. The devil

assembles the hosts of the infernal regions, and tells them
that a Buddha is about to appear. Three onslaughts he
makes on the lone man seated beneath the tree; the
legions of hell, myriads upon myriads, to the number of
800,000,000, riders upon elephants and camels, cavalry,
infantry, chariots, flag-bearers, cannibal-spirits armed
with arrows, spears, and clubs, the dragons riding on black
clouds; all with mighty shouts, and flashing lightning
and hail storms: thus onwards Mara leads Hades in battle
array. The leader cries, "One man, what can you do?
Get out of the way!" He brandishes a sword, and says,
"I'll cut you in two." The recluse waved his hand, and
there were earthquakes, at which elephants, camels, horses,
chariots, dragons, and spirits fled in dire confusion, and
bows and spears covered the ground. Some of the army
of darkness escaped to the mountains, some to the caves,
while Mara and a portion of his legions prostrated themselves before Buddha.

Attaining to Buddhaship.—Seated beneath the Bodhi-
tree, the *Ficus religiosa*, he remained steeped in a sort
of ecstatic meditation during the whole night. "He
forced his mind as the night wore through to a strict
sequence of thought, and as morning dawned the light
he so long sought broke upon him, and he reached the
goal of absolute intelligence; freed from the bondage
of sense, perception, and self, he has broken with the
material world and lives in eternity." Thus by a purely
human process the Prince Imperial of India found the
light, and painfully won his way to Buddhahood; now
no longer man, he is Buddha, The Enlightened, The
Awakener.

The Heart of Pity.—It is recorded in his youth that the royal prince, going out to witness a ploughing match, "seeing the tired oxen, their necks bleeding from the yoke, the men toiling beneath the mid-day sun, and flocks of birds devouring the insects in the upturned soil, his heart was filled with grief, as a man would feel who saw his own household bound in fetters." And with increasing years grew his compassionateness, his "countenance glowing with the burning passion of love" to a world of woe. Who can live on the plains of Asia and not sympathise with suffering humanity? During twoscore years he entered the hovels of the poor and was familiar with distress and want; the burden of the labourer "toiling for leave to live" rested as a load upon his back; the wails of the mourner, the groans of the sick, and the cries of the orphan filled his ear; the suffering world so vast, the "agony of earth" so great, creatures in bondage, "caught in this common net of pain and woe," lay upon his heart; the spectacle of misery, crime, decay, desolation, and death rose before his eyes.

"To reign as a great king, to be courted by the high and feared by the low, to be rich in the spoils of the world, all seemed to him contemptible. The honour to which he aspired was to redeem the countless millions that would be born into the world from their sins and sorrows, and guide them in a way leading to peace." "Through the soft strains of the musicians he heard the groans of sorrow; his eye looked beyond the fantastic movements of nautch girls under the glitter of the lamp, to the moans of those in darkness; beyond the perfumes of his garden he perceived the nausea of death; beyond the pride of life and the pomp of kings floated visions of decay and dissolution, of ghastly suffering and never-ending bondage."

Buddha stated his object in leaving his palace as four-fold. 1. To save suffering creatures. 2. To be as a lamp and medicine to those in blindness and darkness. 3. To teach men not to live for self. 4. Seeing all creatures as if bound to the wheels of the three worlds, like a thread coiled round and round, to unloose them. Perhaps at times his pity was carried to an extreme. Mara says to Buddha, "Will you not have a heart of pity and save my life?" Buddha, merciful as a father, comforted the devil.

His Manhood.—"When God through the absurdities of polytheism was pushed out of view, the substitute was Buddha, the perfect sage, the model ascetic, the patient and loving teacher, the wonder-working magician, the acknowledged superior of gods and men."

"He is a world-born man, who washes away his sins, like others, by penances, offerings, and the teaching of some enlightened instructor. He is not said to create the universe, nor to act as the judge of mankind. He is simply a teacher of the most exalted kind, who, by superior knowledge, passes out of the metempsychosis, and gradually attains the Nirvana. His attitude towards his disciples is simply that of an instructor, not an authoritative superior. In fact, the character ascribed to Buddha is rather that of a saviour than that of a god. The object of his life and teaching is to rescue living beings from their misery."

The Tola of Mustard Seed.—Kisagotami, three years

since a bride, rejoiced in a first-born son, but just as his
pattering feet were making glad both heart and home, he
was taken sick, grew worse and worse, and the anxious
mother, fearing to lose her precious boy, carried him
clasped to her bosom, seeking healing from physicians.
Some one said, "Ask the holy man with the yellow
robe if there be cure for thy son." She, prostrate, prays,
"Lord and Master, what medicine will heal my child?"
Said he, "Go fetch a tola (two ounces) of mustard seed,
but take it not from any hand or house where father,
mother, child, or slave hath died." The sad face went
from door to door, and all had the handful of mustard
seed to give, but when she asked, "Hath death e'er
entered this abode?" the reply would come, "Lady, what
is this you ask? The dead are very many and the
living few." Father or mother, husband or wife, son or
daughter, had thence been borne to the funeral pile.
Leaving the cold treasure in the forest, broken-hearted,
Kisagotami comes again to Buddha. "Hast thou pro-
cured the mustard seed?" "Great Sir, I could not find
a single house where none had died." Shakyamuni
said, "You thought you alone had lost a son; the law of
death reigns over all creatures. I seek the secret of
that curse,—*bury thou thy child.*" There was no balm
in Gilead, there was no physician there.

All Flesh.—The scheme of Buddha was all-embracing.
It was not designed merely to emancipate man from
sorrow, but all that hath life and breath. Constantly
reiterated was his teaching about "all creatures," "all
living things," "all sentient beings." Men and beasts,
birds and fish, reptiles and insects, are all on an equal

basis. His maxim was, "All the animal kingdom are born free and equal." The soul of a dog was like the soul of a man, the soul of a flea equal to the soul of a prince. If there was one marked characteristic of his ministry, it was that he accounted himself the Saviour of the lower animals.

Ascending to Heaven.

It is recorded that after his six years' fast he thought it time to take a bath. An angel pointed his finger to the earth, and it became a pool.

After his purification the water was taken up to Heaven, and all the fish and tadpoles ascended to Paradise. He bathed in order to save them.

Animal Sacrifices.—When passing through a distant kingdom, he saw hundreds of sheep driven along. Buddha inquired " Where are these sheep being driven ? " The answer was, " The king's mother is sick, and he will offer this flock in sacrifice to Heaven." He follows, obtains the ear of the king, and discourses on taking life. " You take animal life to save your mother's life ; to sacrifice a hundred years is not equal to mercy ; sacrifice is as fornication ; the murder of a sheep and the murder of a man are equal crimes ; if a man in worshipping the gods sacrifices a sheep and so does well, why should he not kill his child and so do better ? " This is the sum of Buddha's views about animal sacrifices. These sentiments seemed to be highly appreciated by the gushing Edwin Arnold, who in the mouth of a bonze thus styles his hero : " Lord Buddha," " Lord and friend," " Ah ! Blessed Lord," " King and high conqueror," " Oh ! High deliverer," " Hailed and honoured," " All honoured," " Incomparable," " Wisest, best, most pitiful," " Ah ! lover, brother, guide, Lamp of the Law."

Æsthetics.—At the birth of Buddha there was music in the air, and at every important event during his life the choirs of the Devas sang, harps were tuned by invisible hands, and sweet voices were heard in the aerial vaults. His historians record that scores of times showers of fragrant flowers from the gardens of Paradise fell along his pathway, so that he then trod on a bed of roses. Light would also often shine round about Shakyamuni. When a youth he sat beneath a tree and glory sat upon his brow. Suddhodana, his father, seeing it, said, " It was like fire upon the mountains, and the moon among the stars." At another time, " His body, bereft of all its jewels, emitted a soft and dazzling light like the beams of the sun piercing through a dark cloud, and spreading all around the brightness of its glory." As he walked, "Glories issued from his body and lighted the road." A halo of golden hue was the only crown which adorned his brow. At any moment the lightning would flash from his fingers ; again his face would be like the sun, and the assembly of his disciples would be lit up as if by a score of electric lights.

Discussions with the Brahmans.—When Buddha left the palace he went to the great teachers of India. It was told the philosopher Alara, that "the son of Suddhodana—the lord of the Shakyas, desiring to escape from sorrow and attain supreme wisdom, bright and glorious as a pillar of gold, his body full of grace and beauty, no other than the great lion among men—is coming."

Alara thus addressed him, "Other kings have forsaken empires, but only when satiated with pleasure, but thou, so young, and in the vigour of youth, to give up the certain enjoyment of royalty and to prefer the hardships of life in a desert, the companion of beasts and the unfettered birds, wonderful indeed is this!"

Shakyamuni replied, " I find that all men are fettered with the chains of birth and death, old age and disease, unable to free themselves, and therefore I am seeking a way of escape. I search for that which is imperishable and permanent."

Alara, "on the general testimony of the Shastars, instructs Buddha that the first condition of religious discipline is that the life be strictly that of an ascetic, and, the mind passing through the various grades of abstraction, the man may at last attain full joy and arrive at a complete deliverance."

Buddha points out that the deliverance is not final, as there is a possibility of returning again from this condition, because there is still the idea of personality, and there still remains the *Ego*,—"I have obtained Nirvana."

Alara says, "This condition of escape that admits of no return to life and its troubles is that of the Great Brahma, whose existence is one of perfect quietude, without beginning, without end, without bounds or limits, no first or last, his operations are inexhaustible, his form without parts or marks, immutable, incorruptible."

"But if this be so," replies Buddha, "what becomes of him when at the end of the kalpa this heaven and earth are burnt up and entirely destroyed,—WHAT THEN BECOMES OF YOUR CREATOR ?"

Alara asks, "What is the system of deliverance after which you look ?"

Shakyamuni replies, "I seek a system in which there shall be no discussions about the senses or their objects, no talk of death or birth, disease or old age, no questions about existence or non-existence, about eternity or non-eternity, in which words shall be useless, and the idea of the boundless and illimitable realized."

The Itinerant.—After he left the Bodhi-tree he travelled on the "circuit," but his circuit embraced India with its many principalities, and Ceylon, going from city to city and village to village teaching. It is remarkable how much work he did in the hamlets. He often sought the forest, and from afar crowds came to listen. His band of immediate followers numbered 1,250, but hundreds of thousands flocked around him as he passed from place to place. He began "a course of public open-air preaching, a perfectly novel thing in his time." He was a John the Baptist, with his alms bowl, shaven pate, and yellow robe, the sensation of that land and age. "His royal appearance and princely bearing, his well-tested self-abnegation, his boundless charity, his skill in persuasion, his originality in teaching, all contributed to his success." Marching at the head of a priestly brigade, *uniform* in their flowing robes of yellow, and armed only with the beggar's bowl, he commanded the attention of the ruling rajahs, several of whom accepted his instructions.

"Leaving Mount Pandara, surrounded by a vast crowd, Buddha advanced steadily onwards, his body perfectly erect, his eyes fixed before him and his garments all strictly arranged, and as he passed through the streets those who were engaged in buying and selling, or others who were drinking in the wine shops, all left their engagements and were wrapped in awe as they beheld Buddha and followed. So also countless women in the city gazed at Buddha from the corners of the doorposts, from the windows, from the balconies, and from the tops of the houses, and as they watched him go from door to door their hearts were filled with unutterable joy, as they spoke to one another, 'Who is this that has come hither, his person so beautiful and so joy-giving as he moves?' 'What is his name?' 'What caste or family does he belong to?' 'Is he brahman or Shaman?'"

Buddha said of himself, "I am no god or spirit, but a

plain man seeking for rest, and so am practising the rules of an ascetic life." He described himself as "the father and mother of his helpless children; their guide and leader along the precipitous path of life; shedding the light of his truth like the sun and moon in the vault of Heaven; providing a ferry-boat for passengers over this vain sea of shadows; as a propitious rain-cloud, restoring all things to life, providing salvation and refuge by directing men into the final path that leads to Nirvana."

His Opponents.—He, like the Judean teacher, came to find a state of formalism among the religionists of India. He was not so much the founder of a new sect as the Martin Luther among the Brahmans, for he "re-modelled every Brahmanical dogma, and placed every Brahmanical doctrine in a new light." The Brahmans opposed him throughout his career, and several times he was summoned to discussions before an Oriental Diet of Worms. The "six teachers," like the scribes and Pharisees, tried on every public occasion "to entangle him in his talk." One secret of his popularity was his pronounced opposition to the powerful caste-spirit in India, and its tyranny in civil life; his asserting the rights of the democracy, and declaring that his religion was a religion of mercy to all.

The Monastic System.—His first disciples were from the fire-worshippers, perhaps the original Parsees, who were converted more by the use of magic than by the power of his logic; whole sects changed their religion and became his followers. He thus "gradually founds a new religion; crowds of fanatic followers gather around him; men of all ranks and all classes, taking the vow of perpetual chastity and voluntary poverty, follow him clad in rags, begging and preaching." His ecclesiastical organization is built upon the idea that the Church is a kingdom of priests, and that only the priests belong to the Church. "As Shakyamuni was the first in time of the founders of monastic communities, so he surpassed them all in the originality of his conceptions, in the success of his system, and in the force of his influence." His "practical genius" was seen in gaining a livelihood for the community by the gifts of kings, the liberality of new members, and the charity of all kindly disposed, and "in a few years India was covered, through the labours of the Buddhist preachers, with flourishing communities of monks," who sat at the feet of their teacher during the rains and the heat, but "in the cool season of the year the Bikshus or religious mendicants were everywhere seen on the roads and in the cities teaching the true path."

As soon as the number reached fifty-six, he scattered them for work, and in his later years enjoined, "Let no two go the same road." He also conferred the power on his priests of receiving men into the priesthood, and gave this formula of faith,—

I take my refuge in Buddha.

I take my refuge in the Law.

I take my refuge in the Church.

Afterwards, when among his followers were many women, he established "an order of sisters of charity," thus giving to women the chance of salvation.

The Wheel of the Excellent Law.—His first public appearance was at the great religious centre of northern India. "I now desire to turn the wheel of the excellent law; for this purpose I am going to Benares to give light to those enshrouded in darkness." He commanded his disciples, "Explain the beginning, the middle, and the end of the law to all men." "Turning the wheel of the excellent law," is the figure of grinding by which the "chaff and refuse are forced from the good flour." "The wheel of doctrine revolved thrice; first, didactic statement, then exhortation, and lastly appeal to personal experience." Buddha said, "I ought to open the gate of the sweet law, who shall first hear it?"

The Ten Prohibitions.—Once in an assembly of all the gods he delivered the ten great and the forty-eight small commandments. 1. Do not take life. 2. Do not steal. 3. Do not commit adultery. 4. Do not lie. 5. Do not drink. 6. Do not slander priests and nuns. 7. Do not praise self. 8. Do not be stingy. 9. Do not get angry. 10. Do not abuse the "three precious ones" (Buddha, the Law, and the Church).

The Deer Park.—The "deer park" at Benares was the chief seat of his school, and here from time to time, during fifty years, he gave the new law to India. The preponderance of his teaching was ethical, and generally spoken in a simple, pointed style. As an author, his chief works were, "The Sutra of the Forty-two Sections," "The Diamond Sutra," "The Sutra of Establishment," "The Lotus of the Good Law," and "The Doctrine of Nirvana," which were discourses written out by his disciples. One of his "Sermons on Wisdom" was delivered to the "Benevolent King," Prasenajit. "At first Buddha appeared like the sun in the east illuminating the tops of the western hills." "The Lotus of the Good Law" marks the time when "his sun reached the zenith and cast no shadow." This was delivered at the close of his public life, and " is regarded as the mellowest and richest of his productions." Buddha said, "I am not to be destroyed, but shall be constantly 'on the mount of instruction;'" *i.e.*, he would live in his teachings.

The Brevity of Life.—Shakyamuni said, " Life was like a tree from whose roots the earth is washed by a stream ; it was like sketching on water, and like the moon in water; like the flight of an arrow, like a deception, and as a dream ; like a bubble, a shadow; like heat, like dew, passing as quickly as a flash of lightning. Sometimes as he spake the hearts of the audience were melted, and they went after him in love.

The Body.—His great text was the vanity of all below ; the body is the seat of evil, the fountain of misery. From the human passions come sorrow ; subdue these, free yourself from all that is human, and then will the root of misery be extirpated. He says, in his Chinese Biography, " Beloved, that which causes life causes also decay and death. The very nature of the body, however pure, involves the necessity of decay and therefore of change. To have a body is the worst of evils; the body is the fountain of misery ; labour, fear, and sorrow are from the body."

He says, " To follow my law there must be faith ; the doctrine is pure and white ; do not forget the fruits; it is better to lose one's life than to do unrighteousness ; do not take life ; do not commit the ten evils, but you must perform the ten good actions ; the good and evil rewards are now in our actions, mouths, and hearts."

Know Thyself.—A party of thirty princes and twenty-

nine princesses were on a picnic excursion, when they met
a person, and though they were not well acquainted with
her, yet they invited her to join them in their pleasure
trip. By-and-by, when they were all asleep, she stole
all their jewellery and made off. They tried pursuit, and
meeting with Buddha asked him " if he had seen a
woman ?" He replied, " Princes, is it best to seek that
woman or to seek yourselves ?" They said, " Of course,
it is best to seek ourselves." To which Shakyamuni
responded, " Then wait a little, and I will preach to you
the law." They became Buddhists.

Birth, Age, Misery, and Death.—His ministry was
devoted to these four topics. The burning question,
How can the essence of birth and death be destroyed ?
His " four truths" were *duka*, misery ; *samudaya*, the
passions as the cause of misery ; *niroda*, the extinction
of the passions ; and *marga*, the path of reformation.
The first stage is meditation ; feeling and seeing will be
cast away, and you will have a happy heart. The second
stage ; you cast away a happy heart, have true thoughts,
and so obtain the root of pleasure. The third stage ;
you cast away misery and pleasure and have pure
thoughts. The fourth stage ; no thought. He asked
candidates for church membership, " Do you know that
seeing, receiving, thinking, doing, knowing, are all of
short duration ?"

The Ego.—Some of Skakyamuni's teachings do not
seem to a careful reader to be very distinct. Buddha
said, " The not thinking, not not thinking place, has it ' I
or has it not ? If without the *Ego*, you cannot say of
it, Not thinking, not not thinking. If there is the *Ego*,

is it the knowing 'I' or the not knowing 'I'? If there is no knowledge it is to be like grass and wood; if there is knowledge, there is something tangible; if it is tangible, it must be defiling, and so the man is not free. Knowledge is the root of the five *yin* (seeing, receiving, thinking, doing, and knowing); by knowledge, thought is begotten; thought begets the sight of the beautiful. Looking at the body you must not consider the body as existing; thus you can leave the *Ego* and also leave the place where the *Ego* dwells. Misery springs from matter; getting rid of matter, a man is set free from misery. Not to think of 'I,' of men, of creatures, of age,—to leave all thought, this is to be Buddha." It is necessary to have a heart fixed on nothing, a heart which dwells nowhere.

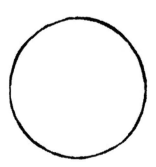

Buddha's Teaching.

He embraced his teachings in a circle—The path is to emptiness, from emptiness to the shoreless region of knowledge, from the shoreless region of knowledge to the useless, from the useless to the not thinkable, from the not thinkable to the not not thinkable, from the not not thinkable to the region of the destroyed, the ceased, the motionless; from the region of the destroyed, the ceased, the motionless, to the not not thinkable, from the not not thinkable to the not thinkable, from the not thinkable to the useless, from the useless to the shoreless region of knowledge, from the shoreless region of knowledge to emptiness, and thus around and around in perpetual motion.

"Can Buddha's words be explained?" asks one. A

disciple replies, " There is no fixed law ; Buddha's law you cannot explain, you cannot take hold of ; it is not law, not not law."

The Previous Existence.—Much of Buddha's talk was about what happened in a previous life. Had he been a teacher of the present generation, some one would have asked if his consciousness testified of this previous existence or was he " drawing on his imagination "? He often spoke of cause and effect, the cause in a life previous to the present, and the effect in this. A happy life resulted from good deeds done before the party lived in mortal flesh ; poverty and suffering because of sin or stinginess in the life gone by. The doctrine of causation runs throughout Buddhistic literature.

An aged man of two hundred years came to Buddha and told him of all his troubles. " I am unfortunate, poor, cold, and hungry. I want to die, but cannot." The sage of India says, " Sins have a root ; in a previous existence you were rich and learned, but you lightly esteemed men, and were unwilling to be charitable. If you wish to know your state in a previous age, look at your estate at present ; if you wish to know your estate when you return to this world, look at your present deeds. Men are poor because when before on earth they would covet and steal. Why now rich ? Because of charitable acts in a previous life." The charity which he insisted on most of all was giving to the priests.

One day as Shakyamuni entered a room, a dog which was hiding under a bed came out barking furiously at him. Shakyamuni said to the dog, " You are protecting money," which remark made the animal very angry ; he lay down and would not eat. The master returning asked the reason why his favourite dog was thus pining away. The servants said, "Shakyamuni has been here." He then went to see the sage to inquire what he had done to his dog. The latter quietly remarked, "That dog is your father." The gentleman rejected the imputation. Shakyamuni says, "If you do not believe me, go and ask the dog where money was hid in a previous life." He did so, and the dog grabbled up the silver hoarded in the earth beneath the bed.

Parables.—The Indian teacher constantly made use of parables. There is a "Book of the Hundred Parables." Over thirty are recorded in his Biography, from which the following are selected.

The Prudent Quail.—Ages ago, there was a certain fowler, who having found a secluded spot where the birds often lighted, proceeded to the place, and making a covering of twigs and branches he shielded himself as he lay in wait. The birds lighting on the top, the fowler slyly put his hand through the branches and captured them. One bird observed that this arbour moved from place to place, while all the other trees stood still, so it kept at a distance from the snare.

At that time I was the wise bird.

"Forget-Favour," the Merchant.—A man named Deputati sent five hundred archers to shoot Buddha. The arrows became flowers. Buddha spoke this parable. A merchant by the name of "Forget-Favour" went in search of pearls. The boat overturned, and a turtle brought the crew to shore on his back. "Forget-Favour" was hungry, and killed the turtle for soup.

I was that turtle, and Deputati " Forget-Favour."

The Mani-Gem.—The Bikshus, his priests, asked, " By what power of resolution and fixed determination the World-Honoured has obtained perfection ? " Buddha replied, " I remember in years gone by that I was a merchant prince who went to sea in order to gather precious gems, and whilst so engaged I obtained one Mani-gem of inestimable value, but I let it fall into the sea and lost it. Then taking a ladle I began with fixed determination to bale out the water of the ocean to recover my gem. The sea-god said, ' How can this foolish man empty the wide and boundless ocean ? ' I replied, ' My resolution shall never flag ; I will bale out the ocean and get my precious gem ; you watch me, and do not grieve and fret at the long delay.' The sea-god, hearing these words, was filled with anxiety for the safety of his realm, and gave me back my gem."

The Cunning Tortoise.—In ancient kalpas, on the banks of the river Paryata, lived a man with a flower-garden, who made wreaths and bouquets for sale. A tortoise at night would come from the water to eat what he found here and there, and mashed down the beds of lovely flowers. In a wicker cage he was entrapped. How shall I escape ? thought he. What device can I adopt ? He addressed his captor with this gatha :

> " I am just from the river and covered with mire,
> Take me to the bank and wash me, I desire,
> Lest the mud on my body, all mingled with sand,
> Should pollute the nice basket you hold in your hand."

The gardener said, " This is good advice, I never thought of that." Immediately he dipped the tortoise in the river, and placing him on a stone flung water on him, when suddenly the tortoise made a dive and escaped, and would not listen to the entreaties of the gardener to return.

I was that tortoise.

The Foolish Dragon.—In years gone by, a dragon living in the great sea saw that his wife's health was not good. He, seeing her colour fade away, said, "My dear, what shall I get you to eat?" Mrs. Dragon was silent. "Just tell me and I will get it," pleaded the affectionate husband. "You cannot do it, why trouble you?" quoth she. "Trust me, and you shall have your heart's desire," said the dragon. "Well, I want a monkey's heart to eat." "Why, Mrs. Dragon, the monkeys live in the mountain forests, how can I get one of their hearts?" "Well, I am going to die, I know I shall."

Forthwith the dragon went on shore, and spying a monkey on the top of a tree, said, "Hail, shining one, are you not afraid you will fall?" "No, I have no such fear." "Why eat of one tree? You cross the sea, and you will find forests of fruits and flowers." "How can I cross?" "Get on my back." The dragon with his tiny load went seaward, and then suddenly dived down. "Where are you going?" says the monkey, with the salt water in his eyes and mouth. "Oh! my dear sir! my wife is very sad and ill, and has taken a fancy to your heart." "What shall I do?" thought the monkey. He then spoke, "Illustrious friend, why did not you tell me? I left my heart on the top of the tree; take me back, and I will get it for Mrs. Dragon." Neptune returned to the shore. As the monkey was tardy in coming down from the tree, the dragon said, " Hurry up, little friend, I am waiting." Then the monkey thought within himself, " What a fool this dragon is ! "

Then Buddha said to his followers, " At this time I was the monkey."

Throwing the Elephant.

Miracles. The White Elephant. — The recorded miracles of the Indian hermit are many. When a boy his father bought a white elephant for him to ride. He grasped it by the trunk, struck it on the neck, killed it, and threw it over the city wall.

In Mid-Air. — At another time, as a pious princess

worships towards the " lion's throne," Buddha and all his
priests, in the full view of the king and his court, came
riding in mid-air on dragons, peacocks, tigers, leopards,
cows, and horses.

The Blind Boy.—There was a stingy father who had
a stingy son. The stingy father after his death returns
to earth, as the blind son of a blind mother, whose
husband sends them out to beg. They go to the house of
the stingy son who is still living. The porter throws him
out of the gate, cracks his skull, and breaks his arm. At
that time Buddha passes; he gives sight to the boy, and
heals his skull and arm. All who heard of this became
charitable.

Healing the Sick.—On another day Buddha comes
to a house where there is a sick man. He flashes light
in the house; the sick man sees the light and is healed.
Buddha discourses on the cause of disease.

The Threads of His Robe.—The dragons came to
Buddha and said they feared they would be devoured by
the kingfishers. Buddha gave them his robe and said,
" Let each take a thread, and the kingfishers cannot
trouble you." The dragons said, " There are not threads
enough," but as he gave it out thread by thread, the robe
remained intact, so he supplied hundreds of thousands.

The Stone.—In his latter days 300,000 mighty men,
hearing that Shakyamuni was about to die, thought they
would go and move a stone out of the road, which would
be in the way of his coffin. Buddha changed himself into
a priest, passed by, and asked, " What are you doing,
children?" " What do you call us children for?" said
they. " If 300,000 of you cannot move a stone, why not

call you children?" "Oh, you are a giant, are you?"
They then asked, "Can you move the stone?" He
took two toe-nails, shook the stone, then threw it over;
blew his breath and turned it into dust; then he resumed
the form of Buddha and preached to this vast assembly.

The Dragons.—Buddha had frequent dealings with
the myriad Neptunes which inhabited the great deep.
Towards the close of his life he appointed the good dragons
as guardians of his law. At times he had famous encounters. Near the beginning of his ministry, when
travelling in a distant land, his host, who was no other
than Kashiapa, the first Patriarch, told him he would have
to put him in a room haunted by a bad dragon. The
guest assured him it made no difference, entered the
apartment, and sat cross-legged. The dragon came out to
see the intruder and smoke issued; from Buddha's body
also smoke issued. The dragon got in a rage and emitted
fire; Buddha also emitted fire, and the two flames
commingling, the house caught fire. The neighbours
came with fire-engines to extinguish it, but their efforts
were unavailing. Buddha used magic, subdued the
dragon, and shut him up in his rice-bowl. His disciples
wondered that he was not burnt, but he said, "I am pure,
fire cannot harm me."

In another state there were female dragons who
associated with poisonous dragons that sent pestilence
and disease. The magicians failing to expel them with
their charms, the king sent for Buddha. The dragons
spit fire, but from Shakya's head went out gold flame
which changed into thousands of Buddhas "in the air,"
—little images on every side. The dragons fled into

Buddha's shadow, but his shadow was sparkling as the
dew. They came and worshipped him.

The Magician.—On one occasion before the assembled
multitude, the "World-Honoured,' as he was officially
addressed, ascended in the air and displayed his
legerdemain. "First he caused a great fire to ascend
from his head and a stream of water from his foot; he
then mixed the fire and water above and below him:

Kapele.

then he sent forth fire from his back and water before
him; then a flame of fire from his right eye and water
from his left; from his right and left ears and right and
left nostrils the same and the reverse; and in the same
manner fire and water from his shoulders, hands, legs,
feet, thumbs, and great toes: all marvellous to behold.
Then flowed from one hair water, and from another
flashed fire. He then sent forth his six glories, and

walked to and fro in the air. The six glories made him appear like pure gold just poured from the crucible, and the glories extended as did the fire and water."

Amusing Incidents. The Fishermen.—Buddha passed by a river, and found five hundred fishermen

The Lions and the Elephants.

trying to pull out a fish. They called a thousand herdsmen to their aid. The fish had a hundred heads,— horse, donkey, deer, tiger, wolf, hog, dog, monkey, and fox. Buddha asked the fish, "Are you Kapele?" The fish replied, "I am." Buddha said, "Formerly there was a Brahman who had a very intelligent daughter, and

he called the priests to be her teachers, but every time
her instructors knew more than she did she called them
stupid as animals, therefore you see her with such a
head." All the convoys asked to be priests.

The Drunken Elephants.—One of the reigning

Rescuing the Little Devil.

rajahs thought he would play a trick on Shakyamuni, so
invited him and five hundred priests to come to the
capital. He made five hundred elephants drunk, who
madly rushed about and tore down houses. The priests
fly over the city. Buddha and Ananda walk; the army
of elephants make an onslaught. Buddha's five fingers

change into five lions, which rush on the elephants, who kneel and weep. The king repents.

The Goose.—The "World-Honoured" on a journey came to a ferry on the Ganges when the river was swollen up to its banks. The ferryman asked him for his toll. Buddha replied, "I have cast away all earthly riches, and look on them as tiles, stone, earth, and mud." "You can't cross this ferry," said the ferryman. Buddha saw a flock of geese flying across without toll. He said to himself, "I will use magic and pass over," whereupon he flew over as a goose.

The Baby.—Mrs. Devil had five hundred sons, who were cannibals, and especially fond of children as an article of diet. The suffering parents came to Buddha, who caught her youngest son, whom she loved most of all, and put him in a rice-bowl. Mara's wife after searching in vain for seven days came and told Buddha. The latter said, "You have five hundred sons, why go mourning and sorrowing after this one? Others have only three or five." After awhile Buddha told her if she would promise to stop the practice of eating other people's little children she might have her boy. The fond mother promised. He then showed her the baby-devil in a cage, and she called her four hundred and ninety-nine sons to take him out. Their united efforts were unavailing, and at last she appealed to Buddha to turn the little fellow loose. Mrs. Devil leading little baby-devil by the hand is sometimes seen in the temples standing near Buddha.

Nanda.—The younger brother of Buddha was named Nanda. Buddha went to his house, shaved his head, and

made him a priest. Nanda, however, kept thinking about
his sweetheart and drawing her picture on the tiles, and
one day when his elder brother was out he ran away.
Buddha followed; Nanda dodged behind a tree; Buddha
caused the tree to be lifted up and caught him. He

Paradise and Tartarus.

took him up to heaven and showed him the sights.
In one palace there were ladies only. Nanda asked,
"Why only ladies and no men?" An angel told him
this palace was reserved specially for him. Nanda ex-
claimed, "Let me stay now; I do want to stay so much."
"Oh no!" said the ladies, "we are heavenly; you are

of the earth ; finish your mortal existence, and then you
may be born in heaven."

Shakyamuni then led little Bud to hell, where he saw
caldrons of boiling oil and men cooking in them ; one
very hot was empty. Nanda asked, " Who is this for ? "
Mara's attendants replied, " For Nanda, because he will
not be a priest." Nanda said to Buddha, " Oh ! do not
talk to me about heaven ; just let me escape this," and
ever after the yoke of the priesthood was an easy one to
him.

The Monastery of Jeta's Garden.—Several incidents in the life of the World-Honoured sage show
that his boasted asceticism was at times in a measure
limited.

Shakya was invited to Shravasti. He said to the rich
noble who asked him, " You have no good house for me."
" I will build you one," said he. Shakya sends a priest
with him, and they select Jeta's garden as the choicest
locality. The price asked by the owner was, " Pave it
with gold." The nobleman paves it, all save a small
plot. A monastery is built, and King Prasenajit receives
Buddha. This place is famous in Buddhist annals as one
of the seats of the new school of religion. Another
incident of the same kind will be given.

The Feast.—A father every twelfth moon and eighth
day gave Buddha and his disciples a feast. On his
death bed he enjoined upon his son to keep up the custom.
Towards the time Buddha sent a priest to inquire about
the prospects. The son was poor, but he sent word,
" Come on," and borrowed one hundred gold cash from
his wife's relatives and gave the dinner. Buddha blessed

him. The next morning he found the coin restored in his money chest.

For Buddha's teachings about women, see Chapter XVI.

The Parrot and the Bull.—The parrot-king asks Buddha to spend a night in his grove, and on receiving

The Parrots' Grove.

his assent went back and told all the parrots to prepare to meet him. The talking-birds flew around all night, and there were no lions, tigers, or wolves to trouble Buddha. The next night the parrot who gave the invitation died and went to heaven. He returned again to worship Buddha and to receive instruction.

At another time, Shakya went near a pond where there were five hundred water-buffaloes and five hundred cow-boys. The latter called to the passer-by not to go that way, as there was a mad bull. The animal rushed at Shakya with a furious roaring. Shakya's fingers became five lions. A circle of fire was around the water-buffalo, and there was no escape. He came and licked Buddha's feet and worshipped; he died that night and went to heaven.

Faith.—Buddha preached to five hundred families of fishermen, but they would not believe. He kept his seat, but duplicated himself into another man who walked across the river towards them. The fishermen asked him how he did it. He said, "The people on the other bank told me Buddha was here, and that the water was only ankle deep. I believed what they said and found it true." Buddha praised the man, and said this stream was only a few miles wide, but that faith would carry one across the gulf of life and death.

Visits Heaven.—Once, while speaking on a mountain in Ceylon, he was said to have been baptized with fire from heaven.

Not only did he travel throughout India and Ceylon, but he also went to heaven and preached to the star divinities and all the assembly of the gods. He said if the evil stars send disease or pestilence upon mortals let the people chant as follows (Sanscrit): and eighty thousand curses will become eighty thousand blessings. He remained in heaven three months, and his light darkened the stars.

Images.—When Buddha was paying this lengthy visit

to heaven, and enjoying the society of his mother, the king
of Oujein missed him so greatly that he made an image
of Buddha.   An angel announced the fact in the celestial
regions, and on three pairs of stairs a heavenly host
accompanied him on his *descension.*   The king brought

The Image-Maker.

on his head the image, and when it was presented to
Buddha it shook hands at him whom it represented.
Buddha formally addressed the image : " After my decease
you will do great things.   I give my disciples into your
hands."   Then standing on the lower step of the heavenly
stairway he turned to the king of Oujein and said, "There

is no one like you bringing gain and happiness on all creatures." The Regent of the skies then spoke to the king and said, "When Buddha was in heaven he was praising the image-maker." Buddha again spoke, "Any one who makes an image, even a finger's length, of gold, silver, brass, iron, stone, earth, wood, glue, varnish, embroidery, silk, or incense; or who will cut, mould, sew, or paint Buddha's image, will have all blessings and escape all sins." This is the second and great commandment of Buddhism.

Relics.—Two merchants visited Shakya. "Oh! Buddha, we are about to separate from you, what shall we venerate as an object of worship?" He stroked his head, and some of the short hairs adhered to his fingers, which he gave to the merchants, saying, "Take these hairs with you." When the brother-merchants received the hairs they were very joyful, and proceeded on their journey.

Ananda asks, "At your death what shall we do with the relics?" Shakyamuni replies, "My body shall be divided like mustard-seed, and one part must be given to heaven, one to the dragons, and one to the spirits." He gives minute directions about his coffin and the cremation with sandal-wood, which the angels would bring. The relics were to be gathered, put in seven precious bottles, and seven pagodas built. These relics would make heaven and earth "a happy field."

After his death eight Indian kings quarrelled over the relics, but the Devas decided that they, the dragons and the kings, must have equal shares.

Death.—The time drew nigh for the aged Patriarch,

toiling under the weight of fourscore years, to die. His last days were full of preaching and itinerating. The last night he spoke to a number of kings who came to pay their farewell respects. Then he asked that a celebrated heretic be admitted, discoursed at length to him, and saw him inducted into the priest's office. Eight million priests were assembled at Benares, and when he told them of his decease, shortly to be accomplished, tears flowed like rain. Devas, dragons, and devils came and asked him not to die. He exhorted the priests to keep his commandments, not to be entangled with business, and to have nothing to do with divination.

His bed was placed in a group of eight Sala trees, and lying on his right side with his head resting on his hand, as represented in the Japanese temples, he spoke his farewell words: "My beloved sons, if any priest becomes unsteady and backslides from Buddha, the Law, and the Church, remember me, have me before your eyes, and do not be discouraged." He added, "My beloved priests, if you continue to retain your reverence for me, tell it to your acquaintance and friends." Ananda said, "Oh! Buddha, in all this vast assembly there is not one priest who has any doubt, therefore they all love and have regard for you." The last words he ever spoke were, "My beloved priests, the state of being (existence) leads to destruction; do you remember this, do not forget this, I charge you."

Ananda asked a priest, "Has Buddha gone to Nirvana?" and was answered, "He has not yet gone, he has only entered on that state where all pain ceases;" thus from one state of contemplation to another, corresponding to the tiers of the heavens, he entered Nirvana.

Cremation.—When he died the trees grew white, the earth quaked, the sea rolled mud, the rivers became dry, the wind blew sand, and heaven and earth wept.

His mother falls from heaven, and when she recovers from the effects of the shock, the coffin lid opens, and

Rising from his Coffin.

Buddha sits up like the lion king emerging from his den, and from the pores of his skin pour forth rays of light which are transformed into thousands of Buddhas. He comforts Maya.

The generous citizens of Benares make a gold coffin for Buddha, but four, eight, and sixteen coolies could not move it. The Devas cause it to rise, it flies over the city, then travels around seven times, and finally settles on the funeral pile.

Kashiapa, who received the Popedom of the Buddhist Church, arrives after the decease of his master, who in

The Feet.

token of recognition sticks his feet through the coffin. Kashiapa rubbed them and wept. The attempts to fire the sandal wood were unsuccessful till fire went out of Buddha's body; the process of cremation was gradually completed, and the shades of night gathered thick o'er Asia's millions.

CHAPTER XI.

THE ORIENTAL BANYAN.

Its Importance.—The children of Shem occupy the largest of the continents, and nearly one-half the population of Asia is influenced by the teachings and rites of Buddhism. A system that has existed for two and a half millenniums, and has succeeded in drawing into the meshes of its Church organisation a large proportion of the human family, and sways at this time the hearts of so many millions, is worthy of attentive consideration. " The history of eastern Asia is the history of Buddhism." Starting in India, it has spread over Central Asia, Ceylon, Burmah, Siam, Annam, Japan, and China. How like the Banyan, their religious tree, which spreads out its branches over hillside and valley, and drops down a twig which itself takes root, and becomes a mighty trunk, stretching out its arms over the plain ; thus one unique tree becomes a forest of foliage, shutting out the face of the sun, so that those who dwell underneath feel none of the warmth and see none of the light which comes down from heaven ! Arnold says, " Forests of flowers are daily laid upon his stainless shrines, and countless millions of lips daily repeat the formula, ' I take my refuge in Buddha.'" He gave, however, unbridled license to his fancies when he penned the lines, "In point of age, therefore, most other creeds are youthful compared with this venerable religion, which has in it the eternity of a universal hope, the immortality of a boundless love, an indestructible element of faith in final good, and THE PROUDEST ASSERTION EVER MADE OF HUMAN FREEDOM."

The Missionary Spirit.—For two centuries Buddhism made little progress, but after the invasion of India by Alexander the Great the new faith was patronized. King Ashoka, the Constantine of the Buddhist Church, B.C. 250, established the first "Board of Foreign Missions" (Dharma Mahamatra), which sent forth enthusiastic preachers, who, "aided by Ashoka's political and diplomatic influence," went clad in rags and with the alms-bowl in hand to all the surrounding countries. The King set an example by sending his own son as a missionary to Ceylon, and forthwith the whole island embraced the faith. "Thenceforth every caravan of traders that left India for Central Asia was accompanied by Buddhist missionaries." There was no mountain too high, no plain too broad, no desert too barren, for these indefatigable zealots; they went everywhere, teaching the doctrines of Buddha. At this early day eighteen Buddhist monks reached China, but failed to plant their religion.

Its Fate in India.—Strange to say, the land of its birth was not the home of its manhood, for it was transplanted to other countries, and is now almost unknown in India. In the second century B.C. the Buddhist Church there was almost destroyed by persecution, "but this very persecution gave a renewed impetus to Foreign Missions, and soon the priests gained a lasting foothold among the Tartar tribes," just as the persecution after the death of Stephen caused the scattered Christians to go everywhere preaching the word.

Introduction into China.—The sacred books of this religion all agree in stating that the Emperor Mingte (A.D. 61), in the visions of the night beheld "an image of gigantic proportions, resplendent as gold," and that he despatched an embassy to go westward in search of this new religion. Whether this is true, or whether it was because in the campaigns of Central Asia the armies brought an image of Buddha, or whether reports had come that a mighty personage had appeared in Judea, we know not, but, it is said, the embassy returned accompanied by an Indian priest, and bringing "The Sutra of forty-two sections." Buddhism, invited by the Emperor, made an easy entrance into this country.

Europe and Asia.—The Buddhist monks travelled to China in the apostolic era. While they went eastward, Paul and his companions journeyed westward. Western Europe became Christian and Eastern Asia Buddhistic. The soil was just as productive along the Pacific as on the Atlantic, and success attended the efforts to introduce the two religions. On the one hand, the first system has had to contend with the rise and fall of empires and ages dark in human learning; the latter has been supported by a stable government, and has flourished amidst a people devoted to letters. Judging a tree by its fruits, what are the comparative results to the two continents in the four departments of religion, education, philanthropy, and progress? Let the reader answer.

Its slow Growth.—The Chinese of the Han dynasty

did not receive the new faith with open arms, but gradually it wormed itself into favour. The first step was translation; after that the monks were engaged in preaching, in collecting funds, in conducting religious services, and in building monasteries. The pioneer work was a slow and tedious process, for this conservative people looked on the swarthy Indians with suspicion, and could not see the practical advantages of the music of the gong and drum, of the fumes of incense, and lighting candles in the day. "It took three hundred years before Buddhism obtained official recognition, and centuries more before the mass of the people was influenced by it." There are some points to be noted:

1. Buddhism is a foreign religion, yet success attended its introduction; and has not Christianity a hundredfold the advantage?

2. It was by preaching the doctrines of the "lion of the law" that Buddhism was made known, and has not the proclamation of the Gospel of the "Lamb that was slain" a mightier power?

3. It took over three hundred years for this vine from India to take root, and many more hundred years before it covered the land,—is not this an incentive to "long patience"?

4. "At the beginning of the sixth century upwards of 3,000 foreign priests were living in China," and why does not the Church, the Church Universal, give us 3,000 ordained men to go two and two to each city in this land?

The Emperors.—A.D. 61. Mingte sent the embassy which brought the priest, the image, and the book.

A.D. 405, the Emperor " gave a high office to Kumarajiva, an Indian Buddhist, and he was commanded to translate the sacred books, and at the present day his name may be seen on the first page of the principal classics." "More than 800 priests were called to assist, and the king himself, an ardent disciple, was present at the Conference, holding the old copies in his hand as the work of correction proceeded." In A.D. 527, " the Emperor was so zealous a promoter of Buddhism that he became a monk and entered a monastery at Nanking." A.D. 558, an emperor of the Leang dynasty, named Wute, commonly called Leang Wute, became a monk and died of starvation. In the year 760, Taetsung ordered a high stage to be erected for reciting " The Sutra of the Benevolent King," maintained many monks, and joined in the worship of hungry spirits. I-tsung, who ascended the throne 860, was devoted to the study of the Buddhist books. During all these centuries the emperors frequently appointed tens of thousands to the priesthood. A.D. 1300, the Emperor used 3,900 ounces of gold in having the sacred books transcribed in characters of gold, and in 1321 Yingtsung had over 300 tons of copper melted to make images and shrines. The Emperor Shunche, 1644, became a monk on the Soochow hills. The distinguished Ka‘nghe, 200 years ago, gave the yellow porcelain tiles now so conspicuous on the roofs of the great temples at Pootoo, and wrote the celebrated letter to the priests. " The last century, the Emperor Keenlung gave the palace of his grandfather at Hangchow to the Buddhists to be a monastery." " A thousand volumes of Buddhist literature were published by the government with public funds, and numberless prefaces to Buddhist works have been written by Emperors." These are a few specimens of the favour given to the Indian religion by the rulers of China.

Confucian Opposition.—During eighteen centuries Confucianism has maintained a determined opposition to the new faith, bringing its absence of religion to bear against the ritual of Buddhism, and placing its practical philosophy in contrast with the fine-spun theories of the Indian sage. Discussions were held between the B.'s and C.'s in the presence of emperors, the latter " putting forth their best literary efforts to nullify the influence" of the former, and every new century has seen new works issued condemning Buddhism. The majority of the Confucianists consider " its history, followers, and dogmas as all equally hateful." They objected to the religion on the ground of political economy, that " the priests eat the bread of idleness and so impoverish the State," " while outside men are ploughing and women are spinning." The leading objection was that the celibacy of the monks, setting aside the relations of father and mother, husband and wife, destroyed the family, which was the miniature of the State. Their sceptical pens were directed against the doctrines of the non-reality of material objects, transmigration, and future rewards and punishments. They said, " The people were led to neglect the old ways taught by the venerable sages of antiquity, which had shed their brightness over the world, and to go astray in the new paths of outlandish error." „ The very nature of monasticism awoke fears in the bosom of statesmen, after about 300 years, when the number of monks and nuns was very great, and the abstraction of so many from the pursuits of agriculture and other industries was considered an evil."

Persecutions.—The first general persecution was A.D. 426, when "an edict was issued, in accordance with which the books and images of Buddhism were destroyed and many priests put to death. To worship foreign divinities or construct images of earth or brass was made a capital crime." The second was in 458, when "a conspiracy was detected in which a chief party was a Buddhist priest." The third, A.D. 714, when 12,000 " priests and nuns were obliged by a despotic government to return to the common world." The fourth, in 845, was the most severe. " By the edict of the Emperor Wutsung, 4,600 monasteries were destroyed, with 40,000 smaller temples. The property of the sect was confiscated, and used in the erection of Government buildings. The copper of images and bells was made into *cash*, and the gold and silver images sent into the public treasury. More than 260,000 priests and nuns were compelled to return to common employments." Buddhism received another check during the fifth general persecution, when Shitsung closed 30,000 establishments.

The Buddhist Travellers.—" The earnestness and vigour of the Chinese Buddhists at that early period is shown sufficiently by the repeated journeys which they made along the tedious and dangerous route by Central Asia to India. Neither religion nor the love of seeing foreign lands are now enough, unless the Emperor commands it, to induce any of the educated class among them to leave their homes."

A.D. 400, Fahien travelled for fifteen years through Tartary, Afghanistan, Central Asia, and Ceylon, and collected the sacred books; on his return he wrote a book of travels. "The extension of the religion that was then propagated with such zeal and fervour very much promoted the mutual intercourse of Asiatic countries. The road between Eastern Persia and China was frequently traversed, and a succession of Chinese Buddhists thus found their way to the parent-land of the legends and superstitions in which they believed."

In 629, the celebrated Hieuntsang set out on his sixteen years' journey, five of which were spent in studying Sanscrit at Magadha. "His unconquerable will, his dauntless pluck. his genius, and, above all, his fervent zeal and purity of life," place him in a high rank among men of religious enthusiasm. His life and travels, with many "moving incidents" and "hair-breadth escapes," is said to be quite entertaining. A popular romance, with accounts of gods and goddesses, fairies and demons, is based on the account of his journeys. Hieuntsang brought with him "115 grains of relics from Buddha's chair, a gold statue of Buddha three feet three inches high," and, it is said, 657 books, which he assisted in translating. This was a favourable period for Buddhism.

Pagodas and Relics.—The primary object of the pagoda is a depository for the relics of Buddha's burnt body. Shakyamuni prophesied that King Ashoka would erect 80,000 pagodas for the relics which are objects of reverential worship to these religionists.

In A.D. 819, the Emperor sent a delegation of man-

darins to escort a bone of Buddha to the capital. This
called forth from the distinguished statesman, Han Wenkung, the celebrated "Memorial on the Bone of Buddha,"

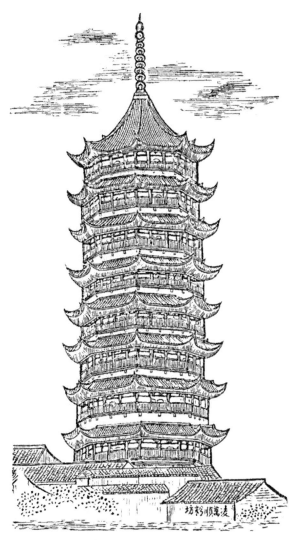

Soochow Pagoda.

which is a standard document among the Confucianists,
and for which he was banished. He was, however, afterwards recalled. "The indignant manner in which Han

Wenkung speaks of the supposed finger-bone of Buddha
is worthy of being imitated by all foes to relic worship."
A thousand years ago this Protestant says, " Buddha has
been dead a long time, and here was the Son of Heaven
bringing this stinking bone of a dead barbarian into the
interior of his palace.   There was not even the preliminary
ceremony of exorcising the noxious demons by whisking
them out with branches of the peach and *lie* trees."
Another Confucianist asks, " What can a bone, or a tooth,
or a nail do for living men ?   If you are hungry these
things cannot feed you, if cold, they cannot clothe you,
and if sick, they cannot cure you."

Confucianists have now turned the pagoda from its
original design into regulators of Fungshuy, or the
influences of the wind and water, by which they obtain
peace and prosperity, longevity and posterity, favourable
seasons and flourishing trade.   The Soochow Pagoda,
erected over a thousand years ago, is now the largest in
the empire ; it is 220 feet in height and 60 feet wide at
the base, tapering up to 45 feet in the ninth story.   It is
in the form of an octagon, and the walls are eight or ten
feet thick.   There is a double wall, or a pagoda within a
pagoda, the steps running between, and as the visitor
ascends a flight of stairs, he has to walk around before
reaching the next steps, making the ascent easy.   There
are seventy-two doors, opening on the verandahs, so it is a
tower full of light, and from every point there are beautiful views of the mountains, the lakes, and the green fields ;
and on beholding the mighty metropolis at the feet,
the densely peopled plain, and the four cities within
sight, the thoughts go out to the many millions within

the range of vision. As there are a hundred large and twenty small images in the pagoda, in every niche and facing every door, and eighty-one idols on the roof, it is a high tower of idolatry.

The Patriarchs.—In some of the temples two men are seen standing on the right and left of Buddha, one with a short white beard and the other with a smooth face; these are Kashiapa and Ananda, the two first Patriarchs. Kashiapa was the head of a sect of fire-worshippers, numbering five hundred, and was converted by seeing Buddha put the dragon into the rice-bowl, recorded in the preceding chapter; his followers also took Shakya as their spiritual guide. It is said he was the means of converting 20,000 to the Buddhist faith. To him was entrusted " the pure secret of the eye of doctrine ; " its symbol ⊔., seen on the breast of Buddha, means 10,000 ; that is, he is in the " possession of 10,000 perfections." This symbol was the " monogram of Vishnu " and the battle-axe of Thor, the Scandinavian god of thunder.

The other image represents Ananda, the second Patriarch, whose name signifies " joy," a cousin of the sage, his constant attendant and " beloved disciple." He never left Buddha's side, who always spoke of him and to him in the tenderest manner. He, with a thousand secretaries, wrote down the dharma or law, which he loved to hear, and to which he had listened so attentively that it was indelibly impressed upon his memory.

Bodhidharma was the twenty-eighth and last of the real Patriarchs. He came from India at an advanced age, was received by the Emperor at Nanking, and afterwards sat with his face to the wall for nine years, and was popularly called, " The wall-gazing Brahman." By the name of Tamo he is constantly spoken of by Buddhist priests. He discouraged the study of the sacred books, and developed the mystic phase of this religion, "being wrapped in thought while surrounded by vacancy and stillness." His picture is seen as he crossed the Yangtse, walking on the water and blowing a tall pagoda out of his mouth. In commemoration of this event he is worshipped by the boatmen on the twenty-eighth day of February.

The Schools.—Buddhism, like other religions, is divided into religious sects ; their lines of separation are clearly marked in Japan, but are scarcely perceptible in China. The two principal schools are the Hinayana and Mahayana, or Schools of Small and Great Conveyance. Buddha is said to have thus described them : " A notable man's house took fire. He brought goat-carts, drawn by goats and deer, to rescue his sons. He afterwards gave them a lofty, broad waggon, drawn by white bullocks. The first are the methods of the Hinayana ; the last that of the Mahayana " or Great Conveyance.

The Hinayana school represents the earlier practical asceticism of Buddhism, when the system was more religious and less philosophical. The Mahayana school was developed by the philosopher Najardjuna, " one of the four suns which illumine the world," who favoured transcendental speculation, and the substitution of mysticism and fanciful contemplation for the rigid rites of the early Church. He says, " The soul has neither existence nor non-existence, it is neither eternal nor non-eternal, neither annihilated by death nor non-annihilated."

The Canon.—Shakyamuni left his teachings in oral form, and, handed down from mouth to mouth, there were many additions, changes, and variations. The sacred books were published as the authoritative teachings of Buddhism, and councils were held to settle points of dispute, but it was not till the fifth century that the whole canon was compiled and published in Ceylon,—this, 1,000 years after the time its founder died. As to the reception of Buddhist literature into China; in the first century the monks brought a few books, and during the fourth an embassy was sent to India to collect works; the travellers brought many volumes, but a complete collection of the Buddhist scriptures was not made till A.D. 1400. What is known as the northern canon, the canon of China and Japan, dates A.D. 1600. The canon of our Scriptures compares favourably. "The Old Testament canon was completed in the time of Ezra; the New Testament canon in the second century." "Besides, we still possess ancient MSS. of the New Testament, some of which were written one hundred years before the first edition of the Buddhist scriptures was undertaken, of which not a single ancient MS. has withstood the ravages of time, and which has never yet been examined critically by either friend or foe."

The Forge of Lies.—As the Buddhists suppose that Ananda held in memory the discourses of Buddha, all the sacred books begin "Thus have I heard" (equivalent in the Bible to "Thus saith the Lord"), as thus he heard Buddha speak. The wholesale interpolations are seen by

the references in Buddha's sermons to Amita, who was unknown for centuries; to Kwanyin, a divinity of later date;
to King Ashoka, to the king of Hades, and to the island of
Pootoo, where Buddhism was planted 1,500 years after his
time. During the succeeding centuries clever priests
would write a book and palm it off as if from the pen of
the sage, and Buddhist writers, no matter at how late a
day, must have the Master's imprimatur. Suppose that
the followers of Luther, in all the ramifications of German

Sand-Waiter.

theological speculation, were to issue their works as if
they were simply the stenographic reporters who delivered
verbatim the discourses of the great reformer, and that
the books represented Luther as their author! This
claiming for Buddha the authorship of the sacred books
stamps Buddhism as a system of falsehoods.

The religious, and many of the moral books of the
Chinese, are received from the gods by a sand-waiter or
kind of planchette. In a room, where there are images,

pictures, and incense, on a table, is placed a waiter with sand in it. From the beam hangs a rope with a horizontal rod, to which is attached a vertical stick, and to this a bird is frequently fastened, in whose mouth is suspended a pen with an iron point. The literary men, who seek an oracular response, hold the ends of the horizontal rod, and when the god or Immortal comes, there is first a verse, then perhaps an answer or a prescription, or sometimes a book, written character after character by the imperceptible movements of the hand. A third party copies on paper, and thus religious books are manufactured.

The Sutra a Fetish.—A fetish is described as a material object, regarded as possessing supernatural powers and influences, which may be controlled by the person possessing the object. Fetishism is practised not only in Africa and Oceania, but also in Asia, one form of it being seen in the Indian religion by the superstitious regard which a Buddhist bestows upon his Sutra or prayer-book. It wards off sickness, cures disease, insures prosperity, and to chant the words is a panacea for every evil. The book may be a family heirloom, and is looked upon as an object of veneration.

Christian Ideas.—It may occur to the reader, that in the name of Buddha's mother, in some of the circumstances attending his birth, in the temptations of Mara, in the offerings of the Eastern merchants, and in some of the incidents of his life, there is a similarity to the Gospel narratives. It is said, however, that the "most ancient Buddhistic books contain scarcely any details of Buddha's life, and none whatever of these events." Also none of these legends can be proved to have existed before the fifth or sixth centuries of our era, 1,100 years after the death of Shakyamuni. Again, before this time the Nestorians had reached Central Asia, and "true to its eclectic instincts Buddhism adopted many Christian ideas, traditions, and ceremonies," and this fully accounts for any similarity between the Indian and Judean narratives. The resemblance is especially seen in the Buddhism of Thibet.

Its Tolerant Spirit.—The followers of the Arabian prophet made their conquests by the sword, and the Moslem faith kindles the fiercest passions of men. Buddhism is the antipodes of Mahommedanism. It has no system of truth for the defence of which its votaries must lay down their lives, and though their idolatry is denounced as false and abominable, the Buddhist meets us with a smile. As the Chinese often say in the chapels, "We say your religion is good, and ours is good too, but you say that the religion of Jesus is the only true religion; we do not think you are as polite as we are;" and on the score of politeness we have to acknowledge that they deserve the medal. "Imprinted upon Buddhism by the master hand of Shakyamuni is the spirit of thorough liberality and absolute tolerance, which has marked its early rise and progress, and which enabled it to adopt the most valuable ideas of all religions it came in contact with, to enter into a compromise with almost every form of popular superstition, and to found and maintain a church without persecuting a single heretic."

Beneficial Effects.—Though Buddhism is the most

gigantic system of idolatry on the earth, yet in the absence of the true it has been beneficial to eastern Asia. It is much better to have a false religion than to have no religion at all. Men in Christian lands who "care for none of these things" are in a worse condition than the devout pagan. Through Buddhism, "countries and peoples shut out by mountains and deserts were brought under the influence of morality," and barbarous tribes "were brought into a state of semi-civilisation, which is the more apparent if we consider in what a savage state all those tribes remained which rejected Buddhism."

The benefits are most apparent in China. Its great sage "clung to the physical, the seen, and the temporal with a tenacious grasp." He took not into account that a reliance upon the unseen was the only possible condition of the soul, and built no temple into which the people could carry their affections and religious instincts; and so through the gap which Confucius left Buddhism entered. "The Chinese in this system found objects to adore of mysterious grandeur; and processions, the ringing of bells, the fumes of sweet-smelling incense, prayers, chants, and music, were aids to their devotion." What if for these 2,000 years China had been left with the cold philosophy of the sage! Its condition would have been tenfold worse. Confucianism has held up morality before the people; Buddhism has kept the flame of religion burning on the altar of their hearts. The translators of Christian books are indebted to Buddhism for much of their religious phraseology.

Revival of Buddhism.—For the ten years previous

to 1864 the Taiping insurrectionists swept through several of the provinces, laying waste its fields and razing the cities. They were iconoclasts, destroying every monastery, breaking to pieces every idol, and putting the priests to the sword, so that twenty years ago an opportunity was given to the Church to enter a land almost, it might be said, without a religion, a temple, a priesthood, or an altar.

The monks commenced the work of rebuilding, and it went on slowly for many years, but during the last two years in Soochow, as well as many other places, there has been a revival of idolatry. It is seen in the rapid rebuilding and repairing of nunneries, monasteries, and temples, and the general air of prosperity attending these sacred places. Many small buildings were unknown to foreigners as temple property till they saw new halls being erected. The priests, both Buddhist and Taoist, now command much money, and the work they do is far more conspicuous and substantial than what is done on private dwellings. For centuries the priests feared to invest money on Pootoo, the sacred isle of the Pacific, but since foreign commerce has driven piracy from the seas the revival of Buddhism and its enterprise in the erection of beautiful temples is there specially manifest, and before many years, throughout the devastated sections of the empire, temples and pagodas will lift their towering heads.

CHAPTER XII.

THE THEOLOGY OF BUDDHISM.

THE leading tenets of the system will be presented very briefly.

Buddhism is Atheistic.—This seems to be a strange charge to make against a religion where there are "gods many, and lords many;" yet in the midst of its outward polytheism theoretical Buddhism is godless, a system of atheism. "Before Buddhism arose, the thinking minds of India saw

> The universe as one stupendous whole,
> Whose body nature is, and God the soul."

From the great Brahma, the uncreated pantheistic deity, who pervades all existence as the life pervades the body, the whole Universe emanates, and into this Brahma it will at last be reabsorbed. Buddha asked Alara, "What becomes of the Great Brahma, when at the end of this kalpa, this heaven and earth . . . are entirely destroyed,—where then is your Creator?" "The idea of a Creator is nowhere mentioned by Buddha; in the course of his religious disputations with the Brahmans he combats their notions of a god, coolly establishing the most crude atheism." Buddha preferred the law of revolution,—a Universe rising into existence and moving onward in its course till it completes the circle, then undergoing a process of dissolution, and after that reconstructed for a new career, and thus again and again in eternal succession as one kalpa ends and another begins.*

"A wise man can never be born in the abode of Brahma" say the Buddhist cosmogonists, "for that deity asserts that he can create heaven, earth, and all things. He being so ignorant as this, no wise man would go to live in his heaven."

Buddhism knows of no first cause, and gives no answer to the question how the Universe came into existence ; yet over two thousand years ago it set up a theory not unlike the system known as Darwinian, save that the latter is adapted to modern civilisation. Many of the modern atheistic philosophers " have drunk more or less of the sweet poison, and taken as kindly as an Asiatic to the Buddhistic opium pipe." Shakyamuni, whom the Buddhists acknowledge to be a man, is exalted to the supreme place in its religious worship. It is the worship of an idea more than of a being, as the theoretical Buddha or Buddhaship is not so much a god as a *state* after death, a state to which all may attain. In this religion " there is the inconsistency of worshipping an *extinct being* such as Buddha is said to have become at his death." To be resolved into Buddha or the Buddha-hood is the hope of the worshipper, so in reality it is the adoration of a vague thought.

---

* A kalpa is "a period of time varying from a few hundred to many thousand years," "not to be reckoned by months and days," "a period during which a physical Universe is formed and destroyed."

Natural Science.—The Buddhist scriptures " have not maintained a wise reticence about natural science." Mount Sumeru, upon which is the palace of Indra, or as it is called in Chinese, " the thirty-three heavens," in height equal to 168,000 yojanas,* in shape like an inverted cone, that is, the base above and standing on its apex, is situated in the centre of the world, and

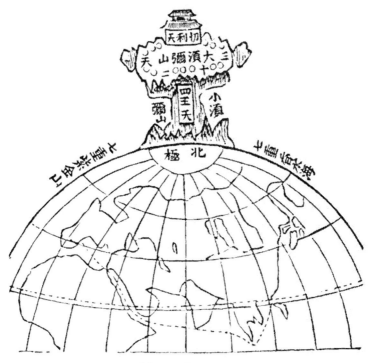

Mount Sumeru.

beneath (as its depth in the *sea* is equal to its altitude) are the innumerable chambers of hell.

To show the ready adaptability of Buddhism to its surroundings, a monk in Soochow who has studied

* The Yojana, the Buddhist sacred measure, is about four miles.

geography sees that the old woodcuts in the sacred books of this central mountain will not answer the present advanced ideas about our globe, so he has issued a pictorial pamphlet, resting Mount Sumeru upon the north pole,—rather a cold region for heaven.   His picture is given.

At the top of the Himalayas is a great lake, which is the common source of all the rivers of the earth.   The earth is in the shape of half a calabash, sloping upwards on all sides to the summit of the Himalayas.   India, not China, is "the middle kingdom," and so "the navel of the earth."   What causes the tides?   "The water flowing through the palace of the dragon assumes a blue colour, and as it enters or issues forth from the palace, causes the fall and rise of the sea."   Why does not the ocean over-flow?   "There are four precious jewels at the bottom of the sea which absorb the waters from the countless rivers."   What gives the sea its brackish taste?   One of the reasons assigned is that "in the middle of the sea is a great fish 9,000 miles in length, and its pollutions cause the salt taste."   What is the cause of earthquakes?   "The earth is placed on water, the water on wind, the wind on space : when the wind is agitated, then the water is moved, and this shakes the earth."

The Great Chiliocosm.—In the sacred books there are cuts with many little circles ; these circles are worlds, and each may by a process of evolution become a system of worlds,—worlds upon worlds filling immensity.   There are little chiliocosms, and a thousand thousand of these make a great chiliocosm.

There are kalpas (indefinite periods of time) of establishment, kalpas of perfection, kalpas of destruction, and kalpas of vacancy, twenty of each ; during the first forty kalpas the universe is gradually brought to perfection, and during the last forty the process of dissolution brings it to its primeval condition. "The great chiliocosm is not perfected by one influence or by one operation, but by countless influences and countless operations." "The physical causes engaged in its periodical formation and destruction are water, wind, and fire." "Supposing the world to be under the eternal law of change, Buddhists give no account of its first origin, not feeling the need of the doctrine of creation."

Its scriptures say, "When the heavens and the earth again began to be, there was no defined substance, neither was there sun nor moon ; but the earth bubbled up as a sweet fountain, the taste of which was like virgin honey." The Devas touched it with their fingers, tasted it, and ate, till they lost their angelic beauty, and became coarse like men. "A great black wind arose, which blew upon the face of the waters and produced the sun and moon. On beholding them come forth, men were filled with joy. From this time began morning and evening, darkness and light, and the revolving seasons." "There was no distinction of male or female, but all were born alike in the world, and from this arose the expression, 'all living things.'" "When men began to desire many things, then the sexes were developed, and from this came the name of man and wife."

The Heart.—The Pantheistic tendencies of Buddhistic philosophy are illustrated by its deification of the heart. A Sutra says, "The heart, as a skilful workman, makes all the different conditions of existence throughout the ten regions of space ; everything in the universe results from the operation of this universal essence."

"The heart is Buddha," is an expression in constant use by the Chinese, which is the same as to say that a man has a divinity within his own bosom, and needs no other lord. The heart is "the inborn Buddha, which belongs to everything that has conscious existence. It is pure and holy, but is overshadowed and shut out from view by the passions. Let every one search for it with introverted eye, and he will need no god or idol to adore, nor any law to control him. Let him uncover the veiled Buddha in his own heart. He will then become his own teacher and his own regenerator." In this language we see another sacrifice, a very acceptable one, to human pride.

An author says, "Heaven and earth with this heart pervade the myriad of things ; man obtains it, and then it is the heart of man; things obtain it, and then it is the heart of things. Grass, trees, birds, and beasts chain it, and then it is the heart of grass, trees, birds, and beasts. This is just the one heart of heaven and earth."

Morality.—On entering Buddhist temples there are found most excellent moral precepts on signboards or fixed in the walls. "Only Heaven is Supreme." "There is but one road to happiness." "Only the good are happy for ever." "Buddha lives in one's heart." "Coming and going, have one heart." "When one prays the heart responds." "The pure heart will excel in intelligence." "Do not deceive." Alas! they are merely engraved on wood and brick, and not graven on the fleshy tablets of the heart. The precepts of Shakyamuni "proceeded from the lips of a man who through a long life was animated by a pure and lofty asceticism." Buddha spoke of the ten evils: murder, theft, and lust belonging to the body; equivocation, slander, lying, and flattery to the speech; and envy, anger, and delusion to the thoughts. The three poisons within the heart are covetousness, anger, and delusion. The five obscurities are envy, passion, sloth, vacillation, and unbelief. Buddha says, " Lust and concupiscence are the sole causes of all the folly and confusion in the world; they are like a person who takes a lighted torch and runs with it against the wind."

" The heart is the busy contriver of the lusts; compose the heart, and these evil thoughts will all be still." "Once get rid of the pollution of the wicked heart," and the life will be correct. " The man who is able to govern his heart and keep it pure, and who perseveres against all obstacles, advances onward; this man, when lust is banished and vice is destroyed, will obtain salvation."

In " The Sutra of Forty-two Sections," Buddha says, " Man having many faults, if he does not repent, but allows his heart to be at rest, will find sins rushing upon him like water to the sea. If a man becomes sensible of his faults, abandons them, and acts virtuously, his sin will day by day diminish and be destroyed, till he obtains full enlightenment." " Who is the great man?" asks the Indian sage. " He who is strongest in the exercise of patience, he who patiently endures misery and maintains a blameless life."

Among difficult things he mentions, " Being poor to be charitable, being rich or great to be religious, to bear insult without anger, to move in the world without setting the heart on it, and to be the same in heart and life." Some of Shakya's words might be written in gold, —"A man who foolishly does me wrong, I will return to him the protection of my ungrudging love; the more evil comes from him, the more good shall go from me; the fragrance of these good actions always redounding to me, the harm of the slanderer's words returning to him."

Some of the charitable institutions in China may probably be ascribed to Buddhism. There are many Buddhist tracts inculcating morality, but it is impossible to tell how much of the light is borrowed. The influence of Buddhist morality is at a minimum, for two reasons; first, the towering ascendency of Confucianism, and second, because the monks, the exponents of the system, do not by their celibate lives recommend the doctrines they profess.

Asceticism.—The life of Shakyamuni has been a practical illustration. The world renounced, the city abandoned, riches given up, fathers cast away, mothers forsaken, brothers and sisters left behind, wife forgotten, children disowned, family deserted, relatives unknown, homeless, friendless, penniless,— this is to be a Buddhist. Neither by command nor precept does it regulate the relations between prince and subject, father and son, or husband and wife. The Church is a body of hermits, a congregation of priests, an army of mendicants. The doctrine of penance is one of its prime tenets.

"Deny thyself," says Buddha. He inculcated the principle of self-denial and the life of self-sacrifice. "The starting-point in his code was the idea of absolute self-renunciation," and in this lay "the path of deliverance from misery." Let us see how this sage speaks of

Love.—Love is the root of birth and death. If love is not broken one is not born in Paradise. Its cords must be broken in two. The canal of love and the sea of sorrow are the same. Love of friends, family, and riches must be broken off before one may become Buddha. If you do not know that love is the root of life and death, you may be chanting while the root grows larger ; before your eyes at home may be parents, wife, children, and riches, and the whole body in a fiery furnace. If you look round and see your children, can you pull up love by the roots ? If you cannot pull up love by the roots, how can you loose the coils of life and death ?

Emptiness.—The Confucianist objects to Buddhism that it is a system of "emptiness," because it denies the consciousness of man and the reality of the external world. When Buddha turned the wheel of the law in the deer garden and "preached respecting the secret and mysterious signs of being," he founded his argument on the assertion that all things are void, all phenomena unreal. He says, "If a man knows that self has no individual nature, then all phenomena will appear to him unreal." The two things the Buddhist desires are, first, "A heart fixed on nothing," and second, "A mind which dwells nowhere."

This phase of Buddhism is illustrated by extracts from the "Heart Sutra," which is chanted by nearly every man, woman, and child in Central China. "Appearance and emptiness are the same ; emptiness and appearance are the same. Appearance is emptiness and emptiness is appearance. Reception, thought, action, and knowledge are empty. The empty substance of all law is not born, is not destroyed, is not clean, is not soiled; it cannot be added to and cannot be destroyed; for this reason—in the middle of emptiness there is no appearance, no reception, thought, action, or knowledge. It is without the eye, ear, nose, tongue, body, and mind. It is without

Meditation.

appearance, voice, fragrance, taste, feeling, law; without limit to sight, without limit to mind, without, without clearness, and without, without clear ending." In the sacred books, there are some examples of

Nihilism.—A wayfarer in the country of Afghanistan knocks at the door of a Brahman family. A young man within answers, "There is no one in this house." The traveller, who was a Patriarch, understood this, and said, " Who is no one ? " The door opened, and the old man foretells the destiny of the youth; he was his successor, the eighteenth Patriarch.

This man, Sangkayasheta, " heard the bells of a temple ringing on account of the wind blowing. His teacher asked him, 'Is it the bells that make the sound, or the wind?' The Patriarch replied, 'It is neither the bells nor the wind, it is my mind.'"

The Emperor Leang Wute at Nanking meeting with Bodhidharma asks, " Which is the most important of the holy doctrines ? " He replies, " Where all is emptiness nothing can be called *holy*." The Emperor says, " Who is this that thus replies to me ? " The speaker answers, " I do not know."

Meditation.—This may be called the " anxious bench " of Buddhism; thus six years sat Buddha in the jungle. Priests are often seen sitting tailor-fashion on a small platform, for hours at a time, thoughtless, motionless. The bonze " must first arm himself with a firm resolve to save all creatures, vowing that he will obtain supreme wisdom." The mat must be placed in a retired spot to be free from interruption, the body composed to a state of perfect quiet, the clothes spread out, the legs properly arranged, the toes of the right foot on the left thigh, and *vice versa*, the palm of the left hand placed in the hollow of the right, the eyebrows hanging down, the eyes slightly opened, and fixed on the end of the nose, the body and heart both fixed, the mind bound down to repose in the middle of the body, the breathings counted to prevent thought, and then the heart is at rest. At this time the soul goes out and wanders at leisure, sometimes even on a journey of a thousand miles, returning at pleasure, so that the priest in these invisible flights sees and knows all that goes on in the county or province.

Kindness to Animals.—Buddhism shows the sympathy for animals that was intended for men. The principle on which it is based is that to eat meat, the root of pity in the heart is broken off. Another reason is that according to the doctrine of transmigration one may be feeding on an ancestor. A third, that all creatures are the sons of Buddha, so a priest is seen using a brush to drive off mosquitoes to avoid killing one; the lice on the body it is not right to destroy, and even hungry spirits Buddha pities as a father. There are societies to receive animals redeemed from the slaughterhouse, canals set apart in which to turn loose fish, where the hook cannot be dropped or the net dragged; hawkers along the streets cry, "Buy this big turtle for $2, and do a meritorious act;" an old mule is treated as tenderly as a grandmother. A man listening to me preaching on Abraham offering up Isaac exclaimed, "And why was it necessary to kill that goat?"

Vegetarians.—A corollary to the tenet of the sacredness of animal life and the wickedness of animal sacrifices is the sin of eating flesh. The Christian religion is called the Ye-su (Jesus) Church, and so those unaccustomed to the sound often ask "if we eat *su*,"—that is, live on a vegetable diet. The monks are vegetarians (though not a few quietly indulge in fish and pork), and object seriously to a dog bringing a bone, by which the temple precincts would be defiled. To be a vegetarian is the method the

laity have of making a profession of the Buddhist faith,
and millions among the women and tens of thousands of
the old men, some for thirty or forty years, have not
tasted meat. It is exceedingly troublesome, for on a visit
to friends they cannot eat rice out of a pot in which flesh
has been cooked. Others are vegetarians certain days
and parts of certain months; as, in honour of Kwanyin,
the first nineteen days of the 1st, 6th, and 9th Moons
are observed; for the "Three Mandarins" the first half
of the 1st, 7th, and 10th Moons are days of fasting; and
for twenty-four days of July almost the whole population
abstain from meats, in honour of the god of thunder.
The candles used in worship are made of the grease of
the tallow-tree, not of beef-tallow, so that Buddhism is
an "anti-fat society." The idea pervading the devotees
of this faith is that by "eating no meat" the heart is
purified, hence the appropriateness of the passage, "Not
that which entereth into a man defileth the man."

Sin.—This is a word which Buddhism has kept alive
in China, but perhaps there is no nation which has less
sense of sin than the Chinese. They confess sin in general,
but deny every particular sin; they acknowledge sin in
the abstract, but refuse to admit it in the concrete; they
say, "Oh! yes, every one must have sins," but the
individual addressed has no personal sin; there is such
a thing as sin in China, but it does not lie at my door.
Sometimes, in answer to the question, "Why are you a
vegetarian?" the reply will be, "Because my sins are
heavy;" or to "Why do you go on pilgrimages?" it is
replied, "To escape from sin;" to "Why do you burn
incense?" it is said, "We all have sins on our bodies," but

oftener men reply, " I have no sin." " But have you never sinned in your life ? " " Oh ! no, I have never trampled on a grain of rice or misused printed paper." " Think, in heedless youth, did you never lie or curse ? " " If I did, I have forgotten it ; I am not conscious of any sin : if I have, I do not know it now, I may know it hereafter." It seems to be universal that all men consider themselves sinless; the " seared conscience " is the habitual accompaniment of age.   The old ladies wear red pants as a sign that they have attained perfection.

The Buddhist idea of sin is more that which brings calamity than what is essentially evil in itself. " How about those who are killed by the thunder ? " is the continual question.   He must be unfilial, or he was a murderer, as was judged of the apostle by the barbarous people of Melita, when a viper fastened on his hand.   If lightning strikes a tree there is a venomous snake hidden at its root.   The missionary has constantly to preach on the Tower of Siloam, and of the blind man about whom the disciples asked, " Master, who did sin, this man or his parents, that he should be born blind ? "   The blind sit by the wayside with the heart-rending cry, " Hell is before my eyes," *i.e.*, the sorrow is like that in the prison of the lost.   Sickness is spoken of as " transgressed disease," and criminals (see Chapter XXVI.) appear in the processions confessing their sins.

Redemption.—" Redemption " is a blessed word that Buddhism has preserved till Christianity came to China,— the same word the people use in redeeming their effects from the pawn-shop.   The idea of redemption in Buddhism is not so much obtaining pardon for sins committed as of being set free from the power of the evil passions. The methods of obtaining redemption are pilgrimages to distant shrines, regularly burning incense, performing meritorious acts, a vegetable diet, saving animal life, and chanting books of prayer, thus renovating one's own heart ; it is thought a definite amount of gifts and worship will gain the removal of a corresponding amount of sin and its attendant suffering.

The idea of grace is in a slight degree kept before the people ; that grace which is " pity in the heart of Buddha, prompting him to teach true doctrine to those who have gone astray, and opening a path for self-reformation and pardon of sins." As in Taoist works the Buddhist element is freely intermingled, " the god of the Taoists is represented as promulgating a gracious decree to remit the punishment of hell for those who repent."

Merit.—The doctrine of salvation by meritorious actions is the bulwark of Buddhism. Do and live is their maxim. The Buddhist is placed " under the unrelenting yoke of the moral law of his own religion, a burden too heavy to be borne."

According to the doctrine of *karma*, " Every act of worship, every Buddhist ceremony, every book of devotion read, every gift to a monastery or a begging priest, every mass for the dead, every invocation of a Buddha or Bodhisattwa, every wish for the good of others, infallibly causes great good, through the necessary operation of the law of cause and effect in the moral sphere."

The doctrine of " causation " or " fate," by which " a man's destiny is determined by the stock of merits or demerits accumulated in previous forms of existence, constitutes Buddhism a system of fatalism," as good actions bring happiness, and bad ones misery. "To do good deeds" is hourly heard as the synonym of duty and religion. The services for the dead are highly meritorious to the living. "Tso kung-teh," "do merit," consists of liturgical services for the departed, to obtain for them better positions in the other world, by which children and friends may, through the priests, the mediators of the dark covenant of Buddhism, add merit unto their ancestors. It is a double-acting machine, by which the departed obtain merit by what is done, and the living obtain merit by doing it.

The Chinese have a work called "The Rules of Merit and Transgression," with an enumeration of almost every conceivable action, stating the commercial value of good deeds in the market of Hades, and the relative scale of punishments for the evil. A good Chinaman often sits down at night and makes out the account for the day, being always sure he has credit in the bank, so that "morality is converted into a vast scheme of profit and loss." To illustrate :—

ACCOUNT OF MERIT.

	Cr.
To pay the debts of a father	10
To worship at a father's burial	50
When rich to marry a deformed girl to whom betrothed when poor	100
To lend an umbrella	1
To build bridges, repair roads, open canals, and dig wells, for every dollar expended . . .	10
To furnish a coffin for the poor	30
To bury a man who has no son	50
To entreat a mother not to commit infanticide .	30

	Cr.
To save a child from infanticide.	50
To save one hundred insects	1
To bury a bird	1
To turn loose animals, for every 10 cents expended	1
To pick up one grain of rice	1
To return what you pick up on the street, for every value of 10 cents.	1
To give 10 cents to beggars	1
For one year not to eat beef or dog meat	5
To publish a part of the Classics	100
To forgive a debt	100
To destroy the stereotype plates of immoral books	300
Purity through life	1000

ACCOUNT OF TRANSGRESSIONS.

	Dr.
To love a wife more than father and mother	100
To listen to a wife against one's own brothers	10
To allow a step-mother to illtreat a first wife's children ; each day	1
To be double-tongued	30
To be insincere	10
To have one bad thought	10
To see immoral theatricals.	10
To dig up a worm in winter	1
To laugh at an ugly person.	3
To soil the page of a book	5
To take meat and wine to a temple	5
To get drunk	5
To be guilty of usury.	100
To counterfeit silver	100
To misuse written or printed paper	50
To cook beef or dog meat	100
To dig up a coffin	100
For a mandarin not to prohibit infanticide	10
To assist in infanticide	50
To drown an infant	100
To publish an obscene book	*measureless.*

The Field of Happiness.—This phrase often occurs in the sacred books, with the design of inducing men to be charitable. The field is the heart, alms the grain; sow the seeds of charity in this life, and you will reap a happy harvest in the next. To the poor, riches will

Transmigration.

be given; to the lowly, office; upon those who desire health, long life, or sons; such are the blessings that will be bestowed.

Transmigration.—The doctrine of metempsychosis is the great central principle of Buddhism. Just as the cross is the emblem of Christianity, so the wheel is the symbol of Buddhism; the wheel of the law turns in this world and the wheel of transmigration in Hades. In this wheel there are six ranks,—insects, fish, birds, animals, poor men, and mandarins. It is not necessary to go in order through the six paths, but one may go from the highest to the lowest, and from the lowest to the highest. All sentient creatures are bound to this revolving wheel.

There is a state of action and reaction between this world and Hades, a system of rewards bestowed, and vengeance taken. A wicked man returns as a beast, but if the beast is killed, his sins are atoned for and the account settled, and he may the next time be a man. There is a state of enmity between the two worlds. If a man goes through life and he does not kill an ant or a fly, then there is no enmity in the other world. The common saying is, "If I am a hog and you a man, and you kill me, in the next life you will be a hog and I a man, and I will kill you."

An early transmigration is thought to be desirable. From ancient times it was the practice of the poor, some years after decease, to burn the coffin and gather up the bones, for want of burial space. Afterwards, as the priests practised cremation, it was said, "One day quicker burned one day sooner returned," so the custom became general in some parts of the land, though the mandarins issue proclamations forbidding it.

Metempsychosis is the faith of every man, woman, and child in China; all believe that they individually have in a previous existence been here upon this earth. They have a proverb, that "the good has the good reward, and the evil the evil reward," but they see many honest men are poor, and that the wicked " flourish as the green bay-tree," so they seek for a theory to cover these different conditions, and find it in the formula, that happiness and misery in this life are the result of good or bad deeds in a previous existence.   Preach against this as the minister may, their minds still revolve around the hub of trans-migration.   It is not simply inlaid in their constitutions, it is so thoroughly interwoven that it is a part of the mental structure of all Buddhists. " Cruelty, covetousness, false-hood, lust, drunkenness, and other vices will heap up a stock of demerit, producing rebirth in some wretched condition of life upon earth, while the opposite virtues will insure a desirable condition."   All say they know of many instances.   A sheep near Soochow was once born with a man's name branded on its side, and did it not have the soul of that man ?   Some years since a man at Hangchow dreamed that outside one of the gates a cow had a calf, which was his father returning.   Rising early and going to a village, he found a young calf; purchasing the cow and calf he led it home, and honoured it as his venerated father.   A few nights afterwards he dreamed that it was not the soul of his father, but that of an enemy, and its retention would bring untold calamities.   On the morrow, the calf was killed.

The greatest hope of a woman is that next time she may be a man ; of a poor man that he may be born rich ; of the wealthy that in a coming age they may be mandarins.   This is an old doctrine of the Brahmans, which Buddha remodelled, and made it the pivot of his system, and this was the sword the Indian prophet wielded with such frightful terror. What a fearful doctrine! Lashed to the wheel of fate, as a man caught in the machinery of a great mill, going round and round, first in the light and then down in the night; now in life, then descending to the shades of death, around and around through ceaseless æons as the revolving wheel turns over and over. There in the temple is the mill with the man going in above and the dog coming out beneath, and here is the picture of the horse entering the man's body as he possesses merit, and so returns a human being. This is a fort at which Christianity must level its heaviest batteries.

The gods strapped to this Wheel.—Buddha, in his great sermon on Mount Sumeru, addressing the pantheon of the skies, said, "O ye gods and goddesses! think not that your estate is permanent and established in heaven; you also must descend and be bound to the wheel of transmigration. and return as men to earth."

Nirvana.—As Heaven offered no safe abode for men or gods, Buddha sought some estate which would be permanent and enduring; that estate is Nirvana, the doctrine of Buddha's old age when his experience was ripe. It is to get outside of the wheel of life and death, so entering Nirvana one escapes from transmigration. It is the repose of the soul, a passionless condition of body and spirit, an absolute rest obtained by the absorption of the soul into itself. The question comes, What does Buddhism teach of this state? One of Buddha's followers asserted, "Nirvana is;" but if it is a state of being, it is a motionless being, where the heart does not beat, the mind does not think, the soul does not act, the life does not live. There is no thought, personality, or identity,—a place where the "I" is lost. It is described as "where the silence lies," a state of "complete silence," a condition of "nothingness," a state of "non-existence." "Nirvana is a state of which nothing can be said, to which no attributes can be given: it is altogether an abstract, devoid of all positive and negative qualities."

If the Chinese equivalents can be relied on, Nirvana means "entire destruction," which is nothing less than annihilation, and it possesses all the qualities we ascribe to annihilation, as it is "the complete extinction of all personal and individual being." In the translations of the Indian Sutras into Chinese, over and over is Nirvana described as "absolute annihilation;" so this great religion of Asia ends "in nothingness as the issue and crown of being."

CHAPTER XIII.

THE WORSHIP OF BUDDHISM.

BUDDHISM as a religion consists not so much in the life of its founder and in its doctrinal tenets as it does in its temple worship, this worship supplying the craving of the heart for a medium by which to express its reverence for the higher powers. The ministers who minister at its altars are

The Priests.—These are known by their shaven heads and yellow robes, which are loose and flowing to allow for spiritual influences; their stockings are large enough for two feet to be put into one. In central and southern China they are like the black crows in number. All religions have ceremonies for setting apart men to the sacred office. Fifty days the candidate for the priesthood is required to spend in special preparation, with severe fasts, watches by night, rigorous penance, and subjected to many hardships. His special seals are the marks above his forehead, for he is branded in twelve spots on his shaven pate by lighted incense, which, burning on his head, leaves an indelible impress. In olden times it was a life of self-denial, but now many " enter the priest's office to eat the priest's bread." Sometimes a priest adopts a boy from a poor family and trains him up as his

successor in the temple service, but often idle tramps and
worthless vagabonds enter the ranks because they have no
employment.   Occasionally the heart is touched by seeing
little boys without their own consent forced into this

Buddhist Priests.

miserable service.   Once we saw a Hangchow man, who
had made a vow on a sick bed to become a priest, tear
his three handsome little sons from their mother, and
put them in a P'ootoo monastery for life.

The bonzes are noted for their idleness. The people speak of them as the "drones in the hive, and not useful as the silk-worm," and despise their lazy habits; for they loiter around except when engaged in temple services or in reading prayers for the dead. In the second place, they are remarkable for their stupidity; the monotone chant not being conducive to mental activity. They have no intellectual tastes. I have asked them at Pootoo, " Why do you not read when you have nothing to do?" Ages gone by they have "abandoned the study of the Sanscrit, and know nothing of the history of their own religion;" their shaven pates with low sloping foreheads do not indicate genius; and it would be hard to find men where the light of reason is so obscured as in many of the monks; yet there are marked exceptions, for we occasionally see those who are noted for zeal, devotion, and learning. Next to stupidity is their cupidity. With the priest it is a question of business, and he never turns aside to philanthropic acts. One illustration will suffice. I said to one of the thousand monks at Pootoo, " I suppose when a priest dies he has a large company to perform masses for his soul?" He replied, "Oh! if he leaves $30 or $40 they will, but if he dies without money he has no funeral." As Buddhism enjoins celibacy the morals of the younger and middle-aged are considered by the masses as questionable.

A common sight is the priest seated beside a table, beating on his wooden fish-head, counting his beads, and chanting the instructions of Buddha with frequent invocations.

The monk has his manual of daily prayer, and the

rules of the order fill several volumes; he is subject to strict discipline from his superiors, though it is not often enforced. When travelling he may stop at a monastery, and is entitled to receive his food. From his prayer-book the following is taken. When he rises in the morning and bows before Buddha he must say,

> " King of the Law, the most exalted Lord,
> Unequalled through the three-fold world,
> Teacher and guide of men and gods,
> Our loving father and of all that breathes,
> I bow myself in lowest reverence and pray
> That thou wouldest soon destroy the power of destiny.
>   To set forth all thy praise
>   Unbounded time would not suffice."

Cremation Jar.

" The monk does not need faith or conviction or zeal. There is no god to worship but Buddha, and he is an uncrowned god in the sense in which Confucius was an uncrowned king." At death he is placed in a sitting

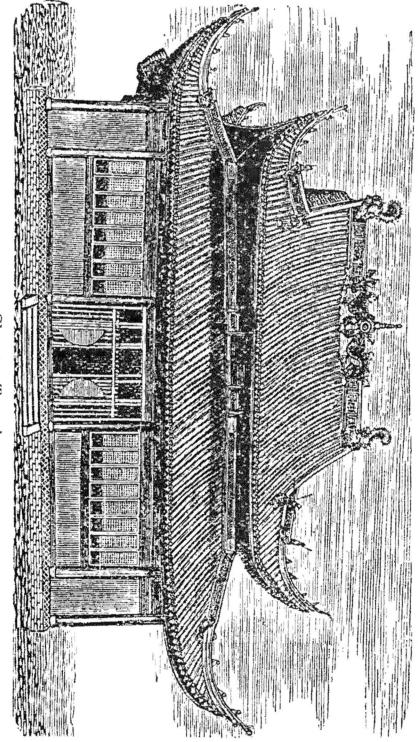

Chinese Temple.

posture in the burial jar, the upper half is fitted on,
faggots are piled around, fire is applied, and soon a handful
of ashes is all that remains.

The Temple.—It is hard for us to divest our minds
of the idea that a Chinese temple is a building of magnificent architecture, but when the visitor beholds the
heavy, cumbrous, barn-like roof, supported by huge pillars,

Four Diamonds.

the floor paved with brick, all above dark and made
darker by the smoke of incense, and sees the mould and
the dirt, he immediately contrasts it in his mind with
the sacred edifices of Greece and Rome. Sometimes a
temple is seen whose proportions please the eye. In the
cities the temples are large, and they are the property
of the Church, but each little village and hamlet has its

house of worship; these last belong to the people, and are controlled by the elders of the village. In front is usually the pond. If a piece of bread is tossed into this, a troop of gold fish rise to the surface.

A Buddhist temple usually consists of three buildings, with paved open courts between; the smallest in front, the second of more importance, while the third is the largest and most important of all.

The Four Diamonds.—On entering the first building, which constitutes the doorway, four gigantic images, two on each side, the guardians of the portal, are beheld. They are called the "Four Diamonds," and were four brothers, named Lee-pure, Lee-red, Lee-sea, and Lee-age. The first, Lee-pure, has a sword which, if brandished, would cause a black wind to spring up, and in the wind ten thousand spears, which would pierce the bodies of men and turn them to dust, the dust so great that men could not open their eyes. After the wind there would be a fire, like ten thousand golden serpents flying around. The third, Lee-red, has an umbrella in his hand, which can shade the universe. Turn it, and there would be earthquakes; open it, and heaven would be chaos, earth darkness, and the sun and moon without light. Lee-sea has a guitar, and when he touches the strings fire and wind issue forth. Lee-age has a bag, and in the bag a little animal like a white rat; turn it loose, and it would be like a white elephant with two wings flying against the enemy. The four brothers were killed in battle, and appointed the guardians of the doorway in Tartarus. There is a sacred book called "The Diamond Classic;" to believe in this work a man must have had the "good root" planted in him ten hundred times ten thousand years ago.   In the second temple is seen

Matreya Buddha. — He is also called "Me-me Buddha" and "The Coming Buddha," and is the Messiah of the Buddhist Church.   He sits tailor-fashion, with the centre of his body very prominent, and in his hand is a

The Coming Buddha.

bag; when he was on the earth the people called him "cloth-bag priest," or "carpet bagger;" his broad, laughing face welcomes the worshipper.   At this time Shakyamuni rules the Church; his successor will be Matreya, and at that time "the earth with its five evils mingled" will be purified.

Just in the rear of Matreya Buddha, back to back, is

Weito.—He was a former disciple of Buddha, and is now the protector of his law. As one of the most handsome of the gods he may be styled, " Apollo ; " he stands facing inwards, with a golden helmet on his head and a rod in his hand, called the " conquering Satan staff."

The Protector.

The third hall is the principal building in the enclosure, and is really the temple itself. There are several groups of three, we see, in the different temples. Sometimes it is Shakyamuni, the god of gods and lord of lords in the Buddhist Church, in the seat of honour, with Kashiapa and Ananda standing on the right and left.

Buddhas of the Three Ages.—Again it is the Buddhas of the "three ages," the "Past, Present, and Future," the three images alike. The central figure is Shakyamuni; the image on the left representing the many Buddhas of the past; the one on the right the Buddhas to come, who will rule the Church, ascending

Long live the Emperor

the throne in regular succession as so many emperors. In front of Shakya is the tablet, "Long live the Emperor!" literally, "The Emperor ten thousand years ten thousand times ten thousand years."

Shakyamuni, Wen-shu, and Pow-hien.—In another temple you will see Buddha in the centre, and Wen-shu and Pow-hien on either side; the first mounted on a green lion, the second on a white elephant, though sometimes it is only the nose and foot of these animals that can be seen; the first is the god of wisdom, the

Eighteen Lohans.

second the god of action; the first is worshipped principally in Shanse, the second in the Sze-cheun province. They are "ancient Buddhas, appearing among men as the helpers of Shakyamuni, who styles the one 'eldest son' and the other 'little boy.'"

If it is a temple for the worship of the gods of Paradise, the central deity is Amita; on the right is the goddess of mercy, and on the left Tashuchi, the triad styled "the three sages of the west." There are also groups of three in the other temples—the "Three Pure Ones;" the "Three Precious Ones;" the "Three Holy Sages;" the "Three Mandarins," and the "Three Mao."

The Eighteen Lohans.—They were originally sixteen, but two have by some means been added. They were distinguished members of the Indian Church, and

Articles used in Worship.

passing through several degrees they attained to the state of perfect saints. The term has a wider signification, and sometimes includes the five hundred sages whose life-size statues are seen in a temple at Hangchow.

The Worship.—The candles used in worship are made of the grease of the tallow-tree. Incense is made by taking the sawdust of sandal wood, making it into a paste, and pressing it through a small hole in an iron machine. It comes out like a wire, which is cut into sections a foot long and sun-dried, then made into

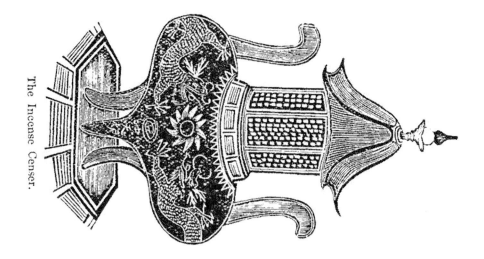

The Incense Censer.

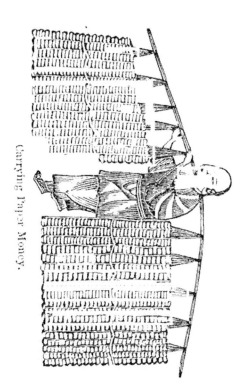

Carrying Paper Money.

bundles the size of the thumb. Sometimes the incense is in sticks.

The paper-money is made of tin-foil beaten very thin. One often sees loads carried along the street and sold at the rate of ten cents for ten thousand, rather a depreciated currency. It generally represents silver, but sometimes it means the gold coin of the other world.

Load of Paper Silk.

There are also paper shoes of sycee, their ancient currency, still used in the north. These, when of solid silver, contain fifty ounces. Paper chopped in little squares is also sold for money. The rolls of coloured paper in the waiter represent silk. The trade in tin-foil or pewter beaten thin is a most extensive one, and gives employment to ten thousands of women. After one of the great feasts men go along the streets and gather up the pewter ashes, purchased at a nominal price; these are reshipped to be manufactured over again, and a second time used in worship.

In the temple court stands a great censer, which upon worship days smokes with the fragrant incense cast in by those who come to adore the god. In front of some temples is a stone laver for washing hands.

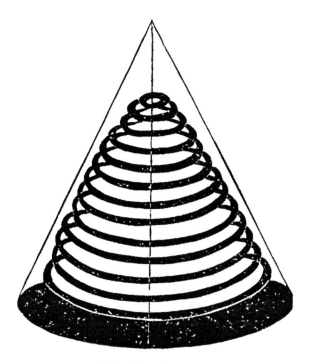

Crinoline Incense.

Often hanging in front of the shrine is incense, in the shape of a crinoline, and this burns for many days.

Oracular Response.—The worshipper kneels before the idol and shakes a bamboo cup in which are many little sticks, till one jumps out; he takes it to the priest, who notes the number, turns to a musty roll, and gives him a prescription for medicine or an answer of the oracle telling whether or no his business will prosper.

Absence of Devotion.—The worship of the heathen lacks all the elements of true devotion, and when in preaching the missionary uses the word " worship," he immediately explains that it does not consist in shaking the clasped hands or in bodily prostrations. The first element of worship is *love*, but how can we love wood,

Inquiring of the Oracle.

mud, and stone ? A second element is *communion*, but what communion can light have with darkness ? Worship is an act of the soul, but " soulless gods make soulless worshippers." When a living man prays to a dead image his heart must become like unto the dead image. "They that make them are like unto them : so is every one that trusteth in them." The worship is debasing, for though they speak of the god as in heaven, yet they maintain that worship without an image is an impossibility; so how can the heart go beyond the tangible and visible? An aged observer says, " The ceremonies performed by the people are as puerile as their offerings are paltry, while they are grievously wanting in the necessary elements of religious worship. We observe

Lighting Candles.

nothing like deep moral earnestness and solemnity in their prostrations at the idol shrine, and the whole is little more than an affair of mere custom or form, which they are satisfied with observing."

The Worshipping Assembly.—One striking feature of heathen worship is the short time spent in the service;

often in five minutes the man has bowed and prayed, cast his lot and taken the answer, left the temple, and returned to his business. This is when on the new and full moon they go, one by one, to the temples. Morning and evening, sometimes five times during the day and

Priests at Worship.

night, the priests of the temple go through with their daily order of service. Again, a family spends a day in worship, or the representatives of a village come in a band, or a goodly company of women meet for special services; how is the worship conducted?

In a Christian assembly the minister is one, here the

priests are many. Without is a busy scene; hawkers of
fruits and cakes, sedans arriving with bundles of paper-
money tied behind, numbers of idlers loafing around, all
jovial as if it were a festive occasion. The great censer
without is smoking with the burning incense, thrown in
as if it were little sticks of wood; the candles are lighted
and stuck upon the nails on the framework in front of the
deity; the brick floor of the temple is covered every few
feet with mats to kneel upon; the priests, attired in their
flowing robes, with the yellow sash thrown across one
shoulder, take their places in front of small tables; devout
women are ranged about the hall; the grum idols sit
facing outwards, and the worshippers stand facing inwards.
The wooden pestle strikes the great bell—Attention,
gods! and the inverted bell is constantly tapped; the
chant commences, and the women at each pause join in
the invocation; the priests prostrate themselves and knock
their heads nine times, while the congregation with
bended knee bow before the altar; the priests march
round and round, tapping small bells, in solemn procession, with eyes almost closed and fixed on the end of the
nose, in number ten or twenty or fifty, and once I saw
one hundred and twenty, winding in and out according to
their inextricable methods of twistification; candles light
up the sombre spectacle, the fumes of incense rise, the
gongs are sounded, fire-crackers explode, paper-money is
burnt, the wooden fish-head is struck with a dull heavy
sound, the brass cymbals clang! clang clang! the voices
commingle, the monotone rises higher and higher, and
gradually almost dies away; at times the chanting is with
the rapidity of a trotting-match, and again solemn and

reverential ; and thus it continues all day, save when the friars enjoy a feast ordered by the lay-sisters from a neighbouring restaurant.

The Three Vows.—Vows form a prominent part of heathen worship; the devotee goes before the idols and makes a vow, and if afterwards it is unfulfilled it is considered the height of wickedness, and must receive the vengeance of the gods. The formula, "I take my refuge in Buddha, I take my refuge in the Law, I take my refuge in the Church," has already been mentioned.

It is in the sacred books sometimes enlarged : "I take my refuge in Buddha, and now pray that all creatures may fully understand the great doctrine and beget the best of hearts. I take my refuge in the Law, and now pray that all creatures may in heart understand the scriptures, and their wisdom become as broad as the sea. I take my refuge in the Church, and now pray that all creatures may, with all the assembly of the faithful, meet with no difficulties."

Prayers.—There are five blessings for which the Chinese pray,—sons, riches, long life, recovery from sickness, and office. The hundreds of volumes of prayers and chants, with the exception of a few little sutras, are used only by the priests. "The prayers are not prayers in our sense" of the word, for "there is nothing but praise and invocation, and that mostly in a brief form." I have read volumes of prayer-books to try and cull out the prayers, but out of a score of such only a few sentences have been obtained; they consist of the pretended words of Buddha, praising the individual god,

and telling of his famous acts. "The prayers are
chanted by the priests, either sitting, kneeling, standing, or marching around," but they "kneel to adore
images, not to pray." Reciting the teachings of Buddha,
they hope, by a sort of magical effect, secret causation,
or reflex influence of the image on their minds, to obtain
the benefits they seek.

The following prayer is selected : " For what they pray
let them have a full answer ; lighten the path of the good
as the sun ; guide the wanderer as with a torchlight ;
scatter sorrow and heat like the cool of the moon ; ferry
the four classes floating along the stream of life as if a
bridge were built ; be as a lifeboat to convey passengers to
the other shore ; subdue infidels as the king of the lions ;
subdue devils as a dragon or an elephant ; protect the
frightened as a relative or a friend ; defend against
enemies as a moat or a city ; save in danger as a father or
mother ; hide the weak like a thick grove." This is not
for use by the people.

In Sanscrit.—In bringing the Indian books to China,
in most cases they did not translate, but merely trans-
literated the litanies syllable by syllable, using the
written character to imitate the sound. A native teacher
can read the printed page, but does not understand
one iota of the meaning, as nearly all of their manuals
of devotion are in Sanscrit ; so it is an "unknown
tongue," verily as "sounding brass" and "tinkling
cymbal." The priests understood the power of prayer,
but as mediators of the dismal covenant they were wise
enough to retain the power in their hands, and not to
make the blessings accessible to all, so " they established

an elaborate ritual, interlarded with Sanscrit phrases," that they might impose upon the people. Perhaps not one in a thousand of the priests understands his own literature.

One of the sacred books gives five reasons for using Sanscrit—1. The words are secrets known only to the Buddhas. 2. Each word has such a breadth of meaning that it cannot be translated. 3. The names of the gods are in Sanscrit, and the repetition in prayer calls on them to protect men. 4. The words are the secret seals of the Buddhas. 5. The mysteries are beyond the power of thought; chant these secret words and there will be hidden benefits.

Prayer for Rain.—Much of the religious worship of the Chinese is summed up in their prayers for rain. In time of drought, when the "heaven is brass and the earth iron," a religious solemnity seems to pervade the land. The mandarins, acting under the double motive of a desire for prosperity and a fear of insurrection, proclaim a fast from animal food, forbid the sale of pork and onions, go to the temples with lighted sticks of incense, call upon the priests to chant prayers, daily go before the gods, and if an answer is not given, the idol is placed in the court under the beams of the noon-day sun, and sometimes the lash is applied to his back. In Soochow, if the usual prayers fail, the south gate is shut, as heat comes from this quarter, and from the hills near the Great Lake a brass image of the goddess of mercy is brought to the city; it is said that she always answers the prayers for refreshing showers. During the official services, the Yamen runners in the temple courts, with twigs of willow, sprinkle water from a jar as an emblem of the falling drops.

The Emperor himself, if the drought be general throughout his dominions, goes to the temples to pray for rain, as during the famine of 1876 he went seventeen times. " In these seventeen days of prayer he did not go from place to place. Having prayed at any temple or altar once, he continued to pray at the same temple or altar until the rain fell. Other temples or altars were added to those at which first he prayed, but the first were not deserted." He ordered an iron tablet to be brought from the dragon-god's well in a distant city to Peking, to be worshipped there. "Two iron tablets had been observed floating upon the water in that well years ago, and were taken out in times of drought, that prayer might be offered to them. The prayer was followed by the rain in a surprising manner." This well is now canonized, and so is one of the deities of China.

During the winter, if no snow falls, the Emperor prays for snow. I have seen the mandarins in Soochow on January 7th, the sky clear and the air balmy, go to the temples and pray for snow.

The manual of prayer for rain contains the names of thousands of dragons, whose names are called, and they each in turn are asked to send fruitful showers. Before the dragon-king the priests say, " In the kingdom which prays for rain, let a great rain descend and fall." "Quickly destroy all trouble and sorrow, quickly send rain and moisten this great earth, quickly protect all the living, quickly destroy the miseries of all creatures ; turn the evil stars to propitious seasons; arise, great pity, and send rain ; destroy the heavy sins of all creatures, so that they may dance for joy."

How solemn are the words of Holy Writ, " Are there any among the vanities of the Gentiles that can cause rain ?   Or can the heavens give showers ?   Art not Thou he, O Lord, our God ?   Therefore will we wait upon Thee, for Thou hast made all these things."

The Buddhist and Taoist Calendar.—This list only includes the common gods of the nation. It is very desirable for every missionary to make an almanac for the local deities of his own city, so that the preaching may be specific and appropriate, not general and desultory. This list corresponds to the Roman calendar of " Saints' Days."

First Moon.

1.—Birthday of " The Coming Buddha."
5.   „   God of Riches.
7.   „   „   Silver.
8.   „   „   Grain.
9.   „   Heaven or The Pearly Emperor.
10.   „   Earth, or The Earth-god, worshipped 8th to 15th.
13.   „   God of Agriculture.   Worshipped 13th to 20th.
15.   „   The Three Mandarins.

Second Moon.

1.—Sun enters his temple.
2.—God of the Precinct (t'udee).
3.—God of Literature.
6.—The Eastern Peak.
8.—Lucky day for chanting.
15.—Laotsze.
19.—Kwanyin.
28.—Worship of Bodhidharma.

THIRD MOON.

16.—God of the Hills.
19.—Birthday of the Sun.
23.—The Empress of Heaven, or Goddess of the Sea.

FOURTH MOON.

1.—Jail-god.
4.—Wenshu P'usa.
8.—Amita.
14.—Dr. Leu Chenyang, the Æsculapius of China.
15.—Shakyamuni Buddha.
28.—God of Medicine.

FIFTH MOON.

1.—Star of old Age.
5.—God of Pestilence. Ancestral worship.
11.—Governor in Hades (corresponding to the Governor of Soochow).
13.—God of War.
18.—Chang, The Heavenly Teacher.

SIXTH MOON.

10.—Leu Hai.
19.—Kwanyin (three birthdays a year).
23.—God of Fire.
24.—God of Thunder. Vegetarians from 1st to 24th.
25.—The Star Ruler.
26.—God of Theatres.
27.—Goddess of the Pole Star.
29.—The Devil.

SEVENTH MOON.

13.—Tashuchi.
15.—Ancestors.
18.—Western Empress Mother.
30.—God of Hades (Titsang). The Devil's Procession.

EIGHTH MOON.

3.—Kitchen-god.
4.—Northern Bushel.
15.—Moon-god.

18.—Bacchus.
22.—Light-Lamp Buddha (Janteng).
24.—Thanking the Kitchen-god.

NINTH MOON.

1—9.—Vegetarians in honour of the Southern Bushel.
13.—God of War.
16.—God of the Loom.
17.—Golden Dragon of the Yellow River.
19.—Kwanyin, the Goddess of Mercy.

TENTH MOON.

1.—Ancestral worship.
3.—The Three Mao.
5.—Bodhidharma.

ELEVENTH MOON.

4.—Confucius.
17.—Amita.
19.—Sun-god.

TWELFTH MOON.

20.—Carpenter's god.
23, 24.—Kitchen-god's ascension.
25.—Buddha's descension.
30.—Receiving kitchen-god.   Worship of Heaven, Earth, and
    Ancestors.

CHAPTER XIV.

CHINESE idolaters may be divided into three general classes, the devout, the sceptical, and the careless. Of the men, the first division includes only a few in the cities, but a large proportion of the peasantry in central and southern China, who believe that the gods are able to help, efficacious in sickness and distress, and who worship with some regularity. The second class are Confucianists, or those influenced by the Confucian tirades against idolatry, who think that Buddhism is "emptiness," the gods mud and stone, the priests drones and hypocrites, the future life uncertain, and who go to the temples once, or a few times, a year; yet even they, in times of sickness and death, and at the feasts, betake themselves to idols. The third class, the careless, is by far the largest. The Chinese mind is practical, worldly-minded in the extreme, and fixed upon the things of this life. They are *this-siders*. The great body of the people look upon religion with indifference; in their hearts they believe in the gods, but in their lives they almost neglect them; "five minutes for prayers," is their motto, and that every two or three months. There is so much

worship in China because the population is so dense, and
not a few are frequently engaged in devotion, but the
average is small.   It is in religion that we see the
" *realism* of the Chinese."

Worship of the Seen.—The formula which embraces
heathenism is *the worship of the seen;* there is a sensible,
tangible object placed before the eyes, and the thoughts
need not go beyond this.   As a man said to me, " We
cannot go up to heaven, so we bring heaven down to us in
the form of an image, and worship it here on the earth."
It is said of Christians, " They do not worship anything
at all; they talk with their mouths in prayer, but they
worship nothing."   Our devotions are spoken of as " worshipping in the void."   The Chinese, like the Jews,
" seek after a sign," and there is probably no doctrine so
absurd in their eyes as that God is a Spirit; and to those
who from their infancy have been taught that the gods
are in the form of men, there is no part of the Decalogue
so difficult to observe as the second commandment.

The gods appear to Men.—There are few questions
so often asked us as, " Does your God ever appear? "
" Does He ever show Himself to men ? "   It is an article
of the nation's faith that the gods are often seen by men;
on the hills during the pilgrim-season, the deity (or a
priest?) is seen walking to and fro with a great lantern;
on the Great Lake, at night, mariners in small crafts
seeking the mouth of the creek say that often a beacon is
seen ahead (not, of course, from the village or a fisher-
man's boat), the god or goddess guiding the boatmen,
who afterwards devoutly pay their vows.   The gods in the
day of battle appear for the protection of the army; also

when a pestilence is sweeping through the camp, or a storm is raging at sea.

From the mirage on the rice-fields sometimes a town is thrown into excitement, and tens of thousands at midnight crowd upon the city walls to behold the silent

Idol Factory.

battle fought by the soldiers of Hades, whose battalions are marshalled on the nightly plain.

The Idol Factory.—The manufacture of images is an important branch of trade, and is generally considered a profitable industry. It is not an art, as where in Italian marble by master-hands the body of man is chiselled in proportions so majestic, so gigantic, that men scarcely

know which most to admire, the sculptor or the statue.
The Chinese figures are misproportioned, grotesque,
and hideous; their faces are grum, frightful, and repul-
sive; if sitting they are awkward and clumsy, when
standing the images are both fantastic and cadaverous.
Why these hideous idols? Christianity teaches of a God
of love; paganism, of deities who will punish the wrong-

Unfinished Images.

doer. The gentler attributes of the Godhead—love, pity,
compassion, gentleness, longsuffering—are little taught
by heathenism.

Walk into one of the shops, with several hundred
images of all sizes, from three inches to ten feet high.
If of wood the head is on the counter, the arm on the
bench, the body on the floor, and the foot on the shelf;
the foot is pinned to the leg, the leg to the body, the

arm to the shoulder, the head to the neck, and lo! it is a god!

Opposite the shop, basking in the sun, there is a line of rough mud daubs, rude and shaggy, drying; for bones they have a framework of wood, mud for flesh, paint for skin, and the heart is made of silver or pewter. Note the hole in the back. A frog, snake, lizard, or centipede is caught and put inside for the soul, and then it is a living deity, and they fall down and worship, and say, "Deliver me, for thou art my God." In the temples you see the large images at every stage of erection; in Wuseih I saw three huge images, made of a framework with laths nailed on, which had waited months for the plasterer.

"Men rely on the gods, and the gods rely on men," is a proverb that reveals the weakness of idolatry. Men rely on the gods for protection, and the gods rely on men for repairs. The shrine is to be guarded, the sacred body shielded, the clothing refitted, the ear mended, the nose replaced, the face gilded, the hand restored, the foot reset, the crown rejewelled, the eyes reballed, and sometimes head, arms, and legs have to be replaced.

I once saw a stone image from which the iconoclasts had clipped nose and ear. Hundreds of worshippers were at the shrine, and as their bodies were prostrate, and incense smoking, workmen were busy restoring the organs of smell and hearing with putty, and in order to give symmetry to the face the whole was burnished with gold.

The images are made of breakable materials; sometimes stone, and very rarely bronze; often of wood, but mostly of mud, which being sun-dried easily crumbles, symbolized by the feet of Nebuchadnezzar's image, part of iron and part of clay, which "the stone that was cut out without hands" brake in pieces.

Large Images.—Large images do not abound in China; some impress the beholder by their size, but a closer examination reveals the fact that the throne or pedestal is ten feet high. Buddha was said to be sixteen feet high, and many images represent him as this height. In Japan there is the celebrated image of Buddha, Daibutz, which is fifty-two feet in height and very broad; it is of bronze. In one of the cities of the metropolitan province there is said to be a bronze image seventy feet high. "In the largest Lama monastery in Peking there is a colossal image of Buddha of wood, also seventy feet in height." There is one at Hangchow cut out of the solid rock, forty feet in height. Another image in the Chehkiang province is "more than a thousand years old, and was cut out of the solid rock by the labour of a father, son, and grandson, requiring the chiselling of three generations. It is an image of the Coming Buddha, the working out of an idea of the artisan devotees that the Coming Buddha would be mighty to save, seventy feet high, and being so majestic in size the sight is very impressive."

The Dedication.—When the idol is taken to the temple, the gong beats in thunder tones, the clarionet sends forth shrill notes, the cymbals clang, and the bells toll, and it is dedicated amidst ceremonies not quite as gorgeous as when the image, ninety feet high, was erected on the plain of Dura. The pupil of the eye is touched by an artist, called "open the light," and

then it becomes a real divinity; before this rite is
performed it is only a toy, which may be handled and
played with; now a god, the people light candles and
incense, bow before the shrine, and witness the theatricals.

Idolatry as an Industry.—The manufacture of images
is an extensive business, but as an idol once bought is
kept for years, it is not as large as the trade in articles
of worship. The tinfoil for paper money is beaten
thin, pasted on bits of paper, and sold in packages.
Candle factories employ a great number of men, as
well as the making of incense. It is often said, " If
we embrace Christianity, what will the large part
of the population engaged in idolatrous trade do?"
Rice is the staple diet, but the number of shops connected with the temples is much greater than those
which sell the staff of life. The candle and incense
shops, the Southern-goods stores, the "variety shops,"
the clothing stores for the dead, the paper-money stalls,
the picture galleries of the gods, with the thousands
of artists employed, the incense stands in front of the
temples, houses, and doors,—all go to show the hold
idolatry has. These symbols of paganism predominate
to the south of the Yangtse.

Building a Temple.—Along the streets a priest is
seen clad in a robe like a patchwork quilt, a picture
of Weito the Buddhist protector on his back, a small
stool in his hand, with which he stops every few rods
and kneels, beating on a fish-head and uttering a shrill
cry; thus he goes for three years, when, being well
known along the streets and his devotion well attested,
he takes a book and collects subscriptions. The monk

who founds a monastery and collects funds for its erection
has his image or tablet placed within, and is afterwards
worshipped.   A short time since, speaking to a priest of
his temple improvements, he said, "This temple I built
on my knees," meaning that he had made the money by

Collecting for a Temple.

reciting masses for the dead.   To erect a temple to the
god of the precinct, a tax is often levied on every store,
as 2 *cash* per cwt. on rice.

A priest erects a thatched hut, sits by his wooden fish-
head, and beats all day and late at night; the old ladies

passing by, get acquainted, and listen to the golden opportunity for obtaining merit now offered, and some one gives him fifty cents. This is conspicuously mounted on a slip of red paper, and soon the whole side of the house tells of the gifts—Mrs. Lee $1; Mrs. Ming $200; Mr. Loh, 25 cents; Hon. Mr. Pan $10; Lady Chang $5, etc., etc. The hut is replaced by a couple of rooms, and gradually, as funds accumulate, never running into debt, section by section and row by row is added. In most of the large temples there is a legend that the timber to erect the buildings was miraculously drawn up out of a well in the court.

The quickest method is by circulating a story of the virtue of the god, as in Soochow a few years since, where the priests pulled up a stone image out of the water, and spread a report that a lady of age and wealth, who was without an heir, had received the desire of her heart. Immediately streams of pilgrims poured towards the shrine, a score at a time bowed before the god, genii-water (which they saw dipped up out of the canal and placed before the god) was sold at threepence a bottle, knives were electrified by rubbing on the stone, ophthalmia and various diseases were brought to the Great Healer, and when asked, " Did you get cured?" the patient would answer, " I am perchance a wee bit, a very little little, almost imperceptibly better;" the booth at first put up was replaced by a substantial building, the carpenters and masons were busy amidst the thronging multitude of devotees, and when the whole was completed, a mandarin, who was of higher rank than the god, coming to worship, the deity became frightened, and his efficacy suddenly departed.

A story is told of a priest who circulated a report that a "living Buddha" was about to arise near his little temple. By night he dug a hole, filled it with beans, placed an image above, covered the earth over, and

Nail Cage.

"poured on water." When the beans began to swell, the ground began to crack, and the people began to gather, when lo! the new Buddha arose; he was received as a messenger from Hades, and his temple was quickly erected.

The Nail Cage A cage is made with nails, sharp and pointed, all around and sticking within, and the outside is covered with locks of different metals. The priest takes his stand inside, speechless and immovable; other priests with gongs go throughout the city and country collecting crowds to witness the prisoner of penance, and the godly are exhorted to buy off a lock,

Hooked into the Arm

set the bonze free, and obtain merit. After three days the excitement becomes intense, and some gold (brass ?) locks go at $50 or $100 apiece.

The Tortures of Buddhism.—Men make vows that they will appear in a procession with a censer weighing five or ten pounds, fastened into the arm by several little brass hooks, so that the flesh is drawn down an inch or two. The stick in the hand is only to aid in holding the arm straight. The pain is excruciating, but a band of the tortured men march all day along the streets with a company of followers to beat gongs.

Stealing Candles.—Behind the candle-rack and in front of the images stands the temple assistant, called the "incense-fire," who receives the candles from the devotee and asks, "Where do you want these placed?" "Oh! light two in the middle and two on each side," is the reply, as the worshipper bows to pray or consult the oracle. The "incense-fire" sticks two on the rack, and, on account of the press of customers, puts the others aside. As soon as the purchaser turns his back the candles are taken from the rack and blown out, and so there is carried on a system of robbery, wholesale and retail, according to the size of the congregation, in the very audience chamber of the god, the whole assembly being witnesses. They say, "We gave the candles with a pious heart, and the god accepts the pious heart, though he does not get the candles."

"Ye worship ye know not what."—Often when a throng is at the temple the question is asked, "What god is this?" The man who has just made nine prostrations answers, "I do not know." "What is the name of the god?" is asked of the devotees, and they answer, "We do not know." When the city gods rotate in office upon a new mandarin taking the seals of government, how is an acquaintance possible? If you ask for the history of the idol, what he was celebrated for, or why they worship, the most indefinite answers are given.

Compendium of gods.—In China there are gods celestial and gods terrestrial, *dei majores* and *dei*

Pantheon.

minores; gods of heaven, and gods of hell; gods of the earth, sun, moon, and stars; of thunder, lightning, wind, and rain; of water, fire, wood, earth, and metal; and of the seas, rivers, mountains, hills, seasons, snow, frost, tides, trees, and flowers. There are Indian gods and Chinese gods; and gods, demigods, Buddhas, Bodhisattwas, immortals, fairies, ancestors, emperors, sages, heroes, warriors, statesmen, dragons, devils, demons, and spirits are worshipped.

Gods in the Clouds.

There are 500 disciples of Buddha, 500 disciples of Confucius, 72 masters, 60 cycle deities, and 36 prime ministers to be sacrificed to. There are good gods and bad gods; city gods and country gods; the gods of the door, the kitchen, the city wall, the theatre, and the prison. The carpenters have their gods and the fishermen theirs; so has the silk merchant and the saloon keeper. Horses, cows, sheep, snakes, and lice have each their presiding deities, and so have fire-crackers and fertilisers. Pestilence, medicine, small-pox, and measles have a host of gods. The eye, ear, nose, tongue, teeth, heart, liver, throat, hands, feet, and skin have each a special god. A bridge, a bed, a compass, happiness, tea, and salt have their presiding deities. At Yangchow there is a temple with 10,000 gods.

Some gods are of stone, others are of wood, clay, and bronze. There are images, pictures, and tablets. There are white gods, black gods, yellow gods, and red gods. The smallest are an inch in height and the tallest fifty feet. A god can be purchased for half-a-cent, and another will cost a thousand dollars. Some are the laughing Buddhas; a few have mild and beneficent countenances, while the great horde have hideous, cadaverous faces, to inspire awe in the worshipper and frighten the impious. The "Pantheon picture" is worshipped on New Year's day. Behind Buddha, facing inwards in the large temples, there is in *basso relievo* a representation of the gods in the clouds, and Neptune rising from the waves of the briny deep.

Places of Worship.—The land is filled with idols. They are to be found in the temple, the monastery, and the nunnery; in the cities, towns, villages, and hamlets; on the streets, at the crossings, and over the gates. The Yamens, stores, workshops, and homes all have them; the door, the main entrance, the hall, the chapel, the chamber, and the roof have their gods; they are seen by the canals and the bridges and on the boats; the shrines in the alleys and the miniature temples on the table are full of them; the picture galleries give an exhibit of celestial beings, and they are "portrayed on the walls" of public halls, and at times the face of a hill is carved with images; they crown the mountain and make holy the cavern, they are worshipped in the valley and under the "green tree."

In the country, meeting an old man, I inquired, "Have you any gods around here?" "Oh, yes," said he. "What gods?" I asked. "The Three Pure Ones." "Any others?" "The god of the fields." "Any others?" "The goddess of Mercy." "My old friend, I am afraid your gods are not a few." "Foreign teacher," was his literal reply, "verily, verily, our gods are ten thousand times ten thousand, and thousands of thousands."

Dei Majores.—Among the hosts of gods the reader would like to have pointed out those most worshipped. Buddha, The Pearly Emperor, Confucius, The Buddhas of "The Three Ages," and The Three Pure Ones, are high deities. Kwanyin, the goddess of Mercy; Kwante, the god of War; Amita, the god of the Western Heaven; Titsang, the god of Hades; King Yama (Yen Lowang), the ruler of Hell, are held in reputation. The gods of Literature, Agriculture, Riches, and Thunder are worshipped often. Of equal rank are the goddess of the Pole Star; the Eastern Peak; Leu Chenyang, the Æsculapius; the Three Mandarins; the triad stars of Happiness, Office, and Age; and last among these twenty high rulers, and by no means the least, is the Devil.

The Abominations.—Heathenism is spoken of as "the images of abomination," "the idols of abomination," and the "abominable idolatries." Pagans are described in the Second Commandment as "them that hate Me," and the sin is so heinous that it is visited even upon the third and fourth generation of idolaters. Because Jeroboam "made other gods," and thus caused "Israel to sin," the extinction of his family became a byword in Judea when they wished to speak of utter destruction. Five times in the New Testament it is said that idolaters are "without," and "shall not inherit the kingdom of God." The exposition of the sin and folly of idolatry, occupying as it does such a prominent position in the sacred Scriptures, would furnish material for a series of discourses in a home pulpit.

CHAPTER XV.

MOUNTAINS, ISLANDS, AND FESTIVALS.

THE sacred mountains in China are truly innumerable, for there is not a towering peak or lofty summit which does not wear Buddha's crown, and the eye of the traveller " is charmed by the picturesqueness of pagodas perched on mountain crags, and monasteries nestling in sequestered dells." Often there is a circlet of temples in the ravines or half-way up the sides of the hills. Save under the Christian dispensation " men universally have connected the worship of the gods with hills and mountains, for they regard their gods as in the air and their abodes as in the heavens ; hence, lofty hills towering to heaven seem to be especially near the gods, and hill-tops the most likely places to reach them with prayer." China has her million mountains, at times the hills rising abruptly from the rice-field plains. Some of the provinces are covered with mountains, and one is described as a " sea of mountains ;" so religion from the high places attracts the dwellers on the plains. Is there a country with more picturesque scenery than this, where mountain and plain, lake and river, give freshness and variety to the view? Landscape gardening has been given almost entirely into the hands of the priests, who have terraced the hills and planted the groves to invite the worshipper to ascend. Only two places of note will be mentioned, the one belonging to the Taoists and the other to the Buddhists.

Mount T'ai.—This mountain is considered by the Chinese as the highest peak in the kingdom, but the barometer gives the headship to others. Its height from the plain is near 4,000 feet, but above the level of the sea it is much greater. It is in the Shantung province in North China, and near the home, school, and grave of Confucius. Mount T'ai is an ancient sacred mountain, for one hundred and twenty successive generations of men have, year by year, ascended this " holy hill." "Shun came here in the first year of his reign, B.C. 2255, presented offerings to Heaven, and sacrificed to the hills and rivers. It is certain that for over 4,000 years Chinese emperors have been accustomed to come here to sacrifice to Heaven, and to worship the mountain, and during all these centuries it has been an object of veneration and worship to millions of people. Perhaps no other mountain on the face of the earth has had an equally remarkable history." There is a large temple in the city which is situated at its base, dedicated to its presiding deity, and thither many pilgrims resort, but to ascend the mountain itself is the object of many a long journey in wheelbarrows over roads frightfully rough. Chinese books say, " Mount T'ai is the chief of the five sacred mountains. Its merit is equal to Heaven, and so it is appointed and called the equal of Heaven, the Benevolent and Holy Ruler. It is Lord of this world, and determines births and deaths, misfortune and happiness, honour and dishonour, things high and great, low and crooked."

The mountain is described as "not an isolated peak, but as having three summits; the central one being the largest and highest." To the north, there is "nothing but hills upon hills, and only the backs of successive ranges of mountains can be seen in the distance." The road for the first mile is graded, so that the rise is gradual, but thence when the eye is uplifted it seems like a stairway to the skies, for there are near 6,000 steps of hewn stone, each fifteen feet in length, leading upward, while "on both sides of the road, far and near, every peak and projecting rock, every cave and ravine, every stream and spring, has its name," and temples without number "line the ascent and crown the summit." During the cold month of February, the pilgrims are from 5,000 to 10,000 daily, and the upward march is continued with an average of 1,000 during the next two months; old men leaning on their staffs, with aged matrons, supported by their grandsons and followed by little children, all conditions and ranks climb this precipitous highway to burn incense on this mountain where their "fathers worshipped." Heathenism makes the mountain sacred, Christianity the home. Mountain worship is limited to time. "Believe Me," saith Jesus, "the hour cometh, when ye shall neither in this mountain, nor yet at Jerusalem, worship the Father."

Pootoo.—The most lovely spot in Far Cathay is the sacred isle of Pootoo, two hundred miles from Shanghai, and sixty from Ningpo, from which latter city, in another direction overland, is reached the far-famed Snowy Valley. The route to Pootoo is among hundreds of islands, great

and small, all mountainous, which compose the Chusan
archipelago, and as the steamer winds its tortuous way
among them, every variety of wild scenery is presented;
now the precipitous rocks and projecting headlands, the
barren knolls and rugged crags; then the mountains
covered with trees, and hills beautifully terraced to the top
with waving fields of grain; or villages nestling in little
bays, or encircled in foliage, lying on the water's edge;
indeed in its approaching views and receding vistas it is
a twin-sister of the inland Sea of Japan.   Pootoo is the
capital of Indo-Chinese Buddhism, and its renown is as far-
famed as the Chinese language is spoken or Chinese literature known.   It is a lofty mountain-island, five miles long,
jutting out in five promontories, having broad roads paved
with flag-stones running over the hills amidst groves and
hedges, and under the overspreading branches of forest
trees; with beautiful beaches, where roll the clear waters of
the mighty ocean, much to the pleasure of the visitor, who
may for a week or two months dwell in the hospitable
monasteries, enjoy the life-giving surf, breathe the health-
restoring air, and be fanned by breezes from across the
trackless Pacific.   Some of the ascents are precipitous, as to
the lighthouse, and some of the paths wind round the cliffs,
with the mountain overhanging and the sea in full view.
There is a deep cave in a rock shaped like a V, which is
called purgatory, probably because the tide rushes into it
with such a thundering sound, dashing the spray upon the
rocks a hundred feet above.   The spectator on the bridge,
gazing down into the dark, seething depths, could almost
imagine it to be the gateway of the bottomless pit.   The
sides of the island are lined with caves and caverns, and

sacred inscriptions are engraved upon the boulders.   There
is the well of the genii, the Indian Pagoda, the furnace for
cremation, and lakes made gay by the white and crimson
lotus.   The temples number one hundred; from the small
building with its solitary occupant to the spacious
monastery having its retinue of bonzes, or up to The
Temple which is in itself a little village, spread out over

The Hermit.

a whole valley.   Some of the sacred edifices are built on
barren precipices overlooking the sea, others stand out
upon the promontories, while the shore, the half-way ascent,
and the lofty summit, all have their temples.   The roofs
of the two large temples of yellow porcelain, an imperial
gift, are in striking contrast with the green of the
surrounding bamboo forests, and glitter amidst the waving

branches of the stately camphor, venerable groves of which surround these old temples, and their overspreading arches impress the beholder with the grandeur and majesty of nature. The whole isle seems truly enchanted, and is made as lovely as Chinese mind can conceive or Chinese skill can execute.

In the one hundred temples are one thousand priests, who own property on the adjacent islands and receive fees from the worshippers, who come on junks and steamers. The last time I was there, a Shanghai compradore paid £160 for the masses to be recited, seven days, for the soul of his father, who died in Canton. Sometimes a liberal patron furnishes a feast to the priests, and it is an interesting spectacle to witness three hundred priests seated in the refectory. The island is governed by two abbots, chosen by ballot, who hold office for three years. No woman can dwell there.

In the spring and autumn pilgrims are numerous, and here the junkmen stop to pay their devotions to Kwanyin, whose throne is Pootoo. For centuries pirates were the terror of the men with the yellow robe, but since foreign commerce has driven these from the high sea great activity has been displayed in sacred architecture.

Theological Seminary.—The priests are an idle, listless class, and care nothing for the library of five thousand volumes. At the lecture the bonzes sat, tailor-fashion, with their books on the table in front, while an attendant passed behind and replenished the tea-cups. The professor, mounted on a high daïs, with a stick of burning incense to mark the length of the lecture (about two hours), expounded the text, and often seemed to think an anecdote was in place, much to the amusement of the sixty priests, though sometimes, it was thought, at the expense of his foreign visitor.

Religion as a Holiday.—In every land, at certain

Theological Lecture.

seasons, religion wears a holiday attire; much more is it necessary in this country, where heavily burdened men and toiling women have so few opportunities for enjoyment. The religious recreations are of three classes, pilgrimages, processions, and theatricals.

Pilgrims.—In Central China, during the soft days of

spring, to the Hangchow temples alone perhaps a million pilgrims resort. Some devotee makes up a party mostly of women, though the men go in great numbers, and charters a boat, in which they pack like sardines, *minus* the oil. They chant their prayers as the boatmen row, go to the mountains, visit the West Lake, so celebrated in poetry, ascend with the mighty army whose badge is a yellow incense bag, talk with the priests, buy a wicker basket and a bamboo chair, and return after a ten days' trip.

Idol Processions.—To every hamlet in the country the god of agriculture, as well as the local deities, must be carried. The most exciting days in Soochow are at the three great feasts—fifth moon, fifth day ; eighth moon, fifteenth day ; and tenth moon, first day—when the mandarins go out with their official trains to offer sacrifice to the wild spirits. About thirty idols are taken out, each with a long retinue, so that the line extends over a mile ; the whole city is out in holiday attire, and the narrow street to the **Tiger Hill** is almost impassable from the dense mass of human beings. In the picture, the gong opens the way, the official signboards of the go follow ; then lictors dragging bamboos, flag-bearers, the great fan, and cavalry move onward ; then come two men with necks twisted, and faces all awry, who walk many miles looking sideways at one another in the face—it is a laughable spectacle. Then come the red umbrellas and streamer-bearers ; and besides these there are criminals in red robes, men with hooks fastened in their arms, to which are suspended bronze censers, riders bearing the credentials and seals of office, coolies carrying trunks,

Idol Procession.

followers with red girdles, men dragging chains, little children carried on a man's head (Cupids), and, most conspicuous, six or eight fat butchers, who, with open breasts, act as the executioners (of Hades), and go panting by; then comes the god in open chair and embroidered robes.

Heathenism Fascinating When the procession

Temple Theatre.

returns at night with lanterns lit, gongs beating, the runners whooping, the idol looking majestic, and the people bowing, one appreciates the magnetism of a crowd, and understands how a pageant may impress, and pasteboard and tinsel captivate.

Theatricals.—Paganism is an amalgam of the Church

and the world ; the theatre is one of its forms of worship, and then the stage actors are the priests. The temples have a stage opposite the sacred shrine, and the picture represents the biennial festival. If men love to go to the theatre, why not the gods ? In the farm villages twice a year, at the religious theatricals, thousands assemble in the open grounds, hucksters and pedlars surround the assembly, the idol is brought out in state, and the scene is a " Vanity Fair." The play days are fixed, so the people go from hamlet to hamlet to attend the shows. In home lands, those who find more delight in the theatre than in the church, are they Christians or are they Buddhists?

CHAPTER XVI.

WOMEN AND BUDDHISM.

THE women of Christian lands, outside the home circle, have three leading sources of pleasure, namely, education, society, and religion. In China, as ignorance takes the place of the first and seclusion of the second, the only spring of happiness which is available to the benighted daughters of Sinim is religion. It is pleasant for them to go to the temples and burn incense, though frequently prohibited by the mandarins, whose proclamations for a few months only can stem the tide of paganism. It is pleasant for a party of neighbours on the idol's birthday to assemble at the nunnery, and have a feast, a social chat, and an all-day chant. It is pleasant for the caged birds of rich plumage twice a year in a boat to visit the temples on the hills, breathe the fresh country air, and gather flowers. In every land religion takes a deeper hold on the hearts of women, in their quiet spheres, than of men, who in the busy marts are subjected to the temptations of the great world without. This is specially true of the women of China, as three-fourths of the worshipping is performed by the gentler sex, and probably seven-eighths of the three hundred or four hundred million dollars spent annually in idolatry are contributed by toiling females, who scarcely have money to purchase coarse food. In their minds there are no sceptical doubts as to the truth of their religion, and in their hearts they love the gentle goddesses, and fear the gods who hold the fire-brand, wield the sword, or hurl the thunderbolt.

Nunneries.—There are from fifty to one hundred nunneries in Soochow, with an average perhaps of a half-dozen nuns to each, quite a number of them youthful, but others aged matrons, who have great influence in the aristocratic families of the city as the spiritual guides of the ladies, and who have power to checkmate a pro-clamation of the Governor by influencing his wife to plead in behalf of their order. As their raiment is similar to that of the priests, and their heads are shaven, it is

The Nun.

hard to tell a nun from a priest. Every day, before the first rays gild the horizon, we are saluted by the dull sound of the mallet on the wooden fish-head, the nuns being paid for an interest in their prayers, and it is supposed they worship before the shrine, whereas on a frosty morn the fish-head is placed beside the couch. Some of these establishments own property which yields an income; some are family nunneries, where a lady of wealth takes the veil, and to one of those in Soochow the Emperor Kienlung gave the " Heart Sutra," written with his own hand ; in some the "vestal fire" (*pah mih ten*) is kept burning ; in others, the inmates eke out a poor subsistence by "beating the autumn wind," *i.e.*, carrying as a present dishes of vegetables at the regular

Goddess.

feasts to the rich, expecting a gift in return ; while still in others the old women have a " Buddha's way," *i.e.*, they meet once a month, and each contributes so much paper money, which is burnt at the death of the first member of the circle.

The Goddesses.—Many of the gods have their wives

in the inner apartments of the temple ; there is the bed,
the bureau, the trunks, and four maids, one to comb the
hair, one to wash the face, one to hand tea, and one to
present the food.   In North China women who recover
from sickness bring a little woman with plaster-of-Paris
face and real hair, place her beside the goddess, and let
her remain three years before burning ; this is to certify
that she will be a servant to the goddess in Hades.
Near our city temple two women, Mrs. Chow and Mrs.
Cash, receive the offerings thrown into the coffer, because
they arrange the hair, wash the feet, and dress the wooden
goddess.   These ladies of the other world are often
worshipped by the sick.

Ancestral Benefits.—" An indirect result of ancestral
worship has been to define and elevate the position of
wife and mother.   All the laws which could be framed for
the protection of women would lack their force if she were
not honoured in the household.   As there can be only
one ' illustrious consort' named on the tablet, there is of
course only one wife acknowledged in the family. . . .
This acknowledged parity of the mother with the father
in the most sacred position in which she can be placed
has done much to maintain the purity and right influence
of woman amid all the degradations, pollutions, and moral
weakness of heathenism."

Buddha's Doctrine of Women.—Thus spake the
founder of the Indian religion : " A woman's body has
many evil things in it ; at birth her parents are not
happy ; rearing her is ' without taste ; ' her heart fears
men ; she must rise early and late, and be very busy ;
she can never eat before others ; her father and mother

begrudge the money to be spent on her wedding; she must leave father and mother; she fears her husband and has times of travail; if her husband curses her she is not permitted to get angry; in youth, father and mother rule; in middle life, her husband; in old age she is at the beck and call of her grandchildren."

The Lake of Blood.—The sacred book most frequently used by the Buddhist priests is the Lake of Blood Sutra. On their knees they chant it for a price paid by the women, as the men have no part in this lake, over which the blackness of darkness broods, where the thirsty have only blood to drink and whose stench ascends to the skies. Every female is born a debtor; a debtor to what? A debtor to the Lake of Blood, and this debt, if not cancelled in this life, must be paid in the world to come. And for what crime do Buddhists consign woman to this fearful destiny? The crime is maternity. Also, those whose light is put out so suddenly in childbirth go immediately to this lake. The soul is filled with horror at this shocking doctrine; the heart sickens at this ghastly spectacle. When we behold punishment following crime, though we shudder, yet our innate sense of justice approves, but the blackest spot on the dark face of Buddhism is that its most terrible retribution is awarded to the innocent, and that to one half of the human family.

The monks by this fill their coffers, for all mothers must pay this debt, and then the lily-boat will ferry them across the lake. The priests tap the temple bell, and within the bell is suspended a paper woman (with a notice of the name, age, day, and hour of death stuck on), and when the bell is struck it causes the woman to move, thus elbowing herself out of the pool; twice a day for forty-nine days they chant, while an assistant beats the bell. At least thirty dollars are paid as a fee. Sometimes to save a woman the Soochowites take a bowl of sweetened water, and cover it with red paper while the monks chant; then the abbot takes his wand, tears the paper, and declares that the woman is saved from the placenta tank—the children and friends drinking the sugared water—by metonomy, the Lake of Blood.

Child's Hat.

The Heathen Mother is very faithful in teaching her children to worship idols, so that the first step in evangelisation is to convert the mother. On the first and fifteenth of every month a mother is seen leading her little toddler before the idol shrine, who is impressed by the majestic appearance of the deity, and draws back in terror, but after he knocks his little head on the mat he is convinced, by the gift of candy or pea-nuts, that it pays to burn incense. The first hat given to a baby is covered with six, twelve, or eighteen little idols; the first play is ı mock sacrifice; the first amusement is to carry the idols in a chair on their little shoulders, and the first lesson in school is to bow before an image or tablet; so that the child, like a fish, swims in the Grand Canal of paganism. On his birthday they worship the goddess of midwives, and also offer sacrifice when he is a month old. When the child is one hundred days old, if a boy, they worship the male star-ruler; if a girl, the female star-ruler. When a year old they worship the star-ruler.

The Dead Child.—There is no Paradise for little ones when called away from earth. The god to whom a parent has an unfulfilled vow claims one as a prize; another is caught by the evil spirits and borne away, while generally they say it is a debtor that demands his price; one to whom he was an enemy in a previous life now seeks revenge, and murders his foe, the innocent little child. Often no coffin is prepared; no funeral service is ever held, and the bones are sometimes buried by a running stream to secure an early transmigration. The death of a boy or girl is simply the blotting out of a star. Does not the broken-hearted pagan mother feel that there is something in a religion with the words, "Suffer little children to come unto Me"?

CHAPTER XVII.

THE HEART OF BUDDHISM.

Buddhism and Roman Catholicism.—The traveller who notes the similarity between these two great systems of faith and worship must on comparison conclude that Romanism is Buddhism prepared for a foreign market,—Buddhism adapted to a Western civilisation. The question troubled the earlier Catholic missionaries, and " Premare ascribed these ceremonies to the devil, who had thus imitated holy mother Church, in order to scandalise and oppose its rites." " To those who admit that most of the Romish ceremonies are borrowed from paganism, there is less difficulty in accounting for the resemblance."

1. In both these systems it is *a worship of pictures and images*, the worship of the seen. As has been said to me, " Hang up a picture of your Jesus, and there will be a thousand of us to worship it in a day." In the cathedrals they bow before each of the pictures hanging around the hall, and suspended to the girdle (in bronze or wood) is the Son of Mary.

2. Both pray in an *unknown tongue;* the Romanists in Latin, and the Buddhists in Sanscrit.

3. Both systems use *candles and incense;* the Catholics

say they do not use " tallow candles " but " angel-candles," *i.e.*, sperm candles.

4. The two religions are alike in having *masses for the dead;* purgatories from which souls may be released by the prayers of the priests.

5. *Rosaries.* Both the Buddhist and the Romanist count their beads.

6. The *vain repetitions.* The substitute for *Ave Maria* is *o-me-to-fuh.*

7. *The celibacy of the clergy.*

8. *Nuns and nunneries.*

9. *The adoration of relics.* The Indian religion has paid no more distinguished honour to Buddha's bones than Rome has given to Peter's.

10. Both religions are based on *systems of merit;* on penance and works of supererogation.

11. Priests from India and France both *adopt the heathen rites of the Chinese.* The proofs in regard to the former are scattered through this work. As to the latter, on a Catholic altar in Shanghai the dragon and cross are united. It is according to the Chinese ideas to worship the Mother of Jesus, but why not the Father? To meet this, the Pope has made Joseph the patron saint of China, so on the scrolls he is designated, " The third man," *i.e.*, Jesus, Mary, Joseph.

12. *Pretended miracles.* The priests of Rome claim miraculous cures, and pretend here to be exorcists.

13. As Rome spends her tens of thousands on *processions,* so does Buddhism.

14. *The worship of saints.* " Chinese demigods are exchanged for foreign saints, with this difference, that

now they worship they know not what, while before
they knew something of the name and character of the
ancient hero, from popular accounts and historical legends."
To see how similar the saints' days of the Catholics are
to the idol birthdays, see the "Buddhist Calendar,"
in Chapter XIII.

Kwanyin in White Robes.

15. *Flower-worship* is
the ornate feature of
each religion; the altars
are alike decorated with
beauteous wreaths and
bouquets of sweetest per-
fume, the woods and the
gardens supplying what
is lacking in the hearts
of the worshipper.

16. *Mary the holy
Mother* finds her perfect
counterpart in *Kwanyin,
the goddess of mercy.*
Let the reader judge for
himself whether Roman-
ism is not simply white-
washed Buddhism.

**Kwanyin, The god-
dess of Mercy** We
come now to the æsthetic in Chinese Buddhism. As Mary
is the guiding spirit of Rome, so Kwanyin is the guardian
angel of the Indian faith. A fact to be noted is that
all false religions have female deities, and exalt their
goddesses; it is because woman's gentle heart is so easily

touched, a mother's tender love being everywhere known, and that a woman is more approachable than a man.

The Thousand-Handed Kwanyin.

Kwanyin was originally a man, but by a convenient metamorphosis he was changed into a lady.

"It would seem to be a fact important in modern Buddhist history, that the most popular of the divinities of this religion should be presented first with male and afterwards with female attributes, and that the change of sex in the images should have been accomplished within the last few centuries."

Fragrant Mountain Liturgy.—A few extracts are given from this work. Kwanyin was the third daughter of a king, beautiful and talented, and, when young, loved to meditate as a priest. Her father, mother, and sisters beseech her not to pass the " green spring," but to marry, and the king offers the man of her choice the throne ; but no, she must take the veil. She enters the " White Sparrow Nunnery," and the nuns put her to the most menial offices ; the dragon opens a well for the young maid-servant, and the wild beasts bring her wood. The king sends his troops to burn the nunnery,—Kwanyin prays, rain falls, and extinguishes the conflagration. She is brought to the palace in chains, and the alternative of marriage or death is placed before her. In the room above where the court of the inquisition was held, there were music, danc-ing, and feasting, sounds and sights to allure a young girl ; the queen also urged her to leave the convent and accede to the royal father's wish. Kwanyin declared she would rather die than marry, so the fairy princess was strangled, and a tiger took her body into the forest. She descended into hell, and hell became a Paradise with gardens of lilies. King Yama was terrified when he saw the prison of the lost becoming an enchanting garden, and begged her to leave, in order that the good and evil might have their distinctive rewards. One of the genii gave her "the peach of immortality." On her return to the terrestrial regions she heard that her father was sick, and sent him word that if he would despatch a messenger to "The Fragrant Mountain" an eye and a hand would be given

Giving-Sons Kwanyin.

him for medicine; this eye and hand were Kwanyin's own, and produced instant recovery.

The Magnet of the Church.—In old Buddhism Shakyamuni was the chief god, and in many temples

he nominally occupies the seat of honour, but now he
is completely eclipsed by the goddess of mercy, as in
Pootoo, where Buddha, six feet high, sits in the rear, and
a gigantic gilt image of Kwanyin stands in front. The
men love her, the children adore her, and the women
chant her prayers. Whatever the temple may be,
there is nearly always a chapel for Kwanyin within
its sacred precincts; she lives in many homes, and in
many, many hearts she sits enshrined. She is the
patron goddess of mothers, and when we remember the
value of a son, we can appreciate the heartiness of the
worship. She protects in sorrow, and so millions of times
the prayer is offered, "Great mercy, great pity, save
from sorrow, save from suffering," or, as it is in the
books, "Great mercy, great pity, save from misery, save
from evil, broad, great, efficacious, responsive Kwanyin
Buddha." She saves the tempest-tossed sailor, so has
eclipsed the Empress of Heaven, who, as the female
Neptune, is the patroness of seamen; in drought the
mandarins worship the Dragon and the Pearly Emperor,
but if they fail, the bronze goddess of mercy from the
hills brings rain. Other gods are feared, she is loved;
others have black, scornful faces, her countenance is
radiant as gold, and gentle as the moon-beam; she draws
near to the people and the people draw near to her. Her
throne is upon the Isle of Pootoo, to which she came
floating upon a water-lily. She is the model of Chinese
beauty, and to say a lady or a little girl is a " Kwanyin "
is the highest compliment that can be paid to grace and
loveliness. She is fortunate in having three birthdays,
the nineteenth of the second, sixth, and ninth moons.

There are many metamorphoses of Kwanyin; of these the four pictures given represent "The Thousand-handed Kwanyin," "The Fish-basket Kwanyin," "The Giving-sons Kwanyin," and "The White-robed Kwanyin."

The Buddhist Saviour.—She is called Kwanyin because at any cry of misery she "hears the voice and removes the sorrow." Her appellation is "Taking-away-fear Buddha." If in the midst of the fire the name of Kwanyin is called, the fire cannot burn; if tossed by mountain billows, call her name and shallow waters will be reached. If merchants go across the sea seeking gold, silver, pearls, and precious stones, if a storm comes up and threatens to carry the crew to the evil-devil's kingdom, if one on board calls the name of Kwanyin the ship will be saved. If one goes into a conflict and calls on the name of Kwanyin the sword and spear of the enemy fall harmless. If the three-thousand great thou-

Fish-Basket Kwanyin.

sand kingdoms are visited by demons, call on her name, and these demons cannot with an evil eye look on a man. If, within, you have evil thoughts, only call on Kwanyin, and your heart will be purified. Anger and wrath may be dispelled by calling on the name of Kwanyin. A lunatic who prays to Kwanyin will become sane. Kwanyin gives sons to mothers, and if the mother asks for a daughter she will be a beauty. Two men—one chanting the names of the 6,200,000 Buddhas, in number like the sands of the Ganges, and the other simply calling on Kwanyin—have equal merit. Kwanyin may take the form of a Buddha, a prince, a priest, a nun, a scholar, any form or shape, go to any kingdom, and preach the law throughout the earth.

Amita and the Western Heaven The most striking difference between northern and southern Buddhism is the doctrine of the Western Heaven and of Amita (Amitahba). It is an innovation of later centuries, probably a thousand years after Buddha, and it is certain that this tenet does not come from India, as this god is unknown in that country and Ceylon. The most plausible theory is that it was borrowed from the Nestorians, whom the Buddhists likely met in Central Asia. In Japan Buddhism is concentrated in the worship of Amita. In China the fronts of the temples have the inscription in great characters, *Na-mo o-me-to-fuh* (Honour to Amita Buddha). There is little homage given by the populace to Shakyamuni compared with what is rendered to this deity, and whole prayer-books and sutras have been manufactured and falsely ascribed to the head of the church as if he were their author. Amita, Kwanyin, and Mahasthama (called Tashuchi, one of Amita's court) form a loving triad, and their images are seen together in the temples of Paradise.

Amita means " boundless light," so called because " his brightness is boundless, and he can illumine all kingdoms. His life, boundless and shoreless, extends through many kalpas." Amita is also called the " boundless-age

Buddha," but his common designation is "the guiding Buddha," the one who directs his followers to a Paradise in the great West.

AMITA.

" See, streaming forth radiance for thousands of miles,
　　Ever sits the compassionate Buddha and smiles,
　　Giving joy to victims of sorrow and strife,
　　Who are saved by his law from the evils of life.
　　All his features of beauty no words can express,
　　For the sands of the Ganges in number are less ;

Amita, Kwanyin, and Tashuchi.

The flowers of the lotus encircle his seat,
As if of themselves they spring up round his feet.
Whoever would enter the home of the blest,
In his innermost thoughts should incessantly rest
On that beautiful form like the moon on high,
When she marches full-orbed through an unclouded sky.
By that halo of light that encircles his head,
On all living beings a radiance is shed ;
The sun at noon-day is less glorious than he,
His compassion resembles a bottomless sea.
His golden arms are outstretched to relieve
The sufferers that weep and the hearts that do grieve ;

His mercy is such as none else can display,
And long years of gratitude cannot repay."

The Magic Name.—In every temple the sound you hear is *o-me-to-fuh;* when you speak to a priest, he utters, *o-me-to-fuh;* the response in prayer is *o-me-to-fuh;* as the monk beats on his fish-head the name is called, *o-me-to-fuh;* as he counts his beads it is *o-me-to-fuh;* as the prayers are read, the women join in *o-me-to-fuh;* as a company of priests assemble at vespers, it is *o-me-to-fuh;* calling the name, they dot the circles on the papers; for every 10,000 times there is one degree of merit obtained. While *o-me-to-fuh* is pronounced, the mind must be fixed on Amita, and the thoughts concentrated on him like a thread running through beads or like an arrow flying to its mark. The effort is to see how many times *o-me-to-fuh* can be called in one breath, and you sometimes hear the priests calling the name at railway speed. Not long since I asked a priest, " How often do you say *o-me-to-fuh* a day ? " and he answered, " Oh, about twenty or thirty thousand times." This is the "vain repetition" of the Buddhist; almost the only prayer the heathen knows is *o-me-to-fuh.*

The Paradise of the West.—The doctrine of the Western Heaven is diametrically opposed to the teachings of Buddha about Nirvana, and proves that the heart could not deal with such abstractions, and that men must have happiness set before them in a more real, substantial form. This Paradise of Amita is not situated within the pale of this solar system. The sacred book says (translated):—Ten million miles to the West there is an earth called Paradise, the home of Amita. Why is it called Paradise? Answer: Because all the creatures born there have no sorrow. There are seven rows of

Western Paradise.

balustrades, seven rows of precious trees around, and seven precious lakes with golden sands. The streets are a compound of gold, silver, pearls, and crystal. There are towers and pavilions adorned with gold, silver, pearls, crystal, and agate. In the lakes are lilies the size of wheels, azure, yellow, red, and white.

Six hours of the day and six hours of the night there is a rain of flowers. The inhabitants gather them in their robes in the morning, take them to other lands to the ten billion other Buddhas, and return, being absent about as long as it takes to eat rice.

The birds of Paradise, variegated in plumage, are famous; white cranes, peacocks, and parrots chant the Buddhist prayers. These birds have no original sin.

In that happy land the three evils are unknown,—not even the names of the three evils are known. Amita, wishing the "law-sound" (our word gospel is "happy-sound") to be constantly chanted, expelled these evils.

If a gentle zephyr blows amid the trees, there are delicate surprising sounds like to 100,000 musical instruments; the listener must necessarily have a heart to chant of Buddha, the Law, and the Church.

THE PURE LAND.

"The pure land of the West, say, what language can tell
Its beauty and majesty? There ever dwell
The men of this world, and the Devas of heaven,
And to each has the same wreath of glory been given.
The secrets of wisdom unveiled they behold,
And the soil that they tread on is bright yellow gold;
In that land of true pleasure the flowers never fade,
Each terraced ascent is of diamond and jade.
The law of great Buddha sung by each bird,
From thicket and grove in sweet music is heard;
The unwithering Upata, fairest of flowers,
Sheds fragrance around in those thrice-lovely bowers.

There, each from the world that he governs, are found,
Assembled in conference long and profound,
The ten supreme Buddhas, who cease not to tell
The praise of the land where the genii dwell :
For there is no region so happy and blest
As the heaven of Amita far in the West.
On the moment of entering that peaceful scene,
The common material body of men
Is exchanged for a body ethereal and bright,
That is seen from afar to be glowing with light.
Happy they who to that joyful region have gone,
In numberless *kalpas* their time flows on ;
Around are green woods, and above them clear skies,
The sun never scorches, cold winds never rise,
And summer and winter are both unknown
In the land of the Law and the Diamond Throne.
All errors corrected, all mysteries made clear,
Their rest is unbroken by care or by fear ;
And the truth that before lay in darkness concealed,
Like a gem without fracture or flaw is revealed."

Born of a Lily.—The beautiful lotus is the flower of Paradise. It is never said, "go to heaven," but to be "born in heaven.' Those who believe must record a vow to be born in the "pure land," at which time a lotus springs up in a pond, and if he is diligent in calling the name of Amita (*o-me-to-fuh*) the flower will flourish, and when he dies a man will be born out of the flower. The exhortation is given in the sutra: At the approach of death, do not fear it; always think this body has many sorrows; it is made filthy by sin, wound round and round; if this dirty body can be thrown off and you be born in a pure land, is it not a happy event? It is like throwing off old clothes and putting on a new suit. If any one will call the name of Amita for seven days with fixed heart, at death Amita with his holy throng will appear before him; his heart will not be turned upside down, but he will be born in Paradise. There are nine ranks among the inhabitants of water-lily purity. The candidate for the lily-birth must imagine

Titsang.

that he is sitting on a lotus-throne, tailor-fashion, that he sees Buddha in his kingdom and hears him preach; he must also have the bright golden image of Amita just before his eyes. This is the Buddhistic account of the "pure land."

The god of Hades.—Above the ten kings of hell is *Titsang*, the god of Hades. The important position he occupies in the pantheon may be appreciated from the fact that he has a shrine in almost every temple, for financially they cannot afford to do without such a valuable deity. His merit was so great that he would have become a Buddha, had he not made a vow to rescue all orphan spirits and devils, so he is still in the regions below engaged in his arduous task. His worship day is the thirtieth of the seventh moon, when his temples are thronged. He sleeps 359 days, and only awakes on his birthday, and if there are only twenty-nine days in that month he quietly turns over for another year's nap. The bitter sarcasm on Carmel's top, "Peradventure he sleepeth and must be awakened," is here too terribly literal. As the god dwells in the regions below, on this fearful night the candles in front of every door are placed on the curb stones; it is called, "Burning the dog-excrement incense."

The Doctrine of Hell.—The Chinese speak of the eighteen tiers of hells, each subdivided into numberless caverns and pits, located beneath the base of Mount Sumeru, and called the "earth-prison." They have the proverb, "The evil has the evil reward;" they have consciences to warn them of coming judgment; and the innate sense of justice to tell them that the wickedness of the wicked ends not at death. The sacred books speak of the "long night" and of the "black books," *i.e.*, with lists of sins. The doctrine of retribution as now possessed by the Chinese aids in teaching the Scripture doctrine. Revelation gives clearness to the subject, but it adds little to the awful nature of future punishment. It only remained for Him who "brought life and immortality to light" to speak of its duration, making it to last as long as the blessedness of the holy. "And these shall go away into everlasting (aionian) punishment; but the righteous into life eternal (aionian)."

The City of Fungtu In the western province of Szechuen there is a city called Fungtu, and in the city temple there is said to be an underground passage which connects with the city of Fungtu in the other world. The temple is said to be closed, but during the Ming dynasty an emperor opened the doors and descended into the cavern. Led by the attendant of the god of war, he passed through the dark passage and came to a city full of light, broad streets, and storied houses; the different departments were presided over by the ten kings, but the visitor was not allowed to go farther than the fifth hall of justice. It is said by the neighbours that at night they can hear the cries of the criminals as they are put to torture in the regions below. The large sutra which gives an account of this city is evidently an Indo-Chinese production; an attempt to combine the Chinese doctrine of the *Yang* and *Yin* with the Indian tenets of the "earth-prison."

The Ten Kings of Hell.—King Yama, the ruler of the dead, the guardian of the prison of the lost, has ten different personifications, all spoken of in Chinese as Yen Lo Wang; the ten to rule over the ten departments of Tartarus. The accounts of the "earth-prison" are chiefly made known by the "Jade Record," which is often printed by benevolent persons and gratuitously distributed. The reader asks, " Why these two assistants with the cow's head and horse's face ? " It is to prevent new arrivals from recognising them, and so to check all attempts at bribery.

The fifth king with an African face was a mandarin of the Sung dynasty, A.D. 1200, by the name of Pao Lungtu, celebrated for his incorruptible integrity. He was first placed over Ward No. 1, but as he had a " resur-

King Yama, Cow's Head and Horse's Face Assistants.

rection rod " by which he could restore men to life, it was feared that many would return to earth without going before the ten courts, so Shangte moved him to Ward No. 5, because the criminals had to remain seven days in each department, and after five weeks the body would be corrupt, and it would be impossible to bring it to life again. King Yama X. rules over the wheel of transmigration.

White and Black Devils.—These are the Marshals of Hades, who are despatched to arrest the dying, seize their souls, and hurry them into the presence of the judge.

White and Black Devils.

The Vision of Hell.—A man at the time of death has all the sins of his life to pass as a panorama before

Looking Homeward.

his eyes; this is called by Buddhists " The vision of hell."

Looking Homeward.—When the soul arrives at the fifth ward it is permitted to go upon a portico, and take a longing glance at the loved ones at home. The friends at the old homestead during the fifth week after the decease spread a feast before dawn, lighting a lantern in the court, the filial son calling, and a friend beside the coffin responding, for if they do not invite the departed he will not go upon the observatory.

The Mirror.

The Mirror.—The first act in Hades is for the man to be taken to the steel-yard, a hook fastened in his back, and his sins weighed; if his deeds of merit outweigh his sins, he is forthwith carried to the tenth department, to return to earth. If it happens the other way, he is taken before a mirror, and there he beholds what he is to be in the next life for the sins of the past—a cow, a dog, an ass, or a reptile. The proverb says, "Before the mirror a good man does not come." Sometimes in the mirror it is a headless cow

The Mill.

The Mortar.

The Chopping-knife.

Pulling out the Tongue.

Sawn Asunder.

Lake of Blood.

and a man that you see. On inquiring the meaning, one is told that the beef is indicting the butcher before the judge for cow-slaughter.

The Undivided Hell.—This is an iron city 18,000 miles in circumference, and the walls 1,000 miles high, of solid iron; fire from above descends, and fire from below ascends; iron dogs spit fire, iron snakes coil around the neck, and iron eagles pluck out the eyes. There are many evil devils, their teeth like spears, their arms like pitchforks, and their eyes like lightning.

Bridge of Snakes.

There is an iron bed 10,000 miles long, and the criminal is stretched its whole length.

The Earth-Prison.—The punishments recorded in the "Jade Record" and other works on future torment give frightful pictures of the tortures of bad men; in many Buddhist temples these are represented by small figures, and in others by life-size images. Men are ground to powder, the dust becoming ants, fleas, and lice; pestled in a mortar, and mashed to jelly in iron mortars; chopped in slices with a knife and hacked to pieces with hatchets; the tongue of deceit and lying

pulled out; sawn asunder; the bones and flesh crushed
by falling mountains; women cast into a lake of blood
(see Chapter XVI.); crossing the narrow bridge and
falling among fiery serpents; the caldron of oil for

Caldron of Oil.

those who waste rice; drunkards with the cangue
and standing on the hands; quack doctors with hands
and feet tied, and a large stone on the back, the fierce

Hill of Knives.

judge administering hot drinks; a man going into the
mill head foremost, with the legs sticking out and a dog
coming out below in the transmigration; a headless
ghost pulling his murderer to judgment; disembowelled;

tossed on a hill of knives ; cast on a lake of ice ; chained to a red-hot cylinder ; iron dungeon, darkness within and fire without ; lashed with burning iron wires ; when thirsty, drinking molten iron ; eating red-hot iron balls : besides, there is the freezing hell, the burning hell, and the hell of bubbling filth.

Men and women, foreigners and natives, old and young, dragons and demons, gods and angels, are all liable to go to the " earth-prison " for their sins.

" The Buddhist hells combine all that is horrible to

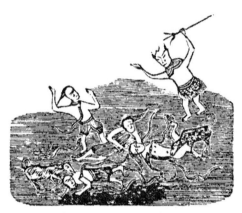

Village of Wild Dogs.

Burning Cylinder.

each of the senses. Every form of torment, mental and physical, that can befall the unhappy violators of a good conscience and of the Buddhist law, are found there. The extremes of cold and heat, cutting, flaying, biting, insulting, and tantalizing have to be endured by such persons according to their deserts. Demons of the most monstrous shapes and most cruel dispositions terrify them in every possible way. All that fire and water, knives and clubs, can by ingenuity be made to do in tormenting, is there done."

Miss Mang's Soup.—Why do not men remember the acts of a previous existence? Buddhism has its answer. Before the metempsychosis, the party is taken to Miss Mang's soup kitchen, and receives a potion which makes him forget all previous events. Miss Mang was a maiden lady of fourscore years; in her youth she was an earnest student of Buddhism and an exhorter; in

Miss Mang's Pavilion.

her old age she was appointed a goddess in Tartarus, and compounds this "forgetful" potion of many different medicines. Scholars arriving at Hades who can repeat the Buddhist chants are beyond the power of King Yama, so they are transferred to Miss Mang's department, return to earth, die just before or immediately after birth, and then they can be brought successively before the ten kings of the dead.

CHAPTER XVIII.

THE GODS OF BUDDHISM.

Janteng Buddha. — Janteng, or the "Light lamp" Buddha, is a fictitious personage who was the teacher of Shakyamuni in a previous existence, and foretold that in a subsequent *kalpa* he would become a Buddha. "The time when this happened was too long ago to be expressed by common Chinese numerals." As the instructor of Shakyamuni in a former life, he occupies with him "the highest rank in wisdom and power." The eighth moon, twenty-second day, is his birthday.

The Dragons. — "The Dragons of the four seas" were four brothers by the name of Yao, who govern the North, South, East, and West seas. "The fabulous dragon of China is a monster with scales like a crocodile and having five-clawed feet. He has no wings, and when he rises in the air, it is by a power he is supposed to possess of transforming himself at pleasure. He can make himself large or little, and rise or fall, just as he chooses. The dragon, which is a flying saurian, seems to be an original Chinese creation." He occupies a prominent place in Chinese mythology; he sends rain and floods, and is the ruler of the clouds.

"Of the scaly reptiles the dragon is the chief," says a native author; "it wields the power of transformation and the gift of rendering itself visible or invisible at pleasure. In the spring it ascends to the skies, and in the autumn it buries itself in the watery depth." "There is the celestial dragon, which guards the mansions of the

The Dragon.

gods and supports them so that they do not fall; the divine dragon, which causes the winds to blow and produces rain for the benefit of mankind; the earth dragon, which marks out the courses of rivers and streams; and the dragon of the hidden treasures, which watches over the wealth concealed from mortals."

The Buddhists count their dragons in number equal to the fish of the great deep, which defies arithmetical computation, and can only be expressed by their sacred numerals. The people have a more certain faith in them than in most of their divinities, because they see them so often; every cloud with a curious configuration or serpentine tail is the dragon: "We see him," say they; the scattering of the cloud is his disappearance. He

King Lee, holding a Pagoda.

rules the hills, is connected with *fungshuy,* dwells around the graves, is associated with the Confucian worship, is the Neptune of the sea, and appears on the dry land. The dragon to China is what the lion and the unicorn are to England, and the eagle to America. The dragon is the emblem on the national flag, it is the crest on Imperial monuments, the design on the Emperor's robes, and the throne of the empire is the dragon-throne.

Holding-Pagoda King Lee.—He was a general of the Shang dynasty. His youngest son, Nacha, went bathing and drowned the dragon's son; the dragon sought revenge on the father, who called his son to account for the murder. Nacha gave his flesh to his father and his bones to his mother, and his soul went to the Great Extreme. The Great Extreme took a lily and made him a body; the mother built a temple in his honour, which his father ordered to be pulled down, whereupon the two got into a fight, and Jantong Buddha took a gold pagoda and cooped Nacha; but as he feared his submission was only temporary he gave the pagoda to his father, who now, as Prime Minister of Heaven, holds the pagoda in his hand and is thus seen in the temples.

The Mother of Buddha.—She has thirty-four arms and eighteen heads; if her chant is repeated 900,000 times, the four burdens will be taken away and the ten evils avoided. Her names are Chente P'usa and Soseihte.

Master of the Lily Lake.—During the Sung dynasty there was a priest collecting for a temple, when, meeting with a tiger, the pious animal offered to be a partner in his firm. Messrs. Priest and Tiger went in company for several years, and the former obtained very liberal subscriptions when the shopmen saw the latter standing guard at the door. After the temple was built, the tiger said to the priest, " You sit here and chant and I will see you have rice," so for a long time he collected food for the friar, and at his death the blood-thirsty denizen of the jungle became lord of the lilies.

Fix-Light Buddha.—As a priest he dwelt on a mountain-top for five hundred years. After he had been there two hundred and fifty years the light in his hair was waving and not fixed, but by the end of the next century it was as bright as gold and remained with a steady effulgence. Shakya called him " Fix-Light Buddha."

Pouhien P'usa.—He is seen in the group with Shakya and Wenshu. At the age of twenty, seeing that the world was false, he became a hermit and afterwards a Bodhisattwa. He is a fictitious character.

The Sombre Maiden.—Hüan Nü. " The Sombre Maiden was, according to ancient tradition, the daughter of Heaven, and was sent to the aid of Hwangte. Post-Buddhist legends appear to have identified this mythical being with Marichi Deva," the personification of light, offspring of Brahma.

CHAPTER XIX.

GODS OF THE PEOPLE.

左坦路頭拍財利布天官
玄君郎郎神牛馬王羊王
壯蛇蟲操蛇之神鈕生娘
王床螳娘之神監北方之基神床子
神方針桂金神力神前福神
南神之行神遊魂神
王田祖司田公婆順風神
神田灯神七十二司河
桥神小兒黄尨神荊
璞玉神花田神丁神
甲年神陽神

God of Wealth.   List of Gods.

God of Wealth.—Yuen-tan is the true god of riches, though he now occupies a secondary place, and the god next mentioned has supplanted him. He lived in the eventful days of Kiang T'aikung, and some of his exploits were riding a black tiger and hurling a pearl which would burst like a bomb-shell. He was overcome by witchcraft: a straw man was made to represent him, and its eyes and heart were pierced with darts; after death he was appointed the god of wealth.

God of Riches.—The picture represents him as sitting in his shrine or little chapel, which is placed on a table in nearly every store and in many homes. There were five brothers, who were "Globe-Trotters," and it is generally said that *Lotow* is in a foreign land. His birthday is the first moon, fifth day, when the merchants spread a feast in his honour, or, as they say, "drink wine to the god of riches." The post-offices and shops are ever opened

God of Riches.

till after this sacrificial banquet is given to him. By his side are two ministers, called " Invite Riches" and "Gain Market," who are considered divinities of no mean rank. For scrolls they have as inscriptions, " Invite Riches says, Where is the lucky place ?" "Gain Market replies, Here it is before your face." The god of riches is regularly and devoutly worshipped by burning incense before the shrine, lighting candles in front of the sign-board, and

placing a cup of wine at the foot of the image. He is
one of the chief among the gods, and it is in his worship
that the streams of covetousness and idolatry flow into
the Great Lake of worldly-mindedness.

Heavenly Mandarin.

The Heavenly Mandarin.—This picture hangs in
numbers of houses. The Heavenly Mandarin in appearance is very handsome, and on his head is the nearest

approach to a crown with which the Chinese are acquainted.

Kitchen-god.—About sixty million pictures of this god are regularly worshipped twice a month. His temple is a little niche in the brick cooking-range; his palace is often filled with smoke, and his majesty sells for one half-

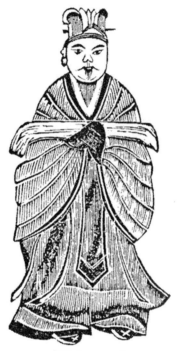

Kitchen-god.

cent. "Every empire has an emperor, and every family has a ruler," is the oft-quoted proverb; the ruler of the family being the kitchen-god. His duties are two-fold; first, he knows intimately the faults of the family and takes account of their sins; second, he stands as a mediator between the family and the Pearly Emperor, so he is an object of fear and honour. He is worshipped at the new and full moon, and he is "thanked" by a feast on the fourth, fourteenth, and twenty-fourth of the sixth month, and twenty-fourth of the eighth. On the twenty-fourth of the twelfth month he ascends to Heaven to report to the Pearly-Emperor, and is received home again on old year's night. His ascension is attained by placing his wee picture in a little bamboo lamp-stand covered with red paper for a sedan chair; this is put on a bundle of rice straw in front of the door, sugar or syrup having first been rubbed on his lips, so that he will only tell sweet things when on high; fire is set to the martyr's

funeral pile, a libation of alcoholic wine adds to the flame, and rice straw is cut small as a substitute for watermelon seeds for him to eat on the way up.

God of Theatres.—Actors worship the god of theatres, to keep from laughing when on the stage.

Theatre-god.

God of Horses and Cows.—He is much worshipped in North China, and pays special attention to the domestic animals. Theatricals are paid for by the owners of stock. The temples are under official patronage. In the temple in honour of these gods the grooms attached to the Yamens worship in order to secure health and mettle to their horses.

Sheep god.—His name is Hwang Tsuping, and he lived near Hangchow in the Kyinhwa district. He told his brother his sheep were on the other side of the hill, but the latter found only white stones. Hwang Tsuping came and cried, "Sheep, get up; sheep, get up," when the whole mountain was covered with his flock. If a shepherd wishes a large flock, or his sheep are feeble, he worships the sheep-god.

God of Snakes.—The image of the snake-god has sometimes a man's head and a snake's body. If a snake is found on the premises the tenant immediately repairs to the snake-god's temple; also he rubs out his tracks with manure. At the feast in the fifth moon they mark

Snake King.

all little children's foreheads with the word "king," and put yellow paint on their legs, as a charm against snakes and centipedes. "Live snakes are still carried in procession in some parts of China, for luck, in honour of the serpent king."

Holding-Snakes god.—He was twenty feet high; a very powerful giant. His father's name was Faith. Wherever he went there was a drought, so studying the subject he became convinced that drought came from the sun, and he must try and destroy the sun. For three months beside the Yellow River he studied the art of flying, and taking a green snake in one hand and a yellow one in the other, he followed the sun in his circuit, but overcome with thirst and heat he died. Afterwards sacrifices were offered to him.

The god of Scorpions is much worshipped in the Honan province. Sometimes a rustic who has caught a

God and Goddess of the Bed.

basket of scorpions for medicinal use feels on his shoulder the touch of an old man, the god of scorpions, who says " Friend, you have taken lives enough, go home." He is very effective in keeping the houses free from the green intruders.

Locust-goddess.—It is said that Kiang T'aikung divorced his wife B.C. 1122, and when she was afterwards killed by lightning he made her the locust-goddess.

Gods of the Bed are worshipped on the wedding day, and on the first and fifteenth of each moon.

Old Man and Woman of the Bed.—By worshipping these two venerable deities, peaceful slumbers will be secured.

Gold-god.—The god of gold is worshipped by all silversmiths and in the jewellery shops.

Tea-god.—He was Loh Yü of the T'ang dynasty. In the north King Lingtsze is worshipped, and in South China Sung Sukung.

Salt-god.—He is the first man who made salt; his name is "World Wood."

Gods of the Compass.—There is a sacrifice in the autumn of the year. For the east it is Keu Mung; south, Choh Yung; west, Suh Seu; north, Yuen Ming.

God of the North Place.—He rules drought, flood, war, famine, and pestilence; as well as prosperous and successful years. His name is Yuen Ming; probably the same as the last mentioned.

God of the Soul.—Lo Yuyang. He obtained the power of releasing his soul and letting it roam at pleasure. He had some interviews with Laotsze.

Gods of Strength.—A class of fabulous beings believed to be superior to men (Gavudas).

God of Happiness.—Every Yamen (governmental residence) has a god of happiness, whose duties are multifarious.

Wang Papa—He is the chief of police in the land of shades. The owners of lost property make application to him for recovery of goods, sometimes sticking a list of valuables on his person. Notices of "Man Lost," with the character "Man" turned upside down, are at times pasted to his clay raiment.

Goddess of Travel.—She was the wife of the Emperor Hien Yuen. The Emperor went on a journey to Mount T'ai to place a handful of earth on the top as an offering to Heaven, and a clod on a clean spot on the level ground as an offering to the mountain, and the Empress dying *en route* he appointed her the goddess of travel.

The Rambling god.—He roams around, and if he hears a quarrel or sees anything wrong, he repairs to the spot; he records the good and bad deeds, and has the power of inflicting immediate punishment.

God of Archery.—He was the first great archer. His name was Emei, now called Suhchang.

God of The Wave.—Wutszeseu was drowned in the River Seu. Merchants on long journeys worship him.

Field-ancestor god.—The divine husbandman, Shin Nung, was the original god of the field, but as he became the god of medicine, his son, Suh Kuin, is considered the field-ancestor god.

God of the Favouring Wind.—He is worshipped by all travellers, especially by those on the Grand Canal, where it crosses the broad bosom of the Yangtsze. This god acts as a kind of insurance agent.

Bridge gods.—They have no images, but rule the spirits of the drowned. When a funeral procession passes over the bridge, the chief mourner, who is the filial son, gets down on his knees and worships the god of the bridge.

Lamp-god.—His name is Ma Chuan. Kiang T'aikung tried to kill him, but three strokes of the executioner's axe did no harm. He tried to burn him, but Ma Chuan fled on the wings of the flame. He borrowed a mirror from the hobgoblins, and it was seen that he was made of fire. The lamp for one thousand years did not go out, so he became a man.

The Forty Masters.—There are seventy-two masters or teachers, who are grouped in one temple, the devotee worshipping the one he wishes to propitiate; of these, thirty-two are physicians and belong to the Medical Chapter; the names of the rest are here given, the numbers corresponding to their position in the temple:—

14, Warding-off-evil Master; 15, Master of gold; 16, Silver; 17, Mitigate calamity; 19, Fortune; 20, Military; 22, Snakes; 23, Magpies; 24, Serpent-Demon; 25, Fortune as you desire; 26, Peace in Heaven; 29, Protect life; 30, To add age; 31, Police; 32, Master of office; 33, Calamity; 35, Horses; 37, Happiness; 38, Sages; 40, Sixty cycles; 41, Palace; 42. Earth; 43, Five quarters of the earth; 44, Grain; 45, Marriage; 46, Literary essays; 50, Water; 51, Mediator to the Eastern Peak; 52, Master of Six Household gods; 54, Thunder; 55, Vows; 56, Canals; 62, Misery; 64, Rewards; 65, Fields; 67, Riches; 68, Grain; 69, Protection; 70, Cursing; 71; Fate; 72, Escaping from evil; 73, Bridges and Boats, 74, Punishments.

The Five or Twenty-five gods.—They are called "The five gods," but there are five groups of five. To prevent murder, five gods; to prevent robbery, five gods; to prevent fornication, five gods; to prevent falsehood, five gods; to prevent drunkenness, five gods.

God of the Rough Gem.—Pien Ho offered a gem in the rough to King Lee, who cut off both his legs, as he thought it was only granite. Afterwards discovering its quality, Pien Ho was appointed by him Gem-god.

Little-boy god.—He is a prophet, and all his predictions are fulfilled, so if a man can inquire of him his destiny, he will avoid all calamity. His residence is at the south pole.

The Yin-dragon god.—He is the essence of fire, and dwells in southern Kiangsu; he has wings, and can fly through the nine heavens; with a brush of his tail on the land, fountains of water spring up.

The Yellow-dragon god. — In the time of the Emperor Shun all the great Mandarins saw him. His scales were resplendent as gold. He gave the Emperor a charm and a chart.

Silk-worm god.—Near Wuseih, a countryman had forty-nine basket-waiters of silk-worms, when seeing a very large silk-worm he chopped it in two, whereupon all his silk-worms died. He knew then he had killed the god of silk-worms. Now worshipped in the silk districts. Near the Great Lake, Madame Silk-worm is worshipped.

God of the Year.—A son of the Emperor Show, named Yin Chow. His father, the abandoned tyrant, killed Yin Chow's mother at the instigation of a concubine, and was about to kill the son, when he fled, and one of the genii took him for a disciple. Afterwards in battle he was defeated, and Janteng Buddha caused two hills to meet and hold him as if in a vice. Kiang T'aikung made him the T'ai-Swuy god. He is one of the fiercest gods in China. Worshipped by the Mandarins at the reception of spring.

Goddess of the Male Principle of Nature.—She

was the Princess Ch'ang Yung of the Shang dynasty. She became an immortal and dwelt on the mountains, and though this maiden lady was aged two hundred, she looked like a damsel in her teens. Walking in the sun she cast no shadow.

Family gods of the Door.—These differ from the door-gods used in front of the Yamens. Their names are Shinto and Yuihleu. There was a peach tree with a limb bent over, thus making an arch, and through this spirits passed and repassed. The two door-gods

Little Boy at the Well.

could subdue these evil spirits, and the Emperor, as his palace was haunted, cut down the peach tree, painted their pictures, and hung them up. The farmers at the new year put them to guard their front doors.

The Ting gods.—The *Ting* gods are six in number: 1, Kwang Chang; 2, Yü Yü; 3, Yellow Devil; 4, Great Cataract (of the eye); 5, Kang Shin; 6, Tunglih. These six assisted the Great Yu in his labours with the floods and streams. Chang, the Taoist Pope, can summon them at his will, and the priests rely on the *Ting* gods to expel demons.   On the land they can subdue tigers and panthers, and in the water overcome dragons.

Little Boy at the Well.—The picture represents a Chinese well, which is generally in the open court of the house.   The well-god, who is a little boy, has no image, but his picture is put beside the well at the new year, and a sacrifice in the form of a feast is made to him.

CHAPTER XX.

GODS OF TRADES.

THE Chinese speak of the "three hundred and sixty trades" as including all their different trades, professions, and business employments. Nearly every one has its patron divinity, related to it as Jubal, "the father of all such as handle the harp and organ," or Tubal-Cain, "an instructor of every artificer in brass and iron," were to their respective arts, but now worshipped as the guiding spirit.

Carpenters' god.—Lu Pan was "a famous mechanician of the state of Lu, said to have been contemporary with Confucius. Wonderful stories are related of his ingenuity; among others it is said that his father

Carpenter's God.

having been put to death by the men of Wu, he carved an effigy in wood of a genius, whose hand pointed in the direction of Wu, where, in consequence, a drought prevailed for the space of three years. On receiving supplications and largess from the men of Wu, he cut off the hand of the figure, when rain at once fell. He is worshipped as the patron divinity of carpenters." Ship carpenters also worship him, as he was the first to build a boat.

Masons' god.—His name is Chang Pan. He was a bricklayer, but afterwards became an immortal. When a house is built they have the two pictures of Lu Pan and Chang Pan, and both the owner of the property and the workmen offer a sacrificial feast and engage in worship. These two gods are worshipped in every carpenter's shop and in the guild halls.

Fishermen's god.—It is said that Kiang T'aikung angled, with a straight hook (if it might be called a " hook "), and a grain of rice for bait, till he was eighty years of age, when he became the premier. Fishermen now worship him.

God of the Net.—Fuhhe is the god of the net ; he watched the spider weave her web and obtained the idea of catching fish, hares, and birds. As in the time of Habakkuk, " they sacrifice unto their net and burn incense unto their drag."

Bacchus.—Tu K'ang was one of the early distillers of wine from rice, and is worshipped in the wineshops and distilleries three times a year, when he is requested to flavour the *samshu* and preserve it from being injured. His picture with the libation is burned in the court in front of the hall, his face being turned to the west to let him go to the Western Paradise. The devotees " hang a sign-board on their faces," as after the sacrificial feast their noses are " red apples " and their cheeks " peach blossoms."

Drunkards worship Lee T'aipeh, who could drink three hundred cups of alcohol at one sitting.

Etee is the "fabled inventor of wine. The Emperor's daughter commanded Etee to make wine, and it was good. She gave it to the Emperor, who, when he had tasted it, poured the liquid upon the ground, sent Etee into banishment, and forbade the knowledge of wine."

Bean-Curd god.—Hwei Nanhwang is worshipped as a paper god, three times a year in the bean-curd shops and in the guild hall. He taught the people how to make bean-curd, and so was a benefactor to his race. Wang Lingan is also said to have first manufactured bean-curd.

God of Barbers.—Loh Yuinshan taught men the art of shaving and hair-cutting, and is now worshipped by the army of barbers who shave the heads, scrape the faces, plait the queues, clean the ears, wipe the eyelids, and thump the backs of the black-haired race.

The Tailors' god.—Hien Yuen. Before his time men wore raiment of fig leaves, and he first taught them to wear clothing.

God of Silk.—His name is See Lingsze, and he is worshipped by the silk merchants and by silk and satin weavers. Before his era men dressed in linen.

Goddess of Embrodiery.—She was the third concubine of Hien Yuen, and was skilled in needlework, so was appointed goddess of the needle and of embroidery. Little girls who take lessons in embroidery worship this goddess.

Ancestor of Jade.—The old women worship him on the nineteenth of the second, seventh, and ninth moons. They write their names on the tinfoil money, place it before the idol and burn it, hoping at death they will get it back.

God of Musical Instruments.—Cha Yung. He is worshipped by drum and violin shops.

Jugglers' god.—Named Keh Sienhung. He could blow a grain of rice out of his mouth and it would turn into thousands of bees. He would call them back and eat them as rice.

God of the Paper Clothing Stores.—The paper clothing stores, which are regular furnishing establishments for the dead, worship their patron divinity.

God of Architecture.—He is worshipped when a new house is built. He is probably the "Yellow Emperor" who "regulated costume, taught his people how to manufacture utensils of wood, pottery, and metal, constructed a palace, which is by some held to have been the first royal residence, and invented a medium of currency."

CHAPTER XXI.

IT is not intended by this heading that all the follies of paganism are collected in this chapter, for this is a book full of its absurdities. The conceits of the human mind in its worship and service of the creature are puerile and ridiculous.

Rain Clothes Dwarf.—His father died when he was an infant, his mother wept herself blind, and he, the son, a dwarf, became a servant. He dresses in shaggy straw clothes, such as the farmers wear in the fields when it rains, and has on his head an umbrella straw hat (nyah mao).

The Monkey-god.—Before heaven and earth existed, or Pankoo lived, there was the monkey. By taking in the flashes of light from the sun and moon, his animal spirits were made perfect, and at one somersault he could travel one thousand miles. His peregrinations were to the Heavenly Palace, the isles of the Immortals, and down to Hades. He stole from the Western Royal Mother the peach of immortality, defeated the generals of heaven in battle, and stirred up a row in the palace of the Pearly Emperor. At length he was captured by Buddha and shut up within a hill, but was released by the famous traveller Hieuntsang.

God of Lice.—In case some reader may doubt the authenticity of this narrative, it may be stated that the temple of the god of lice is within three hundred yards of the author's chapel. He was a famous general, who commanded a besieged city, and was so busy day and night that he could not change his raiment, and consequently he was covered with " grey-backs," which, as the natives say, are generated by perspiration in

Lice-god.

the pores of the skin; these swarms of little creatures gradually " drank his blood," acting as an enemy's sword to the warrior. He was canonized as the god of lice. When our neighbours make a raid on their bodily attendants, they wrap them up in paper and put them under the censer, and the god whisks them to the paradise of insects. When one of the lower classes is seen sitting in the sunshine examining his clothes, and making a hearty meal off the multitude of insects which he finds, we do not wonder that the god of lice is worshipped in this country.

Punch and Judy god.—As fond as the black-haired race is of Punch and Judy, it is not surprising that the large number who play with these wooden men and women should desire a patron for their theatricals. His name is Chen Ping, who was the minister of Han

Kaotsu, and first used a wooden man at the siege of Peh Ten.

God of Fire-crackers.—Named Leedien. In the mountains of the west there is a giant devil over ten feet high, at the sight of whom men grow faint. Leedien found that the popping of fire-crackers would frighten him away, hence they are considered a protection from evil spirits, and are not so much intended for boys to use in sport as for an article of heathen worship.

God of Cruelty.—He was called "Two Worlds." After death he was a monster of cruelty. Hankaotsu appointed him the god of cruelty.

The Chinese sometimes go before the city god, and tell him of any difficulty they have had with another, and ask him to adjudicate it after death.

God of Revenge.—There is nothing so sweet to the Chinese as revenge, and this stands in contrast with many excellent national traits of character. The god of revenge is a *straw man*. When a house has been robbed, or a man has a personal enemy, there is resort to witchcraft. A straw image of the enemy or the thief is made and daily worshipped; needles are stuck in the eyes, blood is made to issue from the nose and ears, the arms and body are pierced, and it is confidently believed that this process will send pains, sickness, and probably death on the object of hatred. The practice is universal in China; I have seen it in this city of Soochow, and recently in Hongkong a man made an application to the courts to bind over his adversary "to keep the peace" and not use witchcraft, as witnesses present proved that he had made a straw image and was worshipping it at his home.

Manure of Goddess.—Tsze Kou was the concubine of Mr. Lee; incurring the animosity of the head wife she was killed, and was appointed by the Ancient Original as goddess of manure. She is much worshipped by the manure hongs.

Goddess of Fornication.—It was told the king that there was a female sprite, with a red skirt, dishevelled hair, arms and feet bare. who, travelling as swift as the wind, was corrupting public morals. She was shot through with an arrow and her flesh became a mountain. She is the goddess of lasciviousness; she has no temple. image, or picture. but in front of houses of ill fame courtesans burn incense before the door and make prostrations in her honour.

Goddess of the Corner.—It is customary for young ladies to apply to this deity to have their fortunes told. After burning incense they take a peck measure turned upside down, with a flower on it; this is for a sedan; then one inquires. "Is Miss Corner at home?" Answer, "No." "Is the second Miss Corner here?" "No." "Is little Miss Corner present?" "Yes." She takes her seat in the peck measure and is carried to the table, on which rice is spread as an offering. One bows and asks of the oracle what her fortune is to be. The peck basket is held over the rice, and the answer is written by a needle attached to it.

God of Shadows.—This divinity can cause a shadow to turn in the opposite direction.

God of Gamblers.—In his hand he holds the dice.

His name is "Wang, the Pure." He was a celebrated gambler, and lost $1,000,000 at the Faro Bank. After that he did not gamble, but when he saw a friend reduced to beggary by gaming, he took him to his home and taught him the science. Wang, the Pure, is the gambler's god. Unfortunately many trust in him and pray to him.

Bad gods.—The majority of the deities in the Chinese pantheon were originally good and great men, who rendered important services to the State or were the people's benefactors, and it is easy to see how they might become demigods in the estimation of the nation. The inquirer, however, meets with the startling fact that not a few of their divinities were the vilest men who have ever wielded power in China. Why is this? The answer is given, that it is well to offer sacrifice to them and keep them quiet, and resting in their own places in Hades, lest

Dice-god.

they might return to earth and disturb its inhabitants—much as if Israel had worshipped Jeroboam and Ahab upon the high places. In many cases the people do not know they were such bad characters. The god of war was a man of blood. The character of the god of wealth was not above reproach. The prison-god was noted for his ferocity. When preaching the other day a man asked, "How about the Five Holy Ones, who ride on their horses over the hills outside the city at night?" I replied, "I do not know anything about them except they are such bad gods, the mandarins have frequently destroyed their temples." The god of small-pox was put in charge of the pesthouse, not as a compliment to his amiability and virtue. Two striking illustrations will be given.

The Emperor Show.—He occupies a high rank in the pantheon, though not worshipped by the people. "He

General Kiang.

was the abandoned tyrant whose downfall brought the dynasty of Shang to a close, B.C. 1123. Wild extravagance, unbridled lust, and the most ferocious cruelty are enumerated among his vices. To please his infamous concubine he constructed vast palaces and pleasure grounds where wild forms of debauchery were practised. According to the legends, he formed a lake of wine, caused the trees to be hung with viands, and set men and women, unrobed, to chase each other before his eyes. The category of his offences against Heaven is summed up in the 'Great Declaration.'" The Emperor Show figures extensively in the "Book of appointing gods."

Kiang T'aikung.—He was said to have been born B.C. 1210, and died B.C. 1120. He is the most celebrated character in the "Book of appointing gods;" a distinguished

Worshipping the Stone Lion.

warrior, and a counsellor to the Chief of the West, "he wielded a valiant sword and slaughtered his enemies; he was, however, as magnanimous as he was brave, for he immediately made the foe weltering in his blood a god. In this way he is the god of Chinese gods. The account of his earthly exploits and heavenly deeds is perhaps the greatest book of marvels ever printed. His picture is pasted on the walls of houses, so that if an inauspicious word is spoken it will be powerless to injure the occupants. He is the pivot of Chinese mythology, and around him the celestial hosts revolve.

The Stone Lion.—In front of every official Yamen there are a pair of stone lions, who guard. as Cerberus, the courts of justice. It is believed that at night they are living lions, and are seen roaming around, so those who live near the Governor's residence in Soochow worship these four-footed creatures.

On the " Absurdities of Polytheism " see Chapters IX., page 129 ; XIV., pages 258, 265, 266, and 270 ; XIX., page 323 ; XX., page 336.

CHAPTER XXII.

Laotsze.—The founder of Taoism as a philosophy, not as a religion, was born probably B.C. 604, in the province of Honan. The details of his life are quite meagre, and in this respect the first Taoist stands in striking contrast with Confucius and Buddha, about whom so much is known, for there are only a few historical morsels, and of the legends several are so evidently Buddhistic that it is not worth while to recount them. It is said that the period of gestation was over threescore and ten years, so the young babe had " the hoary head as a crown of glory" and his face was wrinkled like an aged man bowed down with years. His official title is "The Great Supreme Venerable Prince;" his name is Laotsze, which means, literally. "Old Boy;" or, judging from some things that are said about him, the "Wild-Western" appellation of "Old Coon" is not inappropriate. "He was appointed librarian by the Emperor, and diligently applied himself to the study of the ancient books, becoming acquainted with all the rites and histories of former times." He became famous as a teacher of philosophy, had a goodly number of students, retired from the haunts of men, and devoted himself to speculation. His followers now speak of his pre-existence, of his deification, and of his " travelling to the West to learn their doctrines, which he embodied in his work ; " his position as the third person in the Taoist trinity and the creator is alluded to in the next chapter.

It is on record that the young teacher, Confucius, B.C. 517, sought an interview with the aged man.   Laotsze

Laotsze.

said to him, " Those whom you talk about are dead, and their bones are mouldered to dust,—only their words are left. Moreover, when the superior man gets his time he mounts aloft; but, when the time is against him, he moves as if his feet were entangled. I have heard that a good merchant, though he has rich treasures deeply stored, appears as if he were poor, and that the superior man, though his virtue is complete, is yet to outward seeming stupid. Put away your proud air and many desires, your insinuating habit and wild will. These are of no advantage to you;—this is all I have to tell you." The youthful sage said to the venerable philosopher that he had sought for the *Tao* for twenty years. He replied, " If the *Tao* could be offered to men, there is no one who would not willingly offer it to his prince; if it could be presented to men, everybody would like to present it to his parents; if it could be announced to men, each man would gladly announce it to his brothers; if it could be handed down to men, who would not wish to transmit it to his children ? Why, then, can you not obtain it ? This is the reason. You are incapable of giving it an asylum in your heart." Confucius, thirty-five years old, did not seem to relish the blunt, or, rather, pointed remarks of old Diogenes, now near ninety. He remarked to his disciples, " I know how birds can fly, fishes swim, and animals run. But the runner may be snared, the swimmer hooked, and the flyer shot by the arrow. But there is the dragon; I cannot tell how he mounts on the wind through the clouds and rises to heaven. To-day I have seen Laotsze, and can only compare him to the dragon."

The Lonely Picture.—Laotsze says of himself, " The world is joyful and merry as on a day of sacrifice. I alone prefer solitude and quiet, and prefer not to pry into futurity. I am like an infant ere it has grown to be a child; listlessly I roam hither and thither, as though I had no home to go to. . . . Have I therefore the heart of a fool ? Confused and dim, while the vulgar are enlightened, I alone am in the dark. Tossed to and fro, like the sea ; roaming without cessation. . . . I alone am doltish as a clown."

" My words are easy to understand, easy to put in practice ; yet the world can neither understand nor practise them. . . . It is only ignorance that causes men not to understand my doctrine. Those who understand me are few."

Tao Teh King.—So thoroughly Confucian is the scholarship of China, that the philosophical literature of Taoism is comparatively limited ; the largest collection of translations yet made is a volume of one hundred pages. The great work of Laotsze is the *Tao Teh King* or " Canons of Wisdom and Virtue," which consists of 5,000 words, or about twice the length of the Sermon on the Mount. It is a very brief discussion ; the style is " meagre and laconic ; " much of it is puzzling and obscure, and not a little is puerile and misanthropic. It is, however, the work of a master mind, and most of it, as is seen in the extracts given, places its author in the ranks of great and good men. A New England writer, to whose view " distance lends enchantment," speaks of it thus : " Nothing like this exists in Chinese literature : nothing, so far as yet known, so lofty, so vital, so restful at the roots of strength ; in structure as wonderful as in spirit ; the fixed syllabic characters, formed for visible and definite meaning, here compacted into terse aphorisms of a mystical and universal wisdom, so subtly translated out of their ordinary spheres to meet a demand for spiritual expression, that it is confessedly almost impossible to render them with certainty into another tongue. . . . It is a book of wonderful ethical and spiritual simplicity, and deals neither in speculative cosmogony nor in popular superstitions. It is in practical earnest, and speaks from the heart to the heart."

The Tao.—The keynote of the *Tao Teh King* is *Tao*, which is the text upon which the ancient preacher discourses, and the term from which Taoism comes. It is used in the first chapter of John to translate the *Logos*; it is often rendered "reason;" it sometimes means the "way;" the word "method" is not a bad version, but perhaps the best yet given is that by the author of "Taoist Texts," where he renders *Tao* by "Nature," or "The Principle of Nature," and this translation seems to throw fresh light upon the work, and certainly is a key that unlocks many of the paragraphs.

It is modestly suggested that in many cases *Tao* might be translated "wisdom," and let the reader put the description of *Tao* and the eighth chapter of Proverbs in parallel columns, and he will be struck by the similarity. In the one case we have Solomon, also an Asiatic, and living three hundred years before the other, with his pen guided by Divine inspiration, describing the *Hhokmah* as "from everlasting, from the beginning or ever the earth was"—but not in such life-like terms as the "beloved disciple" spoke of the *Logos*, for he had seen the "Word made flesh," and beheld Him "full of grace and truth"—and on the other hand the pagan philosopher, whose far-seeing mind was striving, as it were, to clothe a vague conception in the habiliments of immortality.

What does Laotsze say in different passages of the *Tao?*

"Its name may be named, but it is not an ordinary name. Its nameless period preceded the birth of the Universe. Having a name it is the mother of all things. The *Tao* is full, yet in operation as though not self-elated. In its origin it is, as it were, the ancestor of all things. I know not whose offspring it is. Its form existed before God was. It is mysterious, recondite, and penetrating. Pellucid as a spreading ocean, it yet has the semblance of permanence. There was something formed from chaos which came into being before Heaven and earth. Silent and boundless it stands alone, and never changes. It pervades every place, and may be called the mother of the universe. I know not its name; but its designation is *Tao*. Heaven is *Tao*, and *Tao* survives the death of him who is the embodiment of it, living on unharmed for ever. The *Tao* of Heaven never strives, yet excels in victory. The *Tao* of Heaven resembles a drawn bow. It brings down the high and exalts the lowly; it takes from those who have superfluity and gives to those who have not enough. The Great *Tao* is all-pervasive; it may be seen on the right and on the left. All things depend upon it and are produced; it denies itself to none. With tenderness it nourishes all things, yet claims no lordship over them."

Again the utterances of the " old moralist and mystic " are misty; " *Tao*, considered as an entity, is obscure and vague. Vague and obscure! yet within it there is Form. Obscure and vague! yet within it there is substance. Vacuous and unfathomable! yet within it there is Quintessential Energy."

The philosopher *Huai Nantsze* thus describes *Tao*:

" *Tao* is that which covers Heaven and supports Earth; its height cannot be measured nor its depth fathomed; it enfolds the Universe in its embrace." "The *Tao* reaches upwards to Heaven and touches the Earth beneath; it holds together the Universe and the Ages, and supplies the Three Luminaries with light." " It is by *Tao* that mountains are high and abysses deep; that beasts walk and birds fly; that the sun and moon are bright and the stars revolve in their courses; that the unicorn roams abroad and the phœnix hovers in the air." " *Tao* is the beginning and end of the visible creation." " *Tao*, in its sublimest aspect, does not regard itself as the author of Creation, or as the power which completes, transforms, and gives all things their shape." "All-pervading and everywhere revolving, *Tao* yet cannot be sought out; subtle and impalpable, it yet cannot be overlooked; if it be piled up it will not be high; if it be added to it will not increase; if it be deducted from, it will not be diminished. Shadowy and indistinct! it has no form. Indistinct and shadowy! its resources have no limit. Hidden and obscure! it reinforces all things out of formlessness. Penetrating and permeating everywhere! it never acts in vain." "Utterly non-existent, *Tao* is yet ever ready to respond to those who seek it."

The Canons of Wisdom and Virtue.—A few extracts from the "Canons of Wisdom and Virtue" is all that the limits of this chapter will permit,—specimens of the best sayings in the book.

1. THE SAGE.—" The Sage's heart is not immutable; he regards the people's heart as his own. The virtue of the sage makes others virtuous." "The sage never departs

from either calmness or gravity. Although there may be spectacles of worldly glory, he sits quietly alone, far above the common crowd."

2. PURITY.—"By controlling the vital force and bringing it to the utmost degree of pliancy, one is able to become as a little child again. By washing and cleansing oneself of that which Heaven alone can see [*i.e.*, secret sins], one may become without one blemish."

3. HUMILITY.—"It is better to desist altogether, than having once grasped [wisdom] to pride oneself on one's self-sufficiency." "To keep oneself in the background when merit has been achieved and fame has followed in its wake, this is the way of Heaven." "The sage does not say that he himself can see, and therefore he is perspicacious. He does not say that he himself is right, and therefore he is manifested to all. He does not praise himself, and therefore his merit is recognized. He is not self-conceited, and therefore he increases [in knowledge]." "He who says himself that he can see is not enlightened. He that praises himself has no merit. He who is self-conceited will not increase [in knowledge]."

4. THE THREE PRECIOUS THINGS.—Compassion, frugality, and modesty. "I prize compassion; therefore I am able to be fearless. I prize frugality; therefore I am able to be liberal. I prize modesty; therefore I am able to become a leader of men." "Now when one is compassionate in battle, he will be victorious. When one is compassionate in defending, his defences will be strong. When Heaven intends to deliver men, it employs compassion to deliver them."

5. GOOD FOR EVIL.—The brightest literary gem of the

old philosopher is when he says of the *ideal man,* " He recompenses injury with kindness." To return love for hatred is the crowning glory of Christianity. and when a sage, with only the light of heaven for a guide. utters such an exalted sentiment. we must assign him a high position in the temple of worthies.

CHAPTER XXIII.

TAOISM AS A RELIGION.

THE philosopher Laotsze had not the slightest intention of founding a religious sect or of establishing a church : his was a school of philosophy, and his followers were simply students who sat at his feet and accepted his system of doctrine. Most religions spring into existence created by the genius of some giant leader, but Taoism was the growth of one thousand years, and in its gradual evolution bears a striking analogy to Rome. Future researches must reveal the rise and progress of this mighty system ; how a band of scholars became adepts in metallurgy, and by degrees were developed into a priestly craft. Ancient China was obscured by countless wild beliefs, which like scattering clouds overshadowed the land ; these, Taoism gathered together, embraced them in her bosom, and thus became a congeries of superstitions. The " priests pander in every possible way to the superstitions of the people, and creeping into their houses 'lead captive silly women.'" " Its mission is not to root out deadly errors or to proclaim precious truths."

Plagiarism.—Taoism is more purely native than Buddhism, and is an attempt to adapt the Indian religion to Chinese civilisation. As the visitor comes to the gate of a Taoist temple he sees two instead of the four guardians; in the great hall they have their trinity, the "Three Pure Ones;" they speak of the "Three Precious Ones," "reason, the priesthood, and the classics;" and the Pearly Emperor is in many respects an ape of Shakyamuni. The sacred books show to what an extent Taoism has plagiarised. The sutras in form, in matter, in style, in the incidents, in the narrative, in the invocations, in the prayers, leaving out the Sanscrit, are almost exact copies of the Buddhist prayer-books. This goes to prove the power of Buddhism, and also that Taoism did not exchange the philosopher's gown for the priest's robe till after it counterfeited the Indian coin.

Alchemy.—The ancient Taoists "sought to transmute the baser metals into gold and silver, and to discover the elixir of immortality." Their writings abound in allusions to "spiritual medicine," "pearly food," and "fountains of nectar." According to the recipe they take several hundred ounces of gold or silver, with red colouring matter, lead and mercury, put them in a crucible with steady fire, and on the forty-ninth day they will amalgamate; then dipping with a ladle and rolling around in a waiter, it rolls into pills. In the time of poverty one of these pills put into lead or mercury will transmute the whole into gold or silver, but after 500 years it loses its virtue, and all who hold the spurious coin will "eat bitterness."

There is another kind called the "gold elixir," a mixture of stone and metals, the extract to be eaten dry and hot. Some of the emperors of the Han dynasty, being desirous of immortality, ate too much, had carbuncles, and were buried in the Imperial tombs.

To become an Immortal.—Instead of the Western Paradise of the Buddhist, Taoism offers immortality to its followers. They call it the *nay tan*, or internal elixir, and in its formation use the "three precious things" in the body of a man—the fecundating fluid, the breath, and the saliva; the first to be drawn upward, the second to be inhaled more than exhaled, and the third to be swallowed. The first unites with the breath, the breath unites with the saliva, and these three form an invisible boy in the body of a man. This immaterial child grows larger and larger, and may go out of the body and return again to its home, but it needs to be protected, as it is liable to be devoured by devils and hobgoblins. When the young spiritual Chinaman becomes as large as the man's body, it can tarry on the earth or depart to the better land at pleasure; if the latter, it goes like the cicada, leaving its shell, and is a heavenly immortal; if it wishes to remain in the world, it becomes one of the *earth genii* and lives for ever.

The Great Extreme.—One of the most familiar objects seen everywhere in picture and engraving is the Great Monad, the "ovum mundi." The philosopher Choofootsze thus speaks of it: "The great extreme is merely the immaterial principle; it is found in the male and female principles of nature, in the five elements, in all things. . . . From the time the great extreme came into operation, all things were produced by transformation. . . . The great extreme has neither residence, nor form, nor place, which you can assign to it. If you speak of it before its development, then previous to that emanation it was perfect stillness; motion and rest, with the male and female principles of nature, are only the descent and embodiment of this principle. . . . It is the immaterial principle of the two powers, the four forms, and eight changes of nature; we cannot say that it does not exist, and yet no form or corporeity can be ascribed to it. . . . It produced one male and one female principle of nature, which are called the dual powers. But from the time of Confucius, *no one has been able to get hold of this idea"*—and, it might be added, no one ever will. This simple cut presents Chinese cosmogony in a nutshell.

The great monad is divided into the dark and light, with a white eye in the dark, and a black eye in

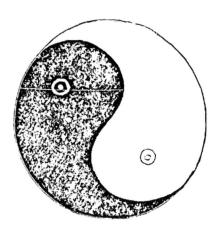

The Great Monad.

the light. These white and black spots show there is a male germ in the female principle, and a female germ in the male principle. Heaven and earth, the sun and moon, light and darkness, hard and soft, are used as illustrations of these inverse powers. This dualistic principle, the male and female principles of nature, by which all things are produced, forms the basis of Chinese philosophy, science, and religion; it is the warp and woof of Chinese thought, teaching, and literature. Let us see its application to polytheism.

Yin and Yang.—*Yang* is the male and *Yin* the female

principle of nature. This world is *Yang*, and Hades *Yin*. Nothing more fully shows the materialistic views of the Chinese than their arrangement of the invisible world; the world of spirits is an exact counterpart of the Chinese Empire, or, as has been remarked, it is " China ploughed under; " this is the world of light, put out the lights and you have Tartarus. China has eighteen provinces, so has Hades; each province has eight or nine prefects, or departments; so each province in Hades has eight or nine departments; every prefect or department averages ten counties, so every department in Hades has ten counties. In Soochow the Governor, the provincial Treasurer, the Criminal Judge, the Imperial Tailor, the Prefect or Departmental Governor, and the three District Magistrates or County Governors, each have temples, with their apotheoses in the other world. Not only these, but every Yamen, secretary, runner, executioner, policeman, and constable has his counterpart in the land of darkness. The market-towns have also mandarins of lesser rank in charge, besides a host of revenue collectors, the bureau of government works and other departments, with several hundred thousand officials, who all rank as gods beyond the grave. These deities are civilians; the military having a similar gradation for the armies of Hades, whose captains are gods, and whose battalions are devils.

" The framers of this wonderful scheme for the spirits of the dead, having no higher standard, transferred to the authorities of that world the etiquette, tastes, and venality of their correlate officials in the Chinese government, thus making it necessary to use similar means to appease the one which are found necessary to move the other.

All the State gods have their assistants, attendants, door-keepers, runners, horses, horsemen, detectives, and executioners, corresponding in every particular to those of Chinese officials of the same rank."

It will not do for the governor of the province to worship the god of the prefect or department, for the governor ranks higher than the god, so at the new and full moon he only worships the governor of Hades. Also the prefect cannot worship the city god of the county-seat, for he is a greater man than this god. The governors in Hades rule over the prefects, who control the county governors, by whom the precinct deities are ruled; these are all gods, worshipped in the same way, but one god differs from another god in glory. Except the few Indian deities, all the gods are Chinamen.

The Manichæans.—The doctrine of the dual principle of nature is Asiatic, and we do not know whether the Chinese obtained it from the Persians or *vice versa*. It troubled the ancient Church. According to Mosheim, " Manes, educated among the Magi and himself one of that number, instructed in all those arts and sciences which the Persians and the neighbouring nations held in the highest esteem, was so adventurous as to attempt an amalgamation of the doctrine of the Magi with the Christian system. . . . He taught, " There are two princi-ples from which all things proceed: the one is a most pure and subtile matter, called *Light*; and the other a gross and corrupt substance, called *Darkness*. Both are subject to the dominion of a superintending being, whose existence is from all eternity. . . . These two beings have produced an immense multitude of creatures, resembling themselves, and distributed them through their respective provinces. The prince of darkness knew not, for a long series of ages, that light existed in the universe; and he no sooner perceived it, by the means of a war that was kindled in his dominions, than he bent his endeavours toward the subjection of it to his empire. The ruler of the light opposed to his efforts an army. . . . The prince of darkness, after his defeat, produced the first parents of the human race. The beings engendered from this original stock consist of a body formed out of the corrupt matter of the kingdom of darkness, and of *two souls*, one of which is sensuous and lustful . . . the other rational and immortal, a particle of that divine light which was carried away by the army of darkness, and immersed into the mass of malignant matter. Mankind being thus formed by the prince of darkness, and those minds which were the productions of the eternal light being united to their mortal bodies, God created the earth out of the corrupt mass of matter."

The Manichæans held to *transmigration :* "Those souls who have neglected the salutary work of their purification pass, after death, into the bodies of animals, or other natures, where they remain until they have expiated their guilt and accomplished their probation."

Rotation.—Chinese mandarins rotate in office, generally every three years, and then there is a corresponding change in Hades. The image in the temple remains the same, but the spirit which dwells in the clay tabernacle changes, so the idol has a different name, birthday, and tenant. The priests are informed by the Great Wizard of the

Dragon Tiger Mountain, but how can the people know gods which are not the same to-day as yesterday?

The gods have Sin.—Men have sins, and why should not the gods? The mandarins lose their official buttons when any disturbance occurs within their territory, so if the gods do not direct aright the affairs of the upper world they deserve removal from authority. It is the right of some of the chief priests of Taoism to judge the gods, and to pass sentence when they permit calamities or pestilence to visit their terrestrial domains.

The gods may marry.—An old lady who was known to be a pious devotee died some years ago in Soochow, and her friends thought it would be very appropriate for her to be a goddess. The priests kindly consented to act as go-betweens, and by their ability to communicate with the other world they found out that the god of diarrhœa wanted a bride. The old lady had been coffined and her remains placed in the tomb, but by means of paper figures, and a paper bridal chair, the ceremonies were conducted just as if she were " sweet sixteen," the priests receiving the usual clergyman's fee.

Promotion.—Chinese mandarins are promoted for distinguished services, and have new buttons given to them ; so the gods may rise from an humble position to one near the Pearly Emperor, who gives them the reward of merit for ruling well the affairs of men. " The correlate deities of the mandarins are only of equal rank, yet the fact that they have been apotheosized makes them their superiors and fit objects of worship."

The gods of State.—These are all distinguished statesmen or warriors. The people say, " How can the Emperor obtain faithful ministers unless they have the hope of promotion after death?" The practical objection to the unity of Jehovah is that " He has not time to attend to minor affairs," and so must be assisted by a host of the *dei minores.* No high mandarin of renown, or member of the royal family, even if it be a prince who has not attained his majority, dies without receiving office in the spirit world. Of this great host of worthies, numbering ten thousand times ten thousand, and who are the tutelary divinities of certain localities, no notice can be taken in this work. The gods of each city must be the special study of the resident missionary. The State gods are continually increasing, for as the graves of earth are filling so are the palaces of the gods, yet the number decreases, for many gods " have their day ; " they rise, flourish, and fade away, " neither have they any more a reward, for the memory of them is forgotten."

Appointing gods.—This rests nominally with the " Ancient Original," the central and highest of the " Three Pure Ones," but as that is indefinite, the nomination is made by the Emperor through Chang, the Heavenly Teacher, who is the Great Wizard, and whose duty it is to furnish the credentials and assign a temple ; professedly the appointment is made by the chief of the " Three Pure Ones," but actually by the Emperor and Pope Chang. There is a *Yin* and a *Yang* appointment, so that the god may receive the sacrifices of a certain section of Chinese territory. In popular parlance the Emperor appoints the gods, which is the fact, as the other is a mere sham ! From ancient times, " wherever popular sentiment seemed to indicate, a new god was

provided, either by the deification of a hero, or the personification of a principle." It will be noted that there
is only *a short step* from *a great man to a little god;*
the difference being almost as imperceptible as it is in
North China between a large donkey and a small mule.
The canonisation is wholesale.

What a claim for the Emperor of the Celestials! Not
only that he is the sovereign of four hundred millions,
but that he is king of the gods; yea, they are constituted
by him and derive their power from him. As of Moab
it may be said, "We have heard the pride of China (he
is exceeding proud), his loftiness and his arrogancy and
his pride, and the haughtiness of his heart."

The Three Periods.—In Chinese mythology there
are three periods when gods were appointed by the ship-
load. The first was in the time of the ancient Emperor,
Hien Yuen, whom Confucius did not regard as an historical individual. The second, the twelfth century B.C.,
in the time of Kiang T'aikung, who deified the heroes
that fell by his sword. The third, the fourteenth
century A.D., when the first Emperor of the Ming
dynasty appointed a multitude of city gods, and thus
expanded the india-rubber system. Thus "an ideal
universe has been peopled with a race of ideal gods."

The Thirteen Boards.—The English language fails
in furnishing a nomenclature for the Chinese Pantheon.
This polytheistic people, not satisfied with having one
god for every separate thing, have devised a system by
which there are several gods ruling in the same sphere,
whose special powers and duties it is impossible for a
foreigner to distinguish or separate. In Peking there

are the six boards of the government; in Heaven the Taoists have made the number thirteen. 1, Board of Thunder; 2, Board of Fire; 3, Board of Riches; 4, Board of Pestilence; 5, Board of Small-pox; 6, Board of the Pole Star; 7, Board of the North and South Stars; 8, Board of all Stars; 9, Board of all gods; 10, Board of Age; 11, Board of the Malignant Stars in Heaven; 12, Board of the Malignant Stars on Earth; 13, Board of the Tsŭ-su P'usa.

The Taoist Creation.—"As Shakyamuni Buddha was the first Buddhist image to be worshipped, so it will appear that Laotsze's image was the first Taoist idol." What were the creative acts of Laotsze? The Taoists say, " At one afflatus he transformed 'The Three Pure Ones.'" Laotsze, the third person in the trinity, "Created the Ancient Original and the Spiritual Precious." Laotsze, preaching to the "assembly of the gods," said, " Before chaos I created all things; I begat heaven and earth, and I carried the female principle on my back and the male principle in my arms. The male air went up and begat heaven, and the female air descended and begat earth. The remainder "of the male air was changed into man, and the remainder of the female air was changed into woman. The two kinds of air by their own power changed into all things.'

In other books the creation of man is ascribed to the Eastern Emperor Kung and the Western Royal Mother. At the dividing of heaven and earth there came first the Primary Man from beyond the heavens, and seeing on earth that there were no men, from his hand went forth five thunderbolts summoning the deities of the five regions. Earth, Wood, Fire, and Water came, and last of all the Golden Mother riding on a fire-coloured cloud, who told him she was asleep in a cloud when she heard his thunder summons. The Primary Man said to the Golden Mother and Duke Wood, "You two represent the male and female principles; on earth there are no men; you create." He gave them a heavenly furnace; the Golden Mother took a ball of clay and put it into the furnace; Duke Wood used dragon thunder, and fanned the flame for seven days; then cracked open the ball, and from it a boy and girl leaped forth, and at one breath of the wind they in an instant became a man and a woman, and so men were created upon the earth.

Variety Temples.—The name of a temple is not always an indication of the god which is there worshipped, for the priests add one image after another, and one shrine after another so that they may accommodate any worshipper,—as the sign to a country store, " Dry goods, groceries, boots, shoes, drugs, clothing, crockery, harness, and general merchandise." Sometimes in one temple there are the Buddhas, the goddess of Mercy, the Three Mandarins, Amita, the Coming Buddha, the Bushel Mother, the Snake-god, the gods of Fire and Thunder, the god of Hades; in all, twenty or thirty divinities.

To Escape the Metempsychosis.—In the city temples there is a room full of the tablets of those who for a series of years served in the procession of the god. At the death of one of them a feast is given by his son to the priests, his tablet is presented before the god, the attendants give three whoops, and the spirit-tablet is whisked into the room. The deceased thus becomes a

Yamen runner to the god in the other world, and is excused from transmigration.

Religious Services for the Living.—The *Tang tsiao* are religious services performed for the dead, as the " All Souls' festival," but more frequently for the living, the form and style of the worship being much the same in both cases. Often it is the " great peace service ; " a number of country villages will send up deputies to join with the priests in solemn worship during several days, to secure tranquillity and abundant harvests, the expenses being defrayed by subscription. Again, it will be a sacrifice to the god of thunder, to protect the waving fields of grain, in which the bakers and restaurant cooks unite. Most frequently it is to the god of fire, the constable of the ward seeing to the worship, and sticking up the two characters *tsai kya* on the doors of contributors ; after a conflagration, those who have escaped the devouring element join in a " protecting peace service." Families often have a private service with a couple of abbots, and seven or nine priests ; in the day they burn charms to invite the gods to be present, and at night the souls of the priests are said to behold Shangte.

The Fairy Crane.—This paper crane is used at funerals, images of it being carried in front of a procession of priests, with the abbot in a chair, and when burnt it is supposed that the departed soul rides to Heaven on the back of the winged messenger.

The fairy crane is also used in services for the living, when it is placed on a table and carried before the image of the Pearly Emperor ; the " bill of forgiveness " is read by the priests, then both the crane

The Fairy Crane.

and the document are burned, and it is supposed that the crane flies to the skies with the written proof that the man's sins are all forgiven.

Sale of Indulgences.—The Taoists have "bills of forgiveness" already printed, which are sold at their "great peace services:" the abbot reads, burns, and pronounces absolution of all past guilt.

Forgiveness Hair-pin.—Old women wear a "forgiveness hair-pin," which is made on "forgiveness-day;" this "forgiveness-day" is only one day in the year, and is indicated by the almanac.

Worshipping Heaven.—This is one of the Taoist services (*kung tsiao*) for the living. A large feast with a variety of fruits and cakes is prepared; also two hundred copper *cash*, and pictures of the Buddhas of the Three Ages and the thirty-six ministers of Heaven · the priests read the "bills of forgiveness," the feast is given to the children, and the *cash* hung as charms around their necks.

Bribery in Worship.—Bribery is an integral part of the government of China; in the appointment of mandarins, in the distribution of offices, and in the halls of justice, money is the ruling power. It would be impossible for materialistic pagans to have any other view of the world to come than that the gods are venal. The money sent to dead friends is to enable them to obtain favours from the Yamen runners of Hades. A striking instance is when large quantities of paper sycee are sent through the provincial treasurer in the temple to the Pearly Emperor, the donor hoping for a quantity of silver to be given in return, just as gold is given to the Emperor (or to the boards) in order to obtain office.

Dreams.—The Chinese, like all other superstitious races, believe in dreams. For example, to dream that a person is dead is a sure sign that he has either left the world or soon will depart. In dreams they consider that the soul goes out on a nightly ramble, even to a foreign land, and sees and hears what seems so plain. The black-haired race locate knowledge and the faculties of thought in the large central part of the body, but with a marked inconsistency all their pictures of dreams represent the vision as entering the top of the head. In ancient times answers to dreams were sought by divination ; now they "pray for a dream," as it is said at Hangchow—in a temple in honour of General Yü of the Ming dynasty—a man goes to the temple, sleeps all night, and asks for a vision to be given him.

There is a proverb,

> " As the thoughts of daylight,
> So are the dreams of night.'

Tree of the Rewards of Good and Evil.— In the city of Fungtu there is a precious tree. Just before the return of the soul to this earth three bows and three arrows are placed in its hands. If the soul shoots the eastern branches of the tree the man will be a Minister of State or great mandarin ; if the southern branches, he will live long and have a strong body ; if the western branches, he will have riches and honour. If he always worships the "Three Precious Ones," is charitable, chants, and does meritorious acts for three generations, he will immediately return to be a man, the governor of the city will give him an arrow, and one of the "Three

Pure Ones" will help him, so that he will not shoot the northern branches.

The Abacus.—In the city temples there hangs a great abacus ; in the shops the abacus is used in the computation of the millions of greasy copper *cash* (filthy lucre), but in the other world it tells of a reckoning of the good and the evil, with their attendant awards and punishments. It is a sermon in wood.

The Tail-cutting Mania.—Taoism is a system fraught with danger to the State for the reason that its whole structure is superstition. It is best illustrated by a

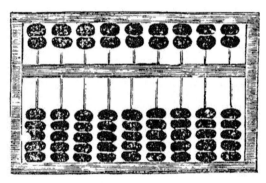

The Abacus.

wide-spread delusion in 1877. The wave passed down the Grand Canal. It was said that parties mysteriously lost their pig-tails as they walked along the street, caused by paper-men flying about, and what so precious to a Chinaman as the national badge. *the queue!* The peasants forsook their houses and slept in the fields or under the trees, fifty or one hundred in a group. Gongs had to be imported, and all night long in every hamlet, was bang, bang, bang! Processions with lanterns, torches, and voices passed from village to village. Afterwards it was said the paper-men could come in through the roof, expand to the size of a cow, and crush the sleeper [evidently nightmare]. In town men kept to the streets all night long. as they were afraid to enter their homes, and the heat, the fright, the demoralization, the excitement, and the wild rumours made the city like a boiling caldron. Three Catholics, innocent fishermen, were accused of having been seen sending off paper-men, and were beheaded.

One night the excitement ran high, for it was reported through the city that two foreigners (the writer and a friend) were on a temple-roof despatching paper-men. Tens of thousands assembled, an excited mob; gongs were beaten, and the crowd would yell, trying to drive away the men who were about to slay all in the city. Two companies of military were marched a mile and a half from the camp and fired blank cartridges, all afraid to injure the "foreign devils" (who happened to be absent from town), lest a shower of paper-men might fall like meteoric stones. After two hours it was found to be the shadows of the trees on the roof in the moonlight.

During the two months of summer that this panic swept through Central China, Taoist priests were busy selling *genii powder*, which in little packages placed in the queue was a charm to frighten away the paper-men. The superstitions of Taoism make the Chinese mind as tinder for the spark, just as an August sun prepares a prairie for the wild-fire.

CHAPTER XXIV.

POPES, PRIESTS, AND TEMPLES.

The First Pope.—The first Taoist pope was Chang Taoling, who flourished in the first century of the Christian era. "Devoting himself wholly to study and meditation, he steadfastly declined the offers made him by emperors, who wished to attract him into the service of the State. Retiring to seclusion in the mountain fastnesses of Western China, he persevered in the study of alchemy and in cultivating the virtues of purity and mental abstraction. His search for the elixir of life was successful, thanks to the instruction conveyed in a mystic treatise supernaturally received from the hands of Laotsze himself."

He was engaged in manipulating "the elixir of the dragon and tiger," when he met a spirit who said, "In the Pesung Mountain is a stone house, where may be found writings of the three emperors and a liturgical book. By getting these you may ascend to Heaven, if you pass through the course of discipline which they enjoin." "He dug and found them. By means of them he was able to fly, to hear distant sounds, and to leave his body. After going through a thousand days of discipline, and receiving instruction from a goddess, who taught

him to walk about among the stars, he proceeded to fight
with the king of the demons, to divide mountains and
seas, and to command the wind and thunder. All the
demons fled before him, leaving not a trace of their
retreating footsteps. On account of the prodigious
slaughter of demons by this hero, the wind and thunder
were reduced to subjection, and various divinities came

Chang Tauling.

with eager haste to acknowledge their faults. In nine
years he gained the power to ascend to Heaven."

"The later years of the mystic's earthly experience
were spent on the Dragon-Tiger Mountain, and it was
here, at the age of one hundred and twenty-three, after
compounding and swallowing the grand elixir, he ascended
to the heavens to enjoy the bliss of immortality."

The Heavenly Teacher.—The name of Chang, the

Heavenly Teacher, is on every lip in China; he is on earth the Vicegerent of the Pearly Emperor in Heaven, and the Commander-in-chief of the hosts of Taoism. Whatever doubts there may be about Peter's apostolic successors, the present Pope, Chang LX., boasts of an unbroken line for threescore generations. He, the chief of the wizards, the "true man" (*i.e.,* "the ideal man"), as he is called, wields an immense spiritual power throughout the land. The family obtained possession of the Dragon-Tiger Mountain in the Kiangse province about A.D. 1000, and the scenery around Pope Chang's rural palace is most enchanting. The present incumbent is a fat jolly mandarin, who lives in pomp and luxury; it is said that he is not a celibate, and he has about "thirty persons constituting his courtiers and high officers." "This personage assumes a state which mimics the Imperial *regime.* He confers buttons like an emperor. Priests come to him from various cities and temples to receive promotion, whom he invests with titles and presents with seals of office."

His power is fourfold. (1) He is the head of a priestly army of a hundred thousand men. (2) He controls the invisible hosts of demons, and is often summoned by emperors and men of countless wealth to rid their houses of these troublesome intruders. "To expel demons he wields the double-edged sword, which is said to have come down, a priceless heir-loom, from his ancestors of the Han dynasty. All demons fear this sword. He who wields it, the great Taoist magician, can catch demons and shut them up in jars. It is said that near his home there are rows of such jars, all of them supposed to hold demons in captivity." (3) The appointment of gods by the Emperor is made through "the Heavenly Teacher," and the rotation of the gods in office is done by him like shifting men on a chess board. (4) But his chief prerogative is in granting

An Audience to the Gods.—On the first day of the moon the one thousand officials in a provincial capital, whether in office or out of office, call on His Excellency the Governor to pay their respects, so at the first of the month Pope Chang holds a levee of the gods. From the heights of Heaven, from the depths of Hades, from across the wide ocean and the distant palaces of the stars, come an invisible host of deified beings, gods and demigods, to present their compliments to the great magician.

Taoist Priest.

The Priests of Taoism The Taoist priests wear blue robes, while the Buddhists wear yellow. They have not shaven pates, but do their hair up in a little knot, and are sometimes spoken of as the "yellow caps." There are two classes of these priests, the one living in the temples and professing celibacy, the other dwelling at home with their families, and wearing the citizen's dress except when on duty. They have not the zeal of the Buddhists (if it be possible to have less), are not employed in daily temple worship, and deal mostly with evil spirits and quack medicines, which makes them deserve the appellation, "a dirty set of fellows."

The Abbot.—The robes of the abbot are of the richest gold embroidery, which make him conspicuous as the chief priest. The ranks are conferred by Chang, the Heavenly Teacher, and are three in number—the Major General or Bishop, " the Praise Church," or Priest, and " the Knowing-Affairs," or Deacon. In a Foo, or Prefecture, there is a nominal ruler over the priests in his department, who is responsible to the civil magistrate for their good behaviour.

Taoist Abbot.

The City Temple, Soochow.—This is the only three-story temple that I have met with ; the temples usually are only on the ground floor, and the monasteries of two stories. It was recently repaired at an expense of $40,000 by the late banker Hu of Hangchow, but his failure left the images simply dry mud instead of covered with gold. The city temple (Yuen Miao-Kwan) is a great temple, surrounded by thirteen large temples. in which there are about three hundred gods, the great religious centre of the Kiangsu province ; the Pearly Emperor occupying the third story, which overlooks the city.

In front is an open court of two acres, on the sides of which are stalls and shops, and in the middle arbours made of matting for tea-drinkers. In the second temple,

City Temple, Soochow.

in a hall that extends 400 feet around the building, is the picture gallery of the city, where native art is displayed. The temple, situated in the centre of the city, is the rendezvous of all pleasure-seekers, who are preceded by a horde of pickpockets and villains, and at times there may be seen hundreds, and even many thousands, of men and boys, priests and beggars, fortune-tellers and gamblers, a motley assembly, calling vividly to mind "the den of thieves" on Mount Moriah. It is a "Vanity Fair," with stalls for chinaware, booths for fancy articles,

Snorter and Blower.

stands for toys, tables for confectionery, and cloths on the ground for a variety of trinkets; also travelling-kitchens, small restaurants, and pea-nut baskets for the weary; and foreign pictures, a miniature engine, jugglers, acrobats, sleight-of-hand performers, gymnastics, women singers, peep-shows, puppet-shows, bear shows,

Punch-and-Judy shows, the horn and the gong, for those who seek amusement.

The Snorter and the Blower.—Hen and Ha. They lived in the time of Kiang-Taikung. If Hen snorted, a typhoon would issue from his nose which would vanquish the foe. If Ha blew a white breath the enemy would wither. They guard the "Hill Door."

The Three Pure Ones.—The centre one is the

The Three Pure Ones.

"Ancient Original," the one on the right the "Spiritual Precious," and the bearded man is Laotsze. It is an evident imitation of Buddhism, which has its three divinities, but two of "The Pure Ones" are imaginary beings, and the third is the Old Philosopher. These are not considered to exercise any power or jurisdiction, but simply to sit back in space, serene and quiet, while the affairs of heaven and earth are directed by the

Pearly Emperor; the Pure Ones like the Mikado of former times, and the Pearly Emperor as the Tycoon or actual ruler of Japan.

The Lantern Pagoda.—During the first moon of

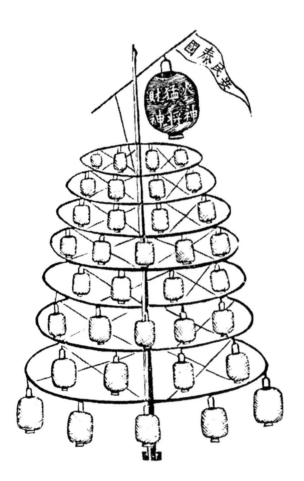

Lantern Pagoda.

the new year there is often erected on the bridges a lantern pagoda, with fifty lanterns, in honour of the gods of riches, fire, and agriculture, and also "to give light to the neighbourhood;" considering light as an emblem of temporal prosperity. These seven-cornered frames of bamboo are drawn up, after the lanterns are lighted, by a rope and pulley like a sail on the mast of a boat. It is a beautiful tower of light, and very attractive. May it be that "the people which sat in darkness saw great light; and to them which sat in the region and shadow of death light is sprung up."

CHAPTER XXV.

The Pearly Emperor.—A prominent fact in pagan systems is that a secondary divinity in the estimation of the people gradually usurps the first place, as is seen in the gods of riches and medicine of Taoism, and in the goddesses of mercy of Buddhism and Romanism. "The Three Pure Ones" are above him in rank, but to the Pearly Emperor "is entrusted the superintendence of the world." To refer to a European monarch as the acknowledged sovereign and the Premier as the actual ruler is not an exact illustration, as the Pearly Emperor has all the power of Heaven and earth in his hands. He is the correlative of Heaven, or rather Heaven itself; his birthday and Heaven's birthday are the same: he is the Jupiter of the Middle Kingdom. Whenever we preach of one supreme Ruler of the universe, there is an immediate reference to the Pearly Emperor, so to dethrone him is to demolish image worship.

His legends are copies of the Buddhistic traditions. The king and queen of the kingdom of Miao Luh were worthy sovereigns. The Spiritual Precious, the second among the Pure Ones. took his jade sceptre and blew his breath upon it, which made it change into a living

being, and in a dream of the night it entered the body
of the Queen, who after a full year bore the Crown Prince.

There is a song the Chinese sing :—

" The Spiritual Precious brought in his hands
The Pearly Emperor from heavenly lands."

Pearly Emperor.

The kingdom prospered during his minority ; he took
all the gold in the Imperial treasury to give alms.   On
his accession to the throne, reflecting that life is a dream,
he gave the sceptre to another, and became a hermit for
a hundred years ; the next two hundred years were spent
in philanthropic acts, and after that he was a pupil of the
Spiritual Precious for three hundred years in the Taoist

scriptures; during the next two centuries Heaven and
earth received his blessings; he then became an humble
immortal, till on his one thousandth birthday he was
made god of Heaven, earth, and men.

This is the poetic account. As a matter of history, the
Emperor Hwei Tsung in the twelfth century conferred
upon a magician, by the name of Chang Ye, the title of
Shangte, The Pearly Emperor, and the people, finding
one deity so much simpler than an abstract triumvirate,
accepted him as their Optimus Maximus. His actual
rule has been about seven hundred and fifty years (some
locate him in the T'ang dynasty one thousand years ago).
He has thirty-six ministers and two chief attendants, one
with three heads and six arms, and the other with four heads
and eight arms.

List of Gods.

Tsusze P'usa.—He is the minister to the Pearly Emperor, who in turn has two assistants, the snake and
the turtle, which are seen by his side. His father was
king of Tsin Luh. He was a precocious youth; at ten
years of age in one glance he understood the classics,
and at fifteen left home. With hair dishevelled he
went to the Snowy Mountains to become a hermit, but
could not endure the cold. On his return he met an
old woman grinding a crowbar. "What are you doing,
old lady?" "Oh! I am grinding this crowbar into a
needle." "But how can you accomplish so arduous an
undertaking?" "Oh! you can do anything with

patience." He returned to the hills for forty-nine years, when he became an immortal. One of his four ministers has a green face and a girdle of bones; is able to control hobgoblins, and can gather the clouds and send rain.

The City gods.—As the government of Hades is the exact counterpart of the government of the Chinese Empire, all the mandarins of the world of night are

Tsusze P'usa.

Chinamen; so the gentry are not only aspirants for temporal power, but they also seek for divine honours, and the generous sovereigns of the land, who also preside over their departed subjects, generally try to gratify their ambition. Each of the sixteen hundred cities has its city god; also the one hundred thousand great market towns each claim a local god, and not a few of the million villages have their village gods, so these gods are a "multitude which no man can number." The mandarins act as governors, judges, magistrates, tax-collectors, and coroners, all combined in one office, so the duties of the city gods are multifarious. These are often taken to the temple of the Pearly Emperor, and an entrance fee from $20 to $100 is paid to the priests for an audience of the god before the king of gods.

Assistants to the City gods.—The work of the

Eastern Peak.

Yamens is mostly performed by the secretaries, so beside the gods are the images of a retinue of secretaries and attendants. There are two principal ones who attend to the lawsuits in Hades, and who decide what grade of punishment should be inflicted, and to which prison of the lost the guilty should be assigned. They are worshipped by all.

The Mediator.—In the first and sixth moons there

are many devotees. If a man wishes to worship the Pearly
Emperor he first adores the Chau-Tseusze, and requests
that deity to obtain for him an audience. On the fifth
of the fifth moon, fifteenth of the eighth moon, and
thirtieth of the twelfth moon, all the gods must be present
at the Pearly Emperor's levee. These gods must first
present themselves at the Mediator's temple, so that he
may obtain tickets for their spirits at the high audience.

The Eastern Peak.—The " Eastern Peak " is Mount
T'ai, and this is the god of that mountain ; his reputation
having rapidly increased during the last century. The
Chinese have not very distinct ideas about the rulers of
Tartarus, so among others he is now considered the " god
of the Judgment Day." At the " Fall Judgment " the
Taoists issue proclamations, calling on all the orphan
spirits to assemble and receive sentence, as he holds in
his hand the awards of good and evil, but he considers
the hypocrite who pays his fee as a good man.

The rank of the Eastern Peak among the long columns
of native gods is as high as the lofty summit of Mount
T'ai among the ranges of Chinese hills. One feature of
his worship in some places differs from others, in that the
temples belong to families and have no priesthood, so the
devotees are both men and women who mingle in the
nocturnal devotions. At a Hangchow temple it has been
computed that $1,000 every night of the worship season
was spent in burning paper money, contributed by the
gentry and by pilgrims. At this time also the sick are
brought for healing, and lunatics in his presence are
cured by the casting out of devils. In this temple the
processions with torches and lanterns, the tinsel and

embroidery, the solemn prostrations and the mimic of a royal pantomime, are as gorgeous as Chinese art can devise.

The Empress of Heaven or Goddess of the Sea.—

She is not only worshipped by "men that go down to the sea in ships," but by millions on land.   In girl-

Goddess of the Sea.

hood she was a Miss Ling, a prophetess whose predictions, whether favourable or adverse, were sure to be fulfilled. "Her brothers, four in number, were merchants. On one occasion when they were absent on a trading voyage, she fell into a deep trance, from which she was aroused by the loud lamentations of her parents, who supposed her dead. On recovering herself she informed them that she had seen her brothers at sea in a violent storm. Shortly afterwards the youngest son returned home and reported the loss of his elder brothers. He stated that during the storm a lady appeared in mid-heaven, and by means of a rope dragged the ship into a safe position. His sister said she had hastened to the rescue of her elder brothers, but while in the very act of saving them was awakened by the cries of her parents."

Afterwards old Mr. Ling was drowned in the sea, and when the affectionate daughter heard the sad tidings she went to the ocean's shore to weep, and her grief being excessive, she threw herself into the foaming deep. Both bodies floated to the shore, and were buried by mourning relatives.

In after years, a mandarin travelling to Corea met with a typhoon, and while all other ships foundered, he saw an angel-lamp guiding his boat. After going about seven hundred miles he landed at an island, and seeing a temple asked what it was, and was told it was Miss Ling's. She is the guardian protectress of the sailor, and in nights of storm holds out an angel-lantern in the sky to guide the almost shipwrecked mariner.

By her side are two assistant gods; one with an eagle eye, who is called "The Telescope Eye" or "The Thousand-Mile Eye;" the other bending forward his ear to hear the propitious breeze, who is called "Favouring-Wind Ear." Recently, in Shanghai, a temple was built on the site of the former railway station. For the Queen of Heaven, see Jeremiah, 44th chapter.

God of Fire.—The god of fire, called the Ho-Lih-Ta-Tee,

has three eyes and a red beard, and is worshipped on the third, thirteenth, and twenty-third of each month. Some two or three centuries ago there was a great conflagration in Soochow, which lasted two or three days. After every method to extinguish the devouring element had been exhausted, the Governor threw his hat, shoes, and clothing in the fire, but without effect: at last he jumped in and was burned to death, and was made the god of fire for this city. He has

God of Fire.

Eight Ministers.—The first holds the *fire bow and arrows*, and wherever an arrow flies there is a conflagration. The second minister holds the *fire-crow*, and on the house where this bird of ill omen alights the insurance companies suffer. The third holds the *fire-rat* in his hand, and walls, garrets, and roofs are not safe from his intrusion. The fourth has the *foot measure* and *fire-spade*; the one to measure the extent of the conflagration, and the other to shovel up sparks. The fifth is the Captain of the " Black Flags." The sixth commands the " fire-engine," from whose hose fire spouts out. The seventh minister holds the red-hot *fire balls*, and the eighth flashes fire from the *fire-mirror*. These are supplicated in the " great fire service " of the eighth month.

God of Pestilence.—The god of pestilence in some

temples has a black face. He was originally a literary man. One day, returning from school, he saw a demon about to blow his deadly breath into a well, and reflecting that this was a public well, and that a multitude would be poisoned, but that if they saw a dead body in the water no one would drink from it, he leaped into the well. He was appointed the god of pestilence, and whenever there is

God of Pestilence.

an epidemic they take him out in a procession. He is one of the four high ministers of Heaven.

The Three Mandarins. - They are much worshipped, especially in North China ; the three rulers of Heaven, earth, and water. The first rules Heaven, the second earth, and the third the seas, lakes, rivers, and canals. Their birthdays occur on the fifteenth of the first, seventh, and tenth moons, and their fasts, two weeks preceding their natal days. The principal time for worship is in August, when the pilgrims of Soochow ascend Mount Seven-Sons ;

on the pleasure boats they gamble all the way going; they ascend to the temple under the burning sun, then descend and have a wine-feast.

The Three Mao.—They are three brothers ruling the three peaks of Mount Mao, and they exercise a commanding influence throughout this section by means of the charms from this sacred mountain, which are sold. The eldest, receiving the drug of immortality, returned

Three Mandarins.

to see his parents. The old man was very angry because his son had remained away so long, and had learned no trade, and took a rod to chastise him. The son assured him he was protected by Heavenly legions; the father smote, but the cane broke in pieces. His younger brothers, who were mandarins, came on an appointed day to see him leave the earth, whereupon he mounted his chariot, rode upon a cloud, and ascended; upon this,

the two brothers resigned their positions, and became, first
hermits, and then genii. The trio were once seen, the
first riding in a tiger chariot, and the other two upon
phœnixes, ascending to see Shangte.

The Five Holy Ones, or, as they are sometimes
termed, "The Five Thoroughfares;" are five brothers, and

Five Holy Ones.

in the temple in the rear are the images of their mother
and five wives. The first of the Ming emperors canonized
them. The witches use their name, and if a pretty lady is
sick they say, "The Five Holy Ones want her for a wife"
(in the other world), and hope to get good pay by telling
how to escape the fate. The temple by the Stone Lake
near this city has been twice destroyed by order of the

Governor, as the influence of these gods was injurious to the public morals, but their popularity is undiminished.

God of Witches.—He stands as a mediator beside the "Five Holy Ones." When one is afflicted with epilepsy the witches say, "The Five Holy Ones call him," and will advise appealing to the god of witches to intercede for him with these deities, and he will get well.

The Horse Duke.—He has charge of the stables of

Western Royal Mother.

the Five Holy Ones, who are noted equestrians, and choose the night for their races upon the hills.

Western Royal Mother.—"A fabulous being of the female sex, dwelling upon Mount Kw'enlun, at the head of the troops of genii, and holding from time to time intercourse with favoured Imperial votaries; the imagination of the Taoist writers of several centuries has been exercised in glowing descriptions of the magnificence of her mountain-palace." Kw'enlun is "a mountain of Central Asia widely celebrated in Chinese legends." It is to Taoism what Sumeru is to the Buddhists, and the descriptions of it are evidently imitations of Hindoo mythology. The Western Royal Mother, " the queen of the genii," who goes at the head of her fairy legions along the terraces where lie " the fields of sessamum," and the " gardens of coriander," and by the borders of the " lake of gems," has had fabulists who have " vied with one another in fantastic descriptions of the wonders of this abode." When she visited her Imperial votary, Han Wute, there were " fairy handmaids that poured out the wines with which the feasting couple were regaled, and discoursed strains of divine melody during the banquet."

The husband of the Western Royal Mother is Muh-Kung, the Lord King of the East. who, " according to Taoist legend, was one of the first beings evolved from chaos," and "it appears probable that the original conception of such a personage arose from the desire to find a mate for the mystic female divinity."

In her gardens is a peach tree, which puts forth leaves once in every three thousand years, and it required three thousand years after this for the fruit to ripen. These were her birthdays, when all the immortals assembled at her palace, and there was a great ecumenical council of the gods, called the " Peach Assembly ; " the occasion being more festive than solemn, for there was music on invisible instruments, and songs not from mortal tongues.

Three Corpse gods.—Men die and become demons ; demons die and become ghosts ; ghosts die and become corpses. The first is a nun with green clothes, the second with white clothes, and the third with red clothes. The first is called Pang Chu, the second Pang Cheh, the third Pang Kiao. These three corpse gods are in the body, and it is necessary to observe, according to the almanac, a watch-night to keep them in, else on that night, if one sleeps, these will go above to tell of his sins.

Day and Night Recorders.—There are these two images in the temples, the one recording the good and the bad done in daylight, and the other taking account of the good and bad thoughts when in bed.

Road god.—On dangerous roads he grants protection from robbers and wild beasts. He is Lih Ling, and aide-de-camp to the god of thunder, appointed because of his speed. The Taoists, speaking of rapidity by metonomy, say, "Lih Ling." He was first an escort to the wife of the Emperor Hien Yuen.

Open Road gods.—These are two tall giants, the one a European, and the other an Ethiopian, by name Yayü and Wanwen, who are drawn on chariots made of boxes with little wheels such as boys improvise for their amuse-ment, and go in front of the coffins of families of man-darins of the first, second, and third rank. They secure the repose of the soul in the coffin, and protect it from any sudden frights of the spirits it may meet on the way to the grave.

White Tiger god.—The Emperor Hien Yuen saw a god riding on a white tiger, and coming to his palace. The Western Royal Mother appointed the White Tiger god as ruler of the world.

Wang Ling Kwan.—In the temple of this god there is a sign-board—"Have you come?" *i.e.*, "I am looking

for you," "You are the very man I want." These three
words in this simple question frighten the man and make
him feel his sins.

The Military Official.—In some of the Taoist services
a small table is placed on a large one, and a bench upon

Wang Ling Kwan.

that, with a dragon tablet on the top. At the window
opposite is a paper mounted horseman, to whom a feast
is offered, and then he is burned; the hypothesis is that
he goes to Heaven on horseback and brings back his
saddle-bags full of good things,—a deified Santa Claus.

CHAPTER XXVI.

MEDICAL DIVINITIES.

THEOLOGICAL works, in discussing the proofs for the existence of God, have presented as an argument, the belief of all mankind, of all lands and races, in beings superior to men, who, in a measure, control their destinies; the argument is from the religious nature of man, that men must have some object to worship and adore.

An equally strong argument may be adduced from the fact that there is a universal belief that invisible agencies control disease, that men seek help from God, or the gods, in times of sickness, and that when the body is suffering with pain it is the special time to offer incense, prayers, and sacrifices. In China, religion and medicine are inseparably connected.

Leu Chen Yang, the Chinese Æsculapius.— nearly every doctor's office there hangs a large scroll portrait of Leu Chen Yang, who was one of the eight immortals, and the most prominent medical divinity of the Chinese, and though several of the gods of this profession outrank him, yet in the amount of practice he receives he has eclipsed them all. He was a Hanlin graduate at Peking, and a mandarin, but retired to the mountains to search for immortality. His birthday is the fourth moon, fourteenth day, and so many go to his temple, that it is popularly called, " Crowd the Divine Immortal." The Governor worships him.

The King of Medicine.—There are four of these gods, or perhaps one with four titles. Desiring to cure

Leu Chen Yang.

the 10,000 different forms of disease, he tasted all kinds of herbs that he might know their virtue. In one day he ate seventy poisons; his body was transparent, so that the effects of the medicines could be seen.

Hien Yuen and Chevah.—To the first of these the Chinese not only ascribe the invention of clothing and architecture, but also of medicine. " He was the first to determine the relations of the five viscera to the five elements, and describe internal and external diseases." Chepah was his assistant in medical investigations, "the author of prescriptions," and "the reputed founder of the art of healing."

Dr. Fox.—Foxes are found in the northern provinces,

Medicine God.   Dr. Fox.

and light literature abounds in legends about this creature, who may become a man or a woman, and practise all kinds of deceit. Houses are frequently haunted by the fox, and both the gentry and peasantry believe that his ingress and exit may be with closed doors. In the Confucian archives in this city, the fox sees to airing the books. Near the Imperial Tailors' Yamen, from which, twice a year, one thousand trunks of embroidered clothing are sent to Peking, is the temple of the fox immortal; if there is a spot of grease on a robe, his glance is equal to benzine for removing it, and the garments are folded and packed before his shrine.

The sick and their friends go to Dr. Fox with every disease, and his is the most celebrated temple in the city for genii prescriptions. The three sides of a large hall are filled with "votive tablets," presented by the devotees on recovery. The "votive tablets" say, "With a pious heart I pray;" "Piety is efficacious;" "Prayer is sure to have its answer."

Dr. Hwat'u.

Just as there are drug stores in every part of the city, convenient for local trade, so there are idol shrines situated in every ward, whose deities have considerable fame in the art of healing, and to whom the people carry all their sicknesses.

Dr. Hwat'u.—This distinguished physician lived in the second century of our era, and "all that is known respecting his career is derived from tradition and romance, in which his wonderful skill and attainments are widely celebrated, and he is said to have been especially successful in surgical operations of a marvellous description."

In his later years he was imprisoned by royal command,

and as the jailer was very kind to the physician, the latter gave him his book of prescriptions. Unfortunately, when the possessor of this legacy attended the state prisoner to the execution grounds, his wife, not knowing the value of the roll, used it in kindling her fire, so it was lost to the world. He stands second in rank among the Heavenly doctors; the people now bow at his shrine, and pray for prescriptions. He is the greatest physician China ever possessed.

Eye god.　　　　　Small-pox god.

The Divine Oculist.—In this country, where ophthal-.ia prevails so extensively, he is worshipped by all who have diseased eyes.

God of Small-pox.—In China from early ages inoculation was practised, or, as it is called, "planting" in the nose; generally when the child is two years old. As the fatality is very great, when the doctor comes to "plant the small-pox" the family go through with extensive religious ceremonies, the god being worshipped with a feast, incense, and fire-crackers.

Liver Complaint and Stomach-ache Genii.—These are beardless young men, who are worshipped by those who have the aforesaid maladies.

God of Measles.—He has a speckled face. Worshipped by those who break out with measles.

God of Luck.—King Wan is the man; they do not call him "god of luck," but "King Wan's luck." Only worshipped in times of sickness. They light three sticks of incense when they go to consult the blind fortune-teller, and three sticks when they return.

God of the Primordial Cause.—T'ai Yih. He lived in the time of the Divine Husbandman, who visited him to inquire about diseases and fortune. He was Hien Yuen's medical preceptor, and Chepah gave him a treatise on physiology and a roll of charms. His medical knowledge was handed down to future ages. He went with the immortals

Goddess of Midwives.

to the Peach Assembly of the gods to meet the Western Royal Mother. In times of sickness to chant seven days, "T'ai Yih, honourable god, save from pain," is a certain panacea.

Goddess of the Womb.—Mang Kinee. She is a pigmy, only three inches in height. Before the birth of a child, if worshipped, everything will be favourable.

Goddess of Midwives.—She is worshipped by the female attendants, and Mrs. Kyien Sen's shrine is in their homes. Both before and afterwards the happy parents offer and pay their vows. Red eggs are used in her worship, which, for good luck, are often stolen by the childless.

The Sleeping Buddha.—The Soochowites, if afflicted with sleeplessness, burn incense to the reclining image of this Buddha, and pat him with their hand to soothe his nerves; if this fails to bring back sleep, "the sweet restorer," they make a bed-quilt to cover him.

The Thirty Teachers.—Among the seventy-two teachers are thirty gods of medicine who are worshipped by those who have the special maladies. The numbers correspond to their positions in the temple.

1, Ruler of Headache; 3, Chills; 4, Liver; 5, Diarrhœa; 6, Dropsy; 7, Cough; 8, Stomach-ache; 9, Colic; 10, The Divine Oculist; 11, The Divine Aurist; 12, Small-pox; 13, Sores; 18, Consumption; 21, Animal spirits; 27, Ague; 28, God of the sickness from losing the soul; 34, Pestilence; 36, To stop the Pestilence; 39, Ruler of the thirteen kinds of doctors; 47, Acupuncture; 48, Hæmorrhage; 49, Criminal Judge of Pestilence; 53, Drugs; 57, Weakness; 58, Dyspepsia; 59, Diseases of hands and feet; 60, Breast; 61, Poison; 63, Toothache.

Gods of the Body.—1, The god of the hair is called Chwang Wa; 2, god of the brain, T'sing Ken; 3, god of the eye, Ming Chang; 4, god of the nose, Yü Lung; 5, god of the ear, K'ung Yen; 6, god of the tongue, T'ung Ming; 7, god of the teeth, Muh Fung; 8, god of the heart, Tan Yuen; 9, god of the lungs, Kao Wa; 10, god of the liver, Lung Yien; 11, god of the kidneys, Yuen Ming; 12, god of the spleen, Chang Tsai; 13, god of the gall, Lung Yao; 14, god of the diaphragm, Tao Kang; 15, god of the nape of the neck, Shang Kien; 16, god of the neck, Yü Nü Kuin; 17, god of the throat, Pah Lien Fang; 18, god of the back, Nü Chah; 19, god of the breast, Hu Pen; 20, god of the ribs, Pih Kya Ma; 21, god of the stomach, Tung Lien Yoh; 22, god of the bowels, Chao Ten Kang; 23, god of the hand, Wen Yin; 24, god of the feet, Chu Tien Lih; 25, god of the skin, T'ang Chang.

Thanking the Earth-god.—Just above the surface of the ground, or just underneath, the earth-god is continually passing along, and sometimes when one plucks a flower, or pulls a spear of grass, or upturns the soil, he meets with this deity in his journeys and interferes with his progress. The next day the man has neuralgic or rheumatic pains in his arms, legs, or back. The fortune-teller informs him that he has interfered with the "earth" or the earth-god; a musician, not a physician, is called in, and a paper-god, three cups of wine, and three kinds of meat are placed on the table; the sick man beats on the wooden fish-head and chants the "Pure Sutra;" the paper-god is burnt and ascends in the smoke: the service is called "burning paper" and "using *cash.*"

The Peasants.—The practice of medicine among the farmers in Central China is mostly confined to idol worship; they seldom go to the drug stores, or apply to the doctors, but first try incense and tinfoil money, for, say they, most surely it is an evil spirit that has brought sickness on the child. One day, in the country, meeting a man with two large baskets of candles and paper money, I asked, " My friend, what are you going to do with all those articles for worship? Sit down on the bridge here and let us talk about it." He says, "I am an old man, fifty-three years of age, I have only one son, a little boy three years old, he has been sick four days, and I want to drive the evil spirit away from him." "Have you called a physician?" "No." "Have you given him any medicine?" "No." This method of curing sickness is universal among the lower classes, and resorted to nearly as much by the gentry.

Dedicated to the Priesthood.—When children are extremely ill, in North China, the parents make a vow that they will give them to the priesthood; the priests of the temple give the boy a hat and a name, and the parents pay the priests a shilling per annum, and when the child is old enough he either fulfils the vow or on his wedding-day he is redeemed by the gift of a donkey as a substitute. Thus long life for delicate children is secured.

Getting a Prescription.—The sick man or his friends go to the temple, light candles and incense, kneel and shake the bamboo cup (as in the picture "Consulting the Oracle," Chapter XIII.), till one of the slips jumps out; the number is noted, and the priest unrolls a musty bundle and hands him a prescription, which is of the most harmless description, for if it does not cure, it will not kill. This grafting of medicine on to religion was first practised by the Taoists, but has been adopted by the Buddhists. "Taoism, as it is popularly believed, is one of the most abject of all the religions that the world has known. There is much in it which is so wretchedly mean, that the examination of it is quite dispiriting, and the reflection often occurs, Can the soul of man sink so low as this?

The Taoist doctors gain their living by a trade no more respectable than that of a gipsy fortune-teller."

The Charmed Water.—This method was said to have been originated by a Honan physician, and is extensively used in various forms. They take a charm, burn it over a cup of water, stir in the ashes, and drink it. It is much used in this city. Buddhist priests, imitating the Taoists but differing in method, do not use the charm, but chant over the water and call it " the great pity water," and " the eight merit water; " there is also " the great pity plaster." The sick often look steadfastly at a cup of water and chant the " Great Pity Sutra," drink it, and get well.

" Healing by prayer or charms formed one of the thirteen departments of medicine in the Great Medical College in the Yuen and Ming dynasties, but during the present dynasty it has ceased to be considered one of the practices." " The practice is neither local, private, wonderful, new, nor hereditary, but exists all over China. It is applied not to single diseases or classes of disease only, but to all cases of medical or surgical practice, with variations according to the seat of the disease, the whim of the quack, or the particular system of the operator. The characters traced to make the charms are various, of various devices and curious symbolical figures, some of which are meaningless; on variously coloured paper, generally yellow or gilt; with coloured inks, red and black being preferred, and prescribed to be burnt, and taken in various ways. In surgical cases the patient sometimes lies flat on his back, and the operator with water or oil describes a charm or a series of circles around the affected part, and applies the ashes of the burnt

charm in various ways." Sometimes the charm is
applied to the affected part by pasting. " For consumption, the charm is to be pasted on both hands and feet ;
for diarrhœa, to be written with vermilion ink, and pasted
over the door ; for colds, to be pasted on the temples ;
for bronchitis, to be eaten ; for ulcers, charms are to be
written over them." When the charm is eaten or applied,
a mystic formula, a kind of prayer,
is repeated by the dealer in charms,
and it is considered that there is " a
spiritual department of healing," and
that "the remedy will be inefficaci-
ous unless the heart be full of
honour to the gods."

The Criminal.

Borrowing Years. — In times
of sickness, when one is nigh unto
death, the physicians having exhausted every expedient and there
remaining no hope, it is customary
for a member of the family to lend
years to the sick relative ; as sons
and daughters may lend to fathers
and mothers ; daughters-in-law to
mothers-in-law ; wife to husband, and younger brother to
elder brother : fathers borrowing life from their sons is
most frequent. The devotee bathes and fasts, goes to
the nearest city temple, and writes out a "life policy,"
certifying that he will take off twelve years from his own
life, and give them to the sick person ; he then goes from
this temple to the temple of the Eastern Peak and burns
the certificate. Our nearest neighbour, a doctor, was at the

point of death ; his son went into the presence of the ruler of Hades and vowed to give his father twelve years ; the next day the old gentleman was much better, and passed four more winters on earth. They can borrow but cannot return.

The Criminal.—At the three feasts of the year you see little boys and young ladies, with their wealth of hair floating over the shoulders, and with red robes, looking very beautiful, handcuffs on their wrists, and chains around their necks, passing to the temples. They are called criminals. During the season they have been sick, and have recorded a vow before the god that if they recover they will appear as criminals in the next idol procession in token of thanksgiving.

Kidnapping Pretty Women.—A few days since, among our nearest neighbours, a boy of twelve summers, the only son of his mother, and she a widow, was standing in his door and looking at an idol procession. That night, with burning fever, he called, "Oh! mother, the god has me by the hand and is dragging me to the temple." The distracted mother went to the shrine, offered dollars of incense, and prayed for the life of the child. Three nights afterwards in the third watch we were awaked by the piercing bitter cries of the lone woman as she wandered in the alleys calling back the soul of her loved boy ; she returned at dawn to find him cold and lifeless.

The most frequent charge is that the god, riding in his chair, and seeing a pretty face, claims her for his bride (perchance not the first) in the world of spirits. The young wife or maiden sickens and dies. Oh! Heathenism, Heathenism ; what a ghastly spectacle of woe !

CHAPTER XXVII.

THE STAR GODS.

" LOOK now towards heaven and tell the stars, if thou be able to number them," and reflect that each star has its own star god, and the reader will have a bird's-eye view of polytheism.

Goddess of the North Star.—As the pole-star guides the mariner, so its presiding deity, called the " Bushel Mother," is the star of hope to the Chinese Church. She has four heads and thirty-two hands, and each hand holds a precious substance ; *e.g.*, the sun's disc, the moon's disc, the five chariots, a spear, a flag, a sword, a pagoda, etc. As Kwanyin is the heart of Buddhism, the Bushel Mother occupies the same relative position in the Taoist religion. Many of the gentry in this city have private chapels where she is regularly adored ; she rules the books of life and death, and all who wish to prolong their days worship at her shrine. Her devotees abstain from animal food on the third and twenty-seventh of every month. She was said to have been born in India, and her books of devotions are in imitation of the Buddhists ; in times of sickness the Taoist priests are invited to implore the favour of the goddess of the pole-star.

Northern and Southern Bushels.—These are sons

of the " Bushel Mother ; " the one dressed in red is the Southern Bushel, and rules birth, and the other in white robes is the Northern Bushel, and rules death.   A young Esau once found them on the South Mountain, under a tree, playing chess, and by an offer of venison his lease of life was extended from nineteen to ninety-nine.

" Bushel Mother."

Shooting the Heavenly Dog.—In the family sleeping apartments hangs a picture of a white-faced, long-bearded man with a little boy by his side, and in his hand is a bow and arrow, with which he is shooting the Heavenly Dog. The dog is the dog-star, and if the " fate" of the family is under this star there will be no son, or the child will be short-lived. Chang Sien is

shooting this dog. "All that is known respecting the
introduction of this name into the Chinese pantheon is
an incident in the history of Mrs. Hwa Jui, who, when
brought from Shuh to grace the harem of the founder
of the Sung dynasty, A.D. 960, is said to have secretly

Shooting the Heavenly Dog.

preserved the portrait of her former lord, the Prince of
Shuh, whose memory she passionately cherished. Jea-
lously questioned by her new consort respecting her
devotion to this picture, she declared it to be the representation of a divine being called Chang Sien, the patron
of child-bearing women."

Happiness, Office, and Age.—This group of star deities is worshipped more than any other, and this scroll hangs in a hundred thousand homes, for besides happiness, office, and length of life, the Chinese only pray for riches and sons. The picture is worshipped at

Stars of Happiness, Office, and Age.

the feast in the reception hall with the usual kneelings and knockings.

Birthday services are of frequent occurrence, especially on the sixtieth, seventieth, and eightieth anniversaries of the natal day. Among merchants, at such a time, the counters are removed from the shop, and the clerks with some near relatives or friends join the proprietor in kneeling and chanting prayers all day long before the character "Age," which is gilt and is four feet high. Sometimes a red scroll with one hundred golden "Ages" hangs before them, to which they present thanksgiving and prayers.

The Cycle gods.—There are sixty years in a cycle, and over each of these presides a special star deity ; a man worships the one which gave light at the time he arrived on *terra firma*, and at each succeeding birthday he lights candles before the image. Around the wall,

"Age."

in life size, stand these sixty grotesque images, and the skill of the idol-makers was put to the test to devise such a large number of different-looking men ; white, black, yellow, and red ; ferocious gods with vindictive eye-balls popping out, and gentle faces as expressive as a lump of putty ; some looking like men and some like women, and in one temple I saw one of the sixty was in the form of a hog. and one like a goose. Here is an image with arms protruding out of his eye-sockets, and eyes in the palms of his hands, looking downward to see the secret things within the earth. See that rabbit, Minerva-like, jumping from the divine head; again, a mud-rat emerges from his occipital hiding-place. and lo! "a snake comes coiling from the brain of another god," —so the long line serves as models for an artist who desires to study the fantastic.

The Twenty-eight Constellations.—Sacrifices are offered to these by the Emperor on the marble altar of

Heaven, and by the mandarins throughout the eighteen
provinces.

1. The Horned constellation is propitious. 2. The Neck
constellation betokens drought. 3. The Bottom constellation is unpropitious; if business is started it will end
in bankruptcy, burial will be followed by suicide in future

Cycle Gods.

generations, marriage by divorce, and a journey by
disasters. 4. The Room constellation is lucky. 5. The
Heart constellation brings lawsuits and imprisonments.
6. The Tail constellation promotes riches and honour.
7. The Sieve constellation brings luck to the family
graves, and the flocks cover the hills. 8. The Bushel

constellation is propitious. 9. The Cow constellation is
the reverse. 10. The Female constellation is worst of
all; sisters are unchaste and brothers are as tigers
and leopards; hobgoblins abound and diseases invade.
11. The Empty constellation does not give abundance.
12. The Danger constellation is fraught with evil.

Paper Gods.

13. The House constellation is fortunate, and so is
(14) the Wall constellation. 15. The Astride constellation
is unlucky. 16. The Mound constellation is propitious.
.17 The Stomach constellation is also propitious.
18. The Mao constellation is unlucky. 19. The End
constellation is fortunate. 20. The Bristling constella-

tion is the same. 21. The Mixed constellation is un-propitious. 22. The Well constellation brings luck. 23. The Demon constellation portends terror. 24. The Willow constellation is almost as bad, and (25) the Star constellation is not much better. 26. The Drawn-bow constellation wings an arrow of peace. 27. The Wing constellation in its aerial flight brings misfortune. 28. The Revolving constellation brings prosperity on its orbit.

Star Worship.—The worship of the stars is carried on in Chinese homes either by astrologers who are invited to conduct the services or by Taoist priests. In times of sickness they have ten paper star-gods, five good on one side and five bad on the other; a feast is placed before them, and it is supposed that when the bad have eaten enough they will take their flight to the south-west; the good are propitiated in the hope that they will expel the evil stars and so happiness may be obtained. The star deities are adored by parents in behalf of their children; they control courtship and marriage, bring prosperity or adversity in business, send pestilence and war, regulate rain-fall and drought, and command angels and demons; so every event in life is determined by the "star ruler," who at that time from the shining firmament manages the destinies of men and nations. Astrology spreads its dread pall over night-cursed China.

Good and Bad Stars.—The "All Stars Board" of divinities was constituted by Kiang T'aikung, who com-missioned his slain generals to be rulers over the thirty-three propitious and the seventy-nine malignant stars.

The Chinese list gives one hundred and twenty-nine lucky and unlucky stars, which with the sixty cycle stars and the twenty-eight constellations, besides a vast multitude of the diamonds in the sky, form a celestial galaxy for terrestrial adoration.

Of the propitious stars are the Sun Star, under which a man will never be poor; the Heaven-forgiveness Star, which old men worship four days of the year, and for which old women wear the " Forgiveness Hair-pin; " the Emperor's Favour-star, adored by all graduates; the Star of Healing, which gives a fine practice to physicians who worship it ; the Orphan Star, which enables a woman to become a man, and the Star of Pleasure, which decides on matches, and has silver cords with which to bind the feet of those destined to be lovers. All Soochowites annually inquire of the astrologers if the Star of Pleasure is to shine upon their home ; under its favouring light the betrothed maiden marries, the widow enjoys uninterrupted health, and the child will have all the embroidered clothes and pretty toys he desires.

飛星嗣皇星尨天星鴟青
庚伐星恩月 德祅星龍吉星
星龍泰尨六星鴦大星
尜尾害六星合月星喰朱

星龍地星綹力星寧玉星

艶黄星兒天星赦旈星武
星旛行星鳥帝星德天星
星尾天星車砲星煮太

List of Propitious Stars.

To worship the unpropitious stars, a lucky day on which the lucky star-gods rule is chosen, that they may accept the sacrifice and drive away the bad stars, so the good and the evil in the celestial abodes are continually at strife as they are within the heart of man. During the sacrifice they put a fish, called the " hen fish," in a tub of water under the table, and suppose that the malignant star rulers enter it and leave, as this fish worships the stars, and should it forget any night to say its prayers, the next day it is trapped. Thus astrology is but a species of witchcraft or demonolatry.

Some of the fierce stars are the Morning Star, which if not worshipped father or mother will die that year; the White-tiger Star, under which misfortune will attend every undertaking, the ruler of which was first killed and then canonized by Kiang Taikung; the Piercing-bone Star, which produces rheumatism; the Balustrade Star, the promoter of law-suits and litigations; the Thief Star, which is "three-handed;" the Three-corpse Star for

抽星 天狄星 血類 牲偶殺 罡鋒 罵刑星 小狗星 捕遊星 白
星滅痘星九 及星撓火星死骨星披耗星勾主星披虎凶
秦次生凶眠生大帶生胶怒生大狐頭歪二故生不肤生岳
宿星凶眠星大帶月殺星月池星葳刑鴛星病尸星勾府星
星又蠶星陰遊星丹被星天破星華欄符星巷猴星吊陳
伏役星破錯星天沉星馬敗星亡益杆星舌吉星火客星
哈星反碎星月空星十殺星大神星罡鬼星計府星騰蛇
尾地峒星陽顧星恢惡星蠶殺星天官索星驛都星金星
空星五差星歲花星狼首星五羅符星大馬星土府星喪
星伏窮星陰刑星大籍星死谷星血耗星羊府星門
胎斷星刀殺星七禍星歲符星地月光星天刀星太

List of Evil Stars.

suicides; the Iron-broom Star of ill fame; the Ten-evils' Star, which sends to prison; the Peach-blossom Star, producing lunacy; the Sackcloth Star, betokening mourning; the Knife Star, an execution; the Five Poor Stars, penury; the Broken Star is for widows; the Floating and Drowning Star for the perishing; and the Male and Female-wrong Star, under which, if a young lady is born, it is absolutely necessary to change her age, for no man would marry her, because her father or mother-in-law would immediately be laid in the grave, but if she puts her birthday in another year, she will not die an old maid.

CHAPTER XXVIII.

THE IMMORTALS.

THE tales of the genii or the immortals found in Chinese books satisfy the national craving for fictitious literature, and might be termed "divine fiction;" it also enables the writer to be *graphic*, as he is not hampered by natural laws, for in an instant he can divest his characters of mortality and let them, invisible and immaterial, soar through space, so that in the descriptions there is a decided air of the marvellous. Let the characters of some noted novelist be canonized, and let men adore and pray to them, and we have what Taoist romance has given to a people longing for something better than flesh and blood. This state of terrestrial immortality the doctors of this religion substitute for the Buddhist Paradise, and to this they invite their devotees, though practically the ranks are full, and it is not supposed that men of this age will attain the joys of the gods of the hills and forests. "The primitive Chinese tales of hermits and genii have perpetuated the recollection of many fabulous and semi-fabulous individuals belonging to the early centuries of the nation's history. Among them are not a few hermits and alchemists, men of rigid morals and having a fondness for solitude, seekers of the plant that confers immortality, and students of the hidden love of mystics, and magicians who under the title of *seen jin* form the mass of the inhabitants of Heaven."

P'eng Lai Islands.—One of the most beautiful cities in China, embowered in trees and with a girdle of hills, is Tungchow, upon the north side of the Shantung promontory, the county seat of the P'eng Lai district. Its poetic name is taken from the promontory overlooking the Gulf of Pechelle, from whence an emperor in ancient days despatched an expedition in search of the P'eng Lai islands, the abodes of the blissful immortals. "These islands, it was believed in the third century B.C., were to be found in the Eastern Sea, opposite to the coast of China. They are all inhabited by genii, whose lustrous forms are nourished upon the gems which lie scattered upon their shores, or with the fountain of life which flows perennially for their enjoyment." This is the Eastern Paradise of Taoists. There is also a mountain in the western province in Szechcun, called Mount Ts'ing Chen, which " is reputed in Taoist legend as one of the sanctuaries of the genii, and it is said to possess seventy-two caves. The Taoist books call this mountain the Fifth-cave Heaven, and describe it as the general place of assemblage for the gods and genii."

Five Kinds of Immortals.—There are five classes of genii or supernatural beings. 1. Demon Immortals; "disembodied spirits, having no resting-place in the abodes either of mankind or the happier immortals, denied alike metempsychosis and eternal bliss." 2. Human Immortals; " men who have succeeded in freeing themselves from perturbation of spirit and the infirmities of the flesh." 3. Earthly Immortals; "human beings who have attained to immortality in the existing world." 4. Deified Immortals; "immortalized spirits who have bidden farewell to earth and have departed to roam among the Three Islands of the blessed." 5. Celestial Immortals; "those who have attained to consummate purity and perpetual life in Heaven."

Han Chunglee.

The Eight Immortals.— The Eight Immortals are favourite characters of Chinese romance, and special objects of adoration. An artistic method is to embroider them on silk and hang as a pair of scrolls. Leu Chen Yang has been noticed in the chapter on Medical Divinities.

Han Chunglee.—This, the first of the genii, is variously placed in the Han and Chow dynasties. As to his appearance, he is full set, corporeally considered, has a red face, long hair, and two bunches of hair on the sides of his head. "He is said to have encountered the Patriarch of the Genii, who revealed to him the mystic formula of longevity and the secret of the powder of transmutation and of magic craft. He eventually became admitted among the genii, and has appeared from time to time on earth as the messenger of Heaven."

T'ih Kwalee.—He was one of the gentry, but one day,

when his " spiritual man " was out roaming around, a wild beast ate his body, so when the spirit returned it found only the skeleton, but fortunately near by was a beggar's corpse, black and lame ; this he took as a substitute for his own body, and always walked with an iron staff, so he was popularly known as Iron-staff Lee, or Mr. Lee with the iron staff. The breath out of the gourd on his back could in the heavens be turned into his original body.

T'ih Kwalee.   Chang Kwulao.

As a philosopher, " he devoted himself wholly to the study of Taoist lore, in which he was instructed by the sage Laotsze himself, who at times descended to earth, and at times used to summon his pupil to interviews with him in the celestial spheres."

Chang Kwulao.—He was fond of legerdemain, "and performed wonderful feats of necromancy." He is said to have been a contemporary of the first emperors, Yao and Shun, and though his years were beyond those of Methuselah, he appeared not over fifty. He made a paper donkey, which by a breath and the sprinkling of water, became a living animal, and could carry him a thousand miles a day. This erratic genius rode backwards to show how the Chinese looked backwards and not forwards.

Han Siangtsze.—He was a nephew of the great scholar Han Yü; left home when a child, and returned on

Han Siangtsze.   Lan Ts'aiho.

the birthday of his uncle, who inquired, "What have you been doing all these years?" He replied, "I have been engaged in transcendental study, and have learned the magical arts." As a proof he dashed a glass of wine on the floor, which was immediately changed into a nosegay; and upon each flower there was a delicate character, making a couplet, which was a prophecy in reference to Han Yü; this was shortly fulfilled. It is said that Han Siangtsze having been carried up to the supernatural peach tree of the genii, fell from its branches, and in descending entered upon the state of immortality.

Lan Ts'aiho.—" A legendary being, usually reputed as a female. She wandered abroad, clad in a tattered blue gown, with one foot shoeless and the other shod, wearing in summer a wadded garment, and in winter choosing snow and ice for a sleeping-place. In this guise this weird person begged a livelihood in the streets, waving a wand

Ts'ao Kwohk'iu.

Ho Sienkoo.

aloft, and chanting a doggerel verse denunciatory of fleeting life and its delusive pleasures," hoping by this means to rectify the conduct of men.

Ts'ao Kwohk'iu.—He was a brother-in-law of one of the emperors of the Sung dynasty. He was known by a bad nickname, which he obtained from his brother. He is one of the characters of Taoist fable.

Ho Sienkoo.—This maiden immortal, "when fourteen years old, dreamed that a spirit gave her instruction in the art of obtaining immortality, to achieve which she was to eat the powder of mother-of-pearl. She complied with this injunction, and vowed herself to a life of virginity. Her days were thenceforth passed in solitary wanderings among the hills, where she passed to and fro as though endowed with wings, returning to her home at night with the herbs she gathered during her lonely pilgrimages. She gradually renounced the use of the ordinary food of

Gods of Marriage.

mortals, and the fame of her wondrous mode of life having reached the Empress Wu, that sovereign summoned her to the court ; but while journeying thither she suddenly disappeared from mortal view. She is said to have been seen once more, in A.D. 700, floating upon a cloud of many colours, and again, some years later, she was revealed to human sight in the city of Canton." This young lady is the last of the Eight Immortals.

Gods of Marriage.—Peace and Union are their appro-

priate names, and they are only worshipped while the
marriage ceremony is being performed. Peace and Union
are two little boys with straight hair, one holding in his
hand a lily, and the other a spherical casket. "Ho" for
peace and "ho" for lily are the same in sound; "heh"
for union and "heh" for casket also sound alike, which
symphony is considered very propitious. In contrast to
this happy combination, on each side hang the dragon and
tiger scrolls as a warning to the happy couple.

The Immortal Ma.—Ma Koo is the only immortal
that Soochow has furnished the pantheon, and his temple
is outside the south gate of the city.

Two Brothers and the Dog.—It is related that Wei
Pehyang, "having devoted himself in a mountain retreat
to the preparation of the elixir of immortality, at length
completed the magic powder, which, by way of experi-
ment, he administered to a dog. The animal instantly fell
dead, but, undismayed, Wei Pehyang himself swallowed a
portion of the drug, and likewise expired immediately.
His elder brother, still confiding in the virtues of the
elixir, next swallowed a dose, with the same result. The
third brother remarking that if this were the result of
the search after immortality it seemed better to leave the
quest alone, went to prepare for the interment of the
bodies. He had scarcely turned his back when Wei
Pehyang, arose, and completing the mixture of his drugs,
placed a portion in the mouth of his brother and the dog,
both of whom at once revived. The two brothers and the
dog forthwith entered upon immortality, and became
enrolled among the ranks of the genii."

The Rosebud Immortal.—During the Sung dynasty

there was a little boy named Lei Hai.   He is represented in the pictures with a string of gold *cash* in his hand and a three-legged frog by his side.   In the processions they make his doll image of rosebuds and seat him on the pole, to which is suspended the great gong, borne by two men, so that he has a happy ride.

CHAPTER XXIX.

AFTER DEATH, THE SEVEN-SEVENS.

WHENEVER the subject of death is mentioned a Chinaman invariably laughs. It is a difficult phenomenon to account for, save on the general principle of *antipodes*, for when we hear that a friend has died the tears naturally fall. They never use the word "death," but substitute an euphemism,—"gone," "passed away," "returned home;" poetically—"travelling by the Yellow Spring," and prosaically, in more common parlance, "stuck up the pig-tail." They avoid every unlucky allusion to the subject, and the Chinese are truly the people "who through fear of death are all their lifetime subject to bondage." With many it is "the great unknown." The preparation for death is often, according to their ideas, attended to. The question is often asked, "Old man, are you prepared for death?" and the stereotyped reply is, "Oh yes, I have my clothes and coffin." "Have you any one to rely on after death?" "Yes, I have a son and a grandson." In many a Chinese parlour you see the old man's coffin standing in one corner and the old woman's in the other; large, black, uninviting places of repose, made of wood three inches thick; in their esteem our neat caskets are "beggar coffins," because the wood of which they are made is so thin.

Do the dead live? There are no religions which pay more attention to the state of the soul after death than do Buddhism and Taoism. The spirits of the departed are in the hands of the living, and it is a convenient way of passing through this world with no care for the life to come, feeling secure that relatives and priests will supply all necessities in the unknown land. There are nearly fifteen special services — think of fifteen funerals! — during the seven-sevens or the forty-nine days after death.

The Corpse.—The body of the dead is laid out, generally in the front room of the house, on boards resting on benches; one foot is placed in a peck basket (to detect any signs of life), paper sycee is laid over the eyes, incense burned at the feet, and a pavilion, like a mosquito net, is made, behind which mourning women utter loud and bitter lamentations. The first ceremony after death is to burn a suit of clothes and a cotton comforter for the departed to use in Hades. As the sick man approaches the dark river his friends make ready quantities of *tiny* or "joss paper," which is burnt when his pulse ceases to beat, so that the soul on entering the other world will not be penniless. "The coffin and burial clothes form most important items in the list of things deemed necessary for the respectability, comfort, and repose of a man in the spirit world. The clothes must be new, with satin cap and boots; the corpse dressed as if for a feast. A man's respectability in the other world is as much affected by his personal appearance as in this life. Hence the relatives and family of a deceased person often impoverish themselves for years, in order to provide a decent burial." A cup of water is placed at the door, to help the spirit to clear its throat.

In some of the cities of North China whenever a death occurs the god of the precinct is informed. The friends take an earthen vessel of millet gruel and sprinkle it about the temple, giving a fee to the priest, who keeps a register of the deaths which occur, and, in a recent cholera epidemic in Tungchow, a person could find out the approximate number of deaths daily by inquiring at the *T'utee Miao.*

The next point requiring attention is the selection of a site for a grave, which brings us to the consideration of

Fungshuy.—*Fungshuy,* literally "wind and water," or "the influences of wind and water," is the most prominent of the superstitions ingrained into the constitution of the Chinese. It does not fall within the limits of this volume to discuss its origin and growth, its wide-spread influence, the rude elements of natural science it embraces, or how it retards progress, forbids railways, closes coal mines, prevents enterprise, checks new efforts at advancement, "interrupts the free thought of the people, and keeps them wrapped in the mummy folds of ancient prejudices." It is only to deal with *fungshuy* as it touches upon the domain of religion, especially the rites practised concerning the dead and the choice of a location for the tomb; in this respect it is a "black art."

1. The first point to be noted is the relation between the living and the dead; the quiet of the one ensuring the peace and prosperity of the other, and the unrest of the dead causing them to wander back home "and avenge

themselves by withholding from the living prosperity and happiness." "It is therefore considered a matter of prime importance in selecting a place for the family grave, that it should be done with reference to conserving the interest and happiness of both parties."

2. The Chinese notice that when cold blasts blow from the north the autumn leaves of the forest fall to the ground, and that nature puts on the attire of death, but when the gentle zephyrs of spring with their genial influences blow from the south the earth is carpeted with grass, the trees put forth their foliage, and the hills are fragrant with flowers, so they infer that baneful influences proceed from the north, and that the south is benign, genial, and animating. Thus the grave to be propitious must be on the southern side of the hill, and the horse-shoe embankment, which surrounds the mound, must have its opening to the south; if it has not the rising bluff in the rear, a cluster of trees will act as a shield.

3. Another point in *fungshuy* is the relation between the five planets and the five elements; the rotary course of Jupiter, Mars, Venus, Mercury, and Saturn find their counterparts in the permutations of wood, fire, metal, water, and earth, by which names these planets are called. With this is the relation between the planets and the hills; the terrestrial being a dim reflex of the splendid scenery of heaven's firmament, and the skill of the *fung-shuy* professor or geomancer lies in being able at a glance to say that this mountain with a flat summit is wood, and the peak jutting clear and sharp is fire,—the tomb must not lie between these two incompatibles.

4. A fourth consideration is the position of the
dragon and the tiger. "The luck-bringing site must
have the dragon on the left and the tiger on the right.
The geomancer must determine by his skill which
elevation is the dragon and which ridge the tiger, and
by his compass the favourable point of conjunction where
the ashes of the dead *requiescat in pace.*"

5. By a grave the course of the rippling brook is
noted, and the direction of the current is taken. "Riches
and rank are personified by the undisturbed flow of the
stream, and if due care is taken by the geomancer, a
perpetual stream of honour and wealth may be expected
to flow into the possession of the family." This is the
element of *shuy* or "water."

6. The element of *fung* or "wind" is equally important. "A grave should not have a hollow near it.
The wind will blow into the grave from that hollow and
gradually disturb the bones and the coffin." In ten
years they will be one-half turned over, and in twenty
years entirely turned over. An outer wind must not
invade the chambers of the dead for fear the family
fortunes will be overturned, so the aim of the geomancer
must be to find a spot where "the cold air which issues
from the earth is hidden, and if there is no hollow there
will be no outlet by which the pernicious wind will
disturb the dead."

7. One of the most unfortunate circumstances is for
a snake or a turtle to issue from the grave; the living
exclaim, "Alas! we are ruined." This is equal to
opium and the Taipings.

8. Geomancy became a profession about A.D. 1200.

The geomancers or *fung-shuy* doctors try to find how the two (magnetic) currents of the earth run, the one male and the other female, the one positive and the other negative, the one favourable and the other unfavourable. The coffin must be placed in the line of

Spreading the Lamps.

these currents, not athwart them, so as not to disturb the repose of the soul. If the Chinese are priest-ridden, they are no less the dupes of the geomancers, for these professionals hold the " keys of the grave." They will say to the elder brother, " If your father is buried this year, it will be propitious to the younger brother but sad for you," and he, of course, will not consent to the burial. The next year is favourable to the elder but destructive to the younger, so the coffin remains at home. The third year they are perhaps short of funds. During the fourth year, it may be, the geomancer finds a plot of ground which he can purchase cheap and sell dear,—*there*·the grave must be. So it is seen that "the filial piety of China is less sincere than is by many supposed; it is more selfish than generous, more calculating than spontaneous, and is deadened by the prevailing desire for riches and rank."

The Four Death Ceremonies. The Lamps.—The Chinese put a carpet on the floor, and on it with rice draw the picture of an immortal. Then they put little hillocks of rice around, 21, 35, or 49 in number, and a lamp on each. This is to give light in Hades. The oil and rice are the perquisites of the priests.

Bathing the Soul.—The priest takes a basin of water, a paper man representing the soul of the deceased, and a willow branch, with which he sprinkles the paper man, then gently wipes with a towel.

Crossing the Bridge.—Chairs and tables piled up form the piers, and the chasm is spanned by a paper bridge. The priests with gongs and cymbals pass under the arch several times, then make the paper man walk over the bridge.

Scattering the Cash.—According to the number of the priests, bunches of *cash* on red cord are placed on a waiter, in the centre of which is a small cake with a flower on it. Each priest takes a string and jerks it so as to scatter the *cash*, which symbolizes the scattering of any unknown enmities in the spirit-world; after this there is a grab game for the copper.

Ornamental Hangings at Funerals. — Paganism delights in the ornate, so when the priests assemble to pray for souls in purgatory the hall is "decorated in a gorgeous manner with temple regalia, emblems of authority in the spirit-world," and ornamented with

Paper Bridge.

embroidered scrolls, the handiwork of Chinese women. The table is covered with red, there are long streamers of exquisite workmanship, the " pleasure-door " is a curtain with needlework of gold, the dragon tablet is of richest silk, a picture of Buddha adorns the wall, while lying around are drums, bells, cymbals, gongs, wooden fish-heads, etc. The Buddhists on the last day have seven crowns for Buddha, five kinds of food, a water-jar, rice-box, file, knife, etc. The Taoists have spirit-tablets, they wave flags and brandish swords, bring a big gong, a big drum, and a big bell, which the people call "the three big noises;" the whole services are much like theatricals.

Tossing the Cymbals.—Funeral services in China are entertaining as well as mournful. The Taoists have

Masses for the Dead.

quite a sleight of hand in tossing up the cymbals and keeping quite a number in the air at one time, which is a pleasant diversion in the midst of sad scenes.

Masses for the Dead Here is the chief source of revenue to heathen religions, and the constant employment of their priesthood, the amount paid being according to the wealth of the family. During the seven weeks, the first and fifth are necessarily Buddhist and the last Taoist, the others at option. Each day a sumptuous feast is ordered from the restaurant for the priests. There are generally five, seven, or nine of them, but if it is a great funeral there may be three hundred priests, who, " attired in richly embroidered imperial robes, march in measured pace, chanting their incantations. This ceremony of getting a man out of purgatory is continued day and night, enlivened at intervals by music and gong." After the services have been continued, the priests in the name of the regents of Hades strike for higher wages, in order to finish the work of emancipation, and when they get them "they return to their work with renewed zeal. The chanting is more energetic, the step is much quicker, and the ringing of the abbot's bell more frequent, and ere the sun sets a fearful din of gongs and fire-crackers announces the deliverance of the captive."

At the Temple.—In the temples an assistant is employed to toll the funeral bell for forty-nine days; it is dark in the land of spirits, but each stroke of the bell causes light to flash in the chambers of Tartarus.

In addition to the masses for the dead, the sons and relatives go to the city temple to burn incense, as the deceased is in the same county in Hades; also on the last day the friends rub the posts of the temple, for fear the gods have stuck the soul of the dead to them.

The Noxious god.—Called the *Sen Shin*, and the time of his worship called the *tsih sen;* the day is fixed two or three weeks after death by the Taoists; this is the most important service during the seven weeks, and is never omitted even by the poorest. The " noxious god," who is in the form of a cock, takes the dead man's soul and brings it back home. One feast is spread for the " noxious god," and another for the returning soul. Upon the bed on which the man died must be placed a full suit of clothes. The evil deity brings the man's soul, and it is the part of the Taoist priests to dismiss the " noxious god " and retain the soul, which after an hour's entertainment is allowed to leave. The day previous all the nails in the house must be covered with red paper, to keep the " noxious god " from hanging the soul upon a nail. See Picture, " The Breath of Death," on page 458.

Remembering the Dead.—Before the body is laid in the coffin, an image of Amita is placed on the table, and a string of *cash* is taken from the god's hand and placed in the hand of the deceased, then the priests and the sons try by prayer to get the lost soul out of sin to the Western Paradise.

Feast to the Soul.—It is made during the first three weeks after death, and it is considered that the dead person alone eats. The picture of the goddess of mercy is on the table, priests and relatives worship and have floral decorations.

A Priest Next Time.—The Buddhists have a service by which men may go to Heaven after the next transmigration. During the forty-nine days, a company of priests hold a five days' worship, when an abbot takes a yellow robe of paper and a paper rice-bowl and puts them in a paper trunk; then the priests march three times around the coffin, and the abbot commands the spirit to be a good Buddhist,—the dead man after the metempsychosis returns a priest, who at death may go to Heaven.

The Last Ceremony is called *hang-hyiang.* On the forty-ninth day they have an abbot to go to the largest temple, whether Buddhist or Taoist, to burn the message to Buddha, or to one of the Taoist gods. The abbot in his official regalia rides in an open chair, preceded by the friends of the deceased, bearers of flags and streamers, a man carrying the "fairy crane," and a company of musicians, and when they arrive at the temple the message to the throne is burnt to inform the gods that the ceremonies are complete. It is done mostly for effect as a street parade. See Chapter XXIII., Picture of the Fairy Crane.

Magic Credentials.—The *luh* is an official passport to travel in the foreign kingdom of Hades. The Taoist priests go to Chang, the magician, and get a supply with which they trade with the people. The rank and title is according to the amount of money paid by the living, and secures freedom from litigation in the other world, as, without this passport, a poor man would be unable to redress wrongs upon one of rank. Sometimes a mandarin's button for the land of shade is purchased during life, but generally the rich obtain it for their friends soon after death. After the credentials are made out the priests perform high mass for the dead, confess the sins of his life, and obtain forgiveness for him, and the credentials are burned. They take the ashes in a yellow bag. go first to the temple of the Water Immortal to worship, and afterwards the yellow bag is tied to the tail of a carp, and he is turned loose in the canal.

Funeral.

Funeral Procession.—When music is heard in the streets, even the natives cannot tell from the sound whether it is a coffin or a bride passing by. The picture represents the procession to the grave, with the banners, gong, red mandarin umbrella, fan, official sign-boards, musicians, Buddhist priests, Taoist priests, happy-spirit pavilion, soul sedan-chair having the tablet within, the lanterns, and the coffin. When the soul sedan returns, the tablet is exchanged for a "divine tablet," which is placed on the "divine seat;" the priests chant words of comfort, and the ceremonies are over.

CHAPTER XXX.

DEMONOLATRY.

THIS chapter does not embrace the whole of the subject, for scattered throughout the book are the views of the Chinese about spirits and demons.

Calling back the Soul.—Often the weird sound is heard during the silent watches of the night of a man calling back the soul of a sick child. *The lost soul!* how fearful are the words to us! With the Chinese the sick frequently *lose their souls.* Passing along the street a foreigner sometimes sees a cloth spread on the ground and some beans thrown on it. An old lady standing in the street calls the child by name, " Ah-do, come back," —a voice upstairs responds, " Ah." Again, a son is sick. The aged mother goes in front with a lighted lantern burning tinfoil money at every corner. The father follows with a basket of the sick boy's clothing and his hat, and utters a piercing wail, " My son, come back, come back ! " At times one is behind the kitchen range and the other is in front. Most frequently one is on the ladder to respond, as in the picture, and the other stands below to call. An insect on the roof is caught, folded nicely in paper, and put beside the sick pillow, and the lost soul is now found! Sickness came from losing it, and recovery follows its return home.

Accompanying the Guest.—Another device in case of sickness, instead of sending for the doctor, is to suppose that there is an evil spirit, who as a guest is stopping within the sick man as at an inn, or, as it is said, "The devil-guest is making a squeeze." To get rid of this troublesome visitor a subtle expedient is resorted

Calling back the Soul.

to. A savoury dish of rice, meat, and eggs is prepared, a lantern lit, and incense and "joss paper" burnt; the food is taken on a waiter into the sick room, which, when the devil-guest smells, it will follow the old servant as she takes it to the corner of another lane, and gives it as a feast to the beggars.

Charms.—The Taoists carry on a busy traffic in charms, which are sheets of paper or placards with a mysterious black scratch on them as if inscribed with a "chicken foot." There are several different kinds of these, and, stuck on the beams of houses, they are effectual in keeping out evil spirits. Towards the close of the year the Taoists sell them from house to house; the best are from the Dragon-tiger Mountain, with the angel-stamp

Accompanying the Guest.

A Charm.

of Pope Chang upon them, and in this section those from Mount Mao are also famous. The charms are used to summon the gods, to expel the demons, to heal disease, and to cleanse the house. Sometimes there are several pasted to one beam.

An official stamp is considered as a powerful warder

against evil influences, and if a child is sick. one is cut from a proclamation and put in its queue to frighten spirits. They sometimes have a scroll of four characters with the Governor's seal upon it. An almanac hung inside a boy's clothing is also a valuable remedy. If there is a corpse lying in the street. a broom is turned upside down in front of every door. In times of sickness

Chung Kw'ei.

the evil spirits hover around, but when the party dies. these leave also. At the birth of children attendant demons throng the room.

Chung Kw'ei.—"An imaginary being, believed to wield powers of exorcism over malignant demons, and frequently depicted as an aged man clad in ragged apparel," and holding a fan to his face to conceal his ugliness. An ancient emperor once saw him going into

a house, and asked him, "What are you going there for?"
He answered, "To catch evil spirits." During the fifth
moon his picture is sold and hung as a charm.

Fifth Moon, Fifth Day.—At this feast a bunch of
sweet flag leaves, rushes, and garlic is hung in the form
of a sword in front of every door; demons can stand a
good deal, but they cannot endure the fragrance of onions.

Lake Lamps.

The fifth moon is a "poison month," and the people all
the time have to beware of devils.

Street Guards.—Little deities, guardians of the peace,
are at every corner and in every niche. Especially where
a street meets a blank wall, it is necessary to have a
stone with an inscription on it, an image, or a tiger's head,
inserted in the masonry to confront the flying spirit and
send it howling down the other way. If a well is opposite
a house a tiger's head is painted on the wall.

Spirit of the House.—When Soochowites move, they

inquire of the landlord if the regular sacrifice has been offered to the " spirit of the residence." The feast is offered on a bench at the door, and it guards the ancestral service from intruding spirits.

Cleansing the house.—If there has been a death in a house, or a suicide, Taoist priests are called to clean the house, not from dirt and filth, but to get rid of all that is unpropitious. In the day the priests chant, and at night an abbot is invited, who stands beside the altar to burn the charms and to summon the regents of the skies. The abbot wrings off the head of a chicken, pours the blood into a cup, and sprinkles it in the halls and courts, and sticks up a charm in every room, lest the family live in perpetual dread.

Floating Water Lamps.—The spirits under the water, or that travel by water, need light, so the priests on a boat put a piece of lighted resin on a little bunch of straw, and the whole canal is beautifully illuminated by these floating lamps; it is a charming night scene.

Paper Clothing Store.—This is the most enterprising business in Soochow, and year by year new goods adorn the counters. The trunks with brass paper locks are filled with every kind of clothing; if for a man, they are mandarin robes, official hat and top boots, with all kinds of underclothes, paper nail boots for the rain, etc.; if for women, their garments are painted as if of the richest embroidery, and are truly very beautiful patterns. The assortment of goods comprises chairs, tables, beds, mosquito nets, bed-spreads, pillows, sedan-chairs, horses, men-servants, maid-servants, cups, tea-pots, basins, writing materials, tobacco-pipes, opium-pipes, fans, musical instruments, clocks and watches, these last such perfect imitations that for years I thought them genuine.

Preparation for Heaven.—Sometimes an aged couple feel that it is time for them to prepare for the other world. A "house," with "many mansions" of reeds and

Paper Clothing Store.

paper, covers a plot of ground; the kitchen, the servants' quarters, the reception halls, and bedrooms are made complete with every article of needful furniture; trunks of clothing and bags of money are piled within; the father leads the daughter and the son the mother, as they with the chanting priests pass around, then the fire is kindled and the paper is quickly consumed, but the reeds must be beaten down with poles: the lurid flames scarcely remind one of the city whose "Builder and Maker is God." The priests furnish title deeds to this property, which must also be committed to the flames.

The "Lily-boat" (South China).

The Bank of Hades.—The priests sometimes give notice by gongs and placards that they will despatch a treasure-boat to Hades; the old women all bring their strings of silvered paper to the boat, which is placed by the canal, till it is full of its precious freight, when, after the amply-rewarded priests march around and chant, it is

Travelling in Hades (North China).

burnt ; a cheque on the Bank of Hades being handed to each one who makes a deposit.

Travelling in Hades.—From the well-watered region surrounding Soochow a man takes a " lily-boat " to travel on the Grand Canal of Tartarus, burning it as he starts on his journey, not like the North American Indian, who places his canoe on the mountain side.

But in North China travelling is done almost entirely by carts, whose axles turn under the body. These carts are without springs, so that they go bump, bump, now in a hole and then against a stone, over roads rough beyond description. The departed soul is thought to travel by the same kind of conveyance in the spirit land, so the mourning family always sends by *combustion*, which is the packet-post between the two worlds, a full-sized paper cart, with paper horses, and from twenty to fifty outriders and gangs of servants, so that the man can make a princely entrance into the hill country of Hades.

Headless Ghosts.—The views of the Chinese as seen above are materialistic in the extreme. Decapitation makes a headless soul in Hades. During the T'aiping troubles as much as $666 was paid for a head to be buried with a body, so as to make a respectable appearance in the other world. " The practice of suspending in public places the heads of decapitated men is as much designed to inspire fear of severe punishment in the other world as of the executioner's knife in this."

Cannot die in the Inn.—The fear of a Chinese to have any one die in his house is so great that a sick stranger will be taken from the hotel and put on the bridge to breathe his last. The busy throng, as it passes carelessly by, casts but a listless glance at the dying form of a fellow-creature. There is not one pitying heart in all the crowd to exclaim indignantly, Who did this act of cruelty? Not one who has enough love toward humanity to pick the sufferer up and let him die comfortably in his home; not one Good Samaritan,— they all "pass by on the other side."

Suicides.—Perhaps there is no other country where this terrible crime is so alarmingly prevalent. The appeals for help to foreigners in an interior city, from the friends of the dying, are frequent. It is often attempted in a fit of passion. Revenge is the object sought, and when "a man is dead he is in the position to avenge himself of all the injuries he may have thought himself the subject." "So prevalent is the opinion that the dead have power over the living, that it is by no means an uncommon tragedy for a person having an irre-

A Pillar to Tranquillize Drowned Spirits.

concilable difficulty with another, to take his life in order to place himself in a position to be avenged." Many a young woman, after a severe beating by her husband or mother-in-law, with a dose of opium goes into the other world that she may return and take revenge on her oppressors. In the examination hall the essay of a literary man may be spoiled by the returning spirit of a woman whose virtue he robbed, and who, on taking the fatal dose, expressed the wish that she might not be transmigrated but remain a suicidal ghost to haunt her deceiver.

Drowned Spirits.—The souls of the drowned are supposed to remain under the water for three years, when they seize some other man, pull him into the water, and escape. Boatmen are in continual dread of these drowned demons, and men sometimes at dusk suppose they see them squatting beside the water's edge. Stone pillars are erected on the unfortunate spots in order to control the souls of the drowned.

Lunacy.—Chinese physicians say that lunacy comes from the phlegm which seals up the orifices of the heart. The Taoists ascribe it to demons, and they are called in; they require the lunatic to drink water with the ashes of a charm in it, and the gods are requested to come and drive away the demon. "The Chinese consider that all mad persons are possessed with a devil, and that the only cure is to make the sufferer prostrate himself before the god called "The Eastern Peak." In Hangchow these unfortunates are locked up at night in a room filled with hideous figures, representing the punishments of hell. In the midst of yells to frighten away the devil within the lunatic's body, and the flames of an immense pile of paper money lighting up the whole court as if it were noon-day, a poor wretch is hurried into the idol's presence and made to prostrate himself. He is pronounced guilty, and a number of blows are ordered; these are bestowed upon a straw figure which is his representative.

Demoniacal Possession.—On this topic what is written is merely tentative. In speaking with a friend on the subject, he asked me, "Will you not obtain some well-authenticated cases?" I assured him that "*well-authenticated cases* on any question did not exist in China." There are, however, some suggestive thoughts on the topic.

1. First, there is a universal belief in this section of the country as to demoniacal possession. This does not prove anything, but as most of their religious errors have a slight basis of truth, it is not impossible that so general an impression might be in a small degree based on facts.

2. Soochow is a witch-ridden city. To the south-east near the hills their number is legion, and outside the north-east gate some years ago the mandarins had to issue proclamations against them, so thoroughly demoralizing was the effect upon the people. They are to be seen calling up spirits from Hades, which descend on the smoke of an incense stick and take possession of the witch's body, so that her words are the words of the departed, and there she sits tossing her head backwards, from side to side, and rolling her eyes wildly as she rants a jargon, partly inarticulate.

"Many women in China at times fall into a trance followed by frenzy, and are consulted as spirit mediums or interpreters of the gods, whose mouthpiece they are supposed to become." "The familiar spirit takes possession of the medium at any moment and without invitation." "Almost every village has one or more spirit mediums, each having his or her familiar spirit. If spiritualism is good, China ought to be one of the most enlightened and holy of countries. But though spirit mediums are so numerous, no practical wisdom has come from the other world through them. While they swarm in China, they fail, as in England and America, to convey any useful knowledge to mankind."

3. There are, outside the city, bad gods who deal with those possessed with devils. One of the most noted temples has twice within a century been demolished by

Exorcising the Demon Fox.

the officials. The forms that demonolatry assume are manifold.

Catching Demons.—In the historical books there are accounts of hogs crying, dragons fighting, stones talking, and of voices in the temples. At the sound of the wind, the rustling of the leaves, or the voice of the birds, the people think there are demons. They call the Taoists to burn the charms, brandish the swords, and call the gods to arrest the evil spirits, and sometimes the affluent ask Pope Chang to despatch a messenger to exorcise the demons.

China the Land of Demons.—The people believe that evil spirits flit hither and thither, so in front of the door there are protection walls to shield the living from the intrusion of the dead. The house walls are built high and the windows open in the courts only, so as to prevent the ingress of spirits; there are no straight passages, for as spirits travel in bee-lines, in order to intercept their progress the passages are zigzag; and there is a succession of screen-doors which meet you at every turn; the object is to build the residence demon-proof. In front of the door lime is often sprinkled in the shape of spears and swords to frighten the invisible intruders. "Thus the Chinese have been taught to consider themselves as constantly surrounded by a spirit world, invisible indeed and inaccessible to touch or handling, but none the less real, none the less influential." They do not consider the inhabitants of the other world as a separate class of beings, but look upon all spirits, demons, and devils, as the souls of dead men; and when they view the dense population of these vast plains, and consider that each Chinaman has three souls, it is no wonder they think, "Seeing we are compassed about with so great a cloud" of demons. Such is the version of Taoism. "The system seems to dog their steps, and let loose billions of malevolent, malignant, and ruthless spirits to trouble them. Though they see them not, hosts of them may be all about them seeking opportunity to inflict some injury, so that to the fanciful mind of a Chinese, a numberless host of invisible beings are about him, concealed at every corner, wandering through the air, and their sounds, weird and eerie, are heard in the darkness of the night as the wind howls about the roof. The dread of spirits is the nightmare of the Chinaman's life." Here it is a ministration of demons, not of angels. He has, not his guardian angel, but his host of invading demons. In times of excitement, when wild alarms disturb the public tranquillity, it is almost equal to that

Breath of Death.

phase of *delirium tremens* when little demons are seen upon the wall and upon the bed, nodding, beckoning, jeering, threatening.

The Breath of Death.—This is the deity they worship as the "noxious god" during the masses for the dead. He comes as the harbinger of evil, and brings swift destruction on his wings.

The Great Feast to Spirits.—The first of the Ming

emperors, who feared, from the numbers of soldiers that
were slain in battle, that there might be a hungry horde
despatched from Hades to hover as a war cloud over his
newly-attained empire, ordered three feasts a year during
April, August, and November to be offered by the

Feasting the Spirits.

mandarins to these deceased warriors, and now it includes
all penniless, orphan spirits. Sometimes the priests take
a bowl of rice and throw it out grain by grain, and this
as food for the dwellers in Tartarus may be turned into
as much as the sands of the Ganges. The throats of the
spirits are small like a hair, but by chanting Buddhist

prayers they will be expanded. The picture represents
a musical entertainment called *fang yen k'eu*, given
to spirits, when the priests blow rice out of their
mouths.

On the thirtieth of the seventh moon, it is supposed

Mara.

that all the spirits in prison, all the devils in hell. are
turned loose; countless myriads coming as swarms of
locusts from the unseen abyss, black, hungry, and
naked, whose motto is "Your money or your life." In
front of every door piles of paper-tinsel are burned,
and it is estimated that at one temple at Hangchow

during two weeks fifteen hundred dollars daily are expended in paper sycee. On this dread night there is

The Devils' Procession.—Mara, the god of lust, sin, and death, comes in two ways,—to frighten and to deceive. The goddess of mercy, pitying the devils in Hades, wished to visit them and bestow her gracious favours upon them, but fearing lest these, so long accustomed to sin, might on seeing her beautiful face have depraved inclinations, and so increase their guilt, she was metamorphosed into the devil king,—also called "the burnt-faced devil king,"—so that none would love, but all would fear. Mara has a green complexion, long tusks, and a frightful face; his paper image is twelve feet high; with two smaller devils, one white and the other black, who as the Yamen runners of Hades receive the souls of the dying, he leads the procession with lanterns and gongs. He comes not now as the "prince of this world," or as "an angel of light," but clad in the habiliments of the prison of the lost. He is worshipped and honoured by a great people, and as he triumphantly enters every city, the rejoicing multitudes that go before and that follow after, cry. Hosanna to the son of darkness; Hosanna in the lowest! and then, in this climax of devil-worship, when Mara is assigned the highest place in the pantheon, an adoring nation bows to him as their high ruler, their accursed guardian, their faithless guide, and their chief divinity.

Conclusion.—Let us follow Him who came to "destroy the works of the devil" in His triumphal entry into Jerusalem, as he paused on Olivet's brow, and as "when He beheld the city, He wept over it." If when He saw the 3,000,000 of Judea, "He was moved with compassion on them, because they fainted, and were scattered abroad, as sheep having no shepherd," should not our pity for this countless people be a hundredfold? As we witness the downward progress of their systems from the school to the temple, from philosophy to demonolatry, and from asceticism to devil-worship, we instinctively cry, "The night is far spent!" the night of superstition and idolatry, and call to the heralds on Zion's towers, "Watchman, what of the night? The watchman saith, The morning cometh!" "The Sun of Righteousness arises."

As a minister was speaking of the "folly of idolatry, and telling the story of God's love," "a white-haired village patriarch" said, "We did not know that this was wrong. Our fathers worshipped thus. *We cannot find the door.*" The Good Shepherd says, "I am the door." The sweet Psalmist of Israel sung, "Their sorrows shall be multiplied that hasten after another god." One day, a year after we came to Soochow, an old lady walked to the chapel leaning upon her staff. She was invited in, and was asked by the missionary's wife, "Who did you come here to see?" She told her story: "I went outside the West Gate to make some purchases, and the shop-keeper's wife, seeing I had such a sad face, asked me what was the matter. I told her that my husband's two sons died during the T'aiping rebellion, and there was left only my youngest boy, who was clerk to a pawn-broker; he was taken sick and died the day after they brought him home, and now in my old age I am all alone; then she said to me, 'If you want comfort, go to the *Yang Yoh Hong*, they have *a doctrine that comforts people.*'" We have had many good things and many bad things said about us, but never a better than this, that "we have a doctrine that comforts people." One morning, going to my chapel, I saw laid out in the front room of a house the icy form of a young maiden of seventeen years, and beside her a little girl weeping and saying, "My golden sister, my golden sister, I do not know where you have gone to!" And many a time has this bitter wail pierced my heart, "My golden sister, my golden sister, I do not know where you have gone to!"

THE END.

INDEX.

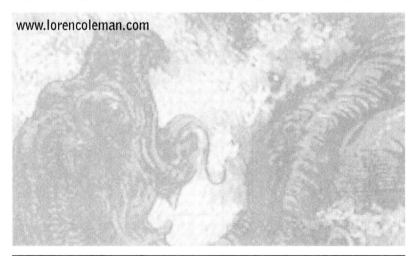

LOREN COLEMAN PRESENTS SERIES
(COSIMO CLASSICS)

Abominable Snowmen, Legend Come to Life, by Ivan T. Sanderson (PB—9781605203331/ HC—9781602068858)

Curious Creatures in Zoology, by John Ashton (PB—9781616409319/ HC—9781616409302)

Curiosities of Natural History, in four volumes, by Francis T. Buckland (PB—9781605205496, 9781605205519, 9781605205533, 9781605205557/ HC—9781605205502, 9781605205526, 9781605205540, 9781605205564)

Dragons and Dragon Lore, by Ernest Ingersoll (PB—9781616409241/ HC—9781616409234)

Gleanings from the Natural History of the Ancients, by Rev. Morgan George Watkins (PB—9781616409203/ HC—9781616409197)

Mythical Monsters, by Charles Gould (PB—9781605204062/ HC—9781605204079)

Natural History Lore and Legend, by Frederick Edward Hulme (PB—9781616409227/ HC—9781616409210)

Oddities: A Book of Unexplained Facts, by R.T. Gould (PB—9781616409296/ HC—9781602068285)

Sea Fables Explained, by Henry Lee (PB—9781616409357/ HC—9781616409364)

Sea Monsters Unmasked, by Henry Lee (PB—9781616409333/ HC—9781616409340)

Snakes: Curiosities and Wonders of Serpent Life, by Catherine C. Hopley (PB—9781616407209/ HC—9781616407216)

The Book of Werewolves, by Sabine Baring-Gould (PB—9781605203355/ HC—9781605201139)

The Dragon, Image, and Demon, Or the Three Religions of China, by Hampden C. DuBose (PB—9781616409388/ HC—9781616409371)

The Dragon in China and Japan, by M.W. de Visser (PB—9781605204093/ HC—9781605204109)

The Great Sea Serpent, by A.C. Oudemans (PB—9781605203324/ HC—9781602060128)

The Romance of Natural History, by Philip Henry Gosse (PB—9781605203348/ HC—9781602060111)

The Unicorn: A Mythological Investigation, by Robert Brown (PB—9781616409265/ HC—9781616409258)

The Werewolf, by Montague Summers (PB—9781616409289/ HC—9781616409272)

Thunderbirds: America's Living Legends of Giant Birds, by Mark A. Hall (PB—9781931044974/ HC—9781605203492)

For more information about Loren Coleman Presents titles, check our website at cosimobooks.com

OTHER CRYPTOZOOLOGY BOOKS
BY LOREN COLEMAN

Monsters of Massachusetts: Mysterious Creatures in the Bay State (Stackpole Books, 2013)

Monsters of New Jersey: Mysterious Creatures in the Garden State with Bruce G. Hallenbeck (Stackpole Books, 2010)

True Giants: Is Gigantopithecus Still Alive? with Mark A. Hall (Anomalist Books, 2010)

Weird Virginia: Your Travel Guide to Virginia's Local Legends and Best Kept Secrets with Jeff Bahr and Troy Taylor (Sterling, 2007)

Mysterious America: The Ultimate Guide to the Nation's Weirdest Wonders, Strangest Spots, and Creepiest Creatures (Paraview Pocket Books/Simon & Schuster, 2007)

The Field Guide to Bigfoot and Other Mystery Primates with Patrick Huyghe (Anomalist Books, 2006)

The Unidentified & Creatures of the Outer Edge: The Early Works of Jerome Clark and Loren Coleman with Jerome Clark (Anomalist Books, 2006)

Weird Ohio: Your Travel Guide to Ohio's Local Legends and Best Kept Secrets with James Willis and Andrew Henderson (Barnes & Noble/Sterling, 2005)

The Field Guide to Lake Monsters, Sea Serpents and Other Mystery Denizens of the Deep with Patrick Huyghe (Tarcher/Penguin, 2003)

BIGFOOT!: The True Story of Apes in America (Paraview Pocket Books/Simon & Schuster, 2003)

Tom Slick: True Life Encounters in Cryptozoology (Linden Press, 2002)

Mothman and Other Curious Encounters (Paraview Press, 2002)

Cryptozoology A to Z: The Encyclopedia of Loch Monsters, Sasquatch, Chupacabras, and Other Authentic Mysteries of Nature with Jerome Clark (Simon & Schuster, 1999)

Curious Encounters: Phantom Trains, Spooky Spots and Other Mysterious Wonders (Faber & Faber, 1985)

Creatures of the Goblin World with Jerome Clark (Fate/Clark Publishing, 1980)

COSIMO is a specialty publisher of books and publications that inspire, inform, and engage readers. Our mission is to offer unique books to niche audiences around the world.

COSIMO BOOKS publishes books and publications for innovative authors, nonprofit organizations, and businesses. **COSIMO BOOKS** specializes in bringing books back into print, publishing new books quickly and effectively, and making these publications available to readers around the world.

COSIMO CLASSICS offers a collection of distinctive titles by the great authors and thinkers throughout the ages. At **COSIMO CLASSICS** timeless works find new life as affordable books, covering a variety of subjects including: Business, Economics, History, Personal Development, Philosophy, Religion & Spirituality, and much more!

COSIMO REPORTS publishes public reports that affect your world, from global trends to the economy, and from health to geopolitics.

FOR MORE INFORMATION CONTACT US AT
INFO@COSIMOBOOKS.COM

➤ if you are a book lover interested in our
  current catalog of books

➤ if you represent a bookstore, book club, or
  anyone else interested in special discounts
  for bulk purchases

➤ if you are an author who wants to get published

➤ if you represent an organization or business
  seeking to publish books and other publications
  for your members, donors, or customers.

**COSIMO BOOKS ARE ALWAYS
AVAILABLE AT ONLINE BOOKSTORES**

VISIT COSIMOBOOKS.COM
BE INSPIRED, BE INFORMED

CPSIA information can be obtained at www.ICGtesting.com
Printed in the USA
BVOW02s1006050116

431757BV00003B/138/P